Build Your Own Expert System

2nd Edition
for the IBM PC and Compatibles

Chris Naylor

Publishers. Wilmslow

HALSTED PRESS a division of **JOHN WILEY & SONS**
New York · Chichester · Brisbane · Toronto

ISBN 1-85058-071-5 (Sigma Press)
ISBN 0-470-20946-1 (Halsted Press)

First published in 1987 by

Sigma Press
98a Water Lane, Wilmslow, SK9 5BB, England.

Printed in Malta by Interprint Limited

Reprinted 1988

British Library Cataloguing in Publication Data

Naylor, Chris
    Build your own PC expert system.
    1. Expert systems (Computer science)
    2. Microcomputers   3. System design
    I. Title
    006.3'3   QA76.76.E95

Library of Congress Cataloguing in Publication Data

Naylor, Chris, 1947-
    Build your own expert system.

    Includes index.
    1. Expert systems (Computer science) 2. Microcomputers
– –Programming. I. Title.
QA76.76.E95N38 1987   006.3'3   87-15006

Distributed in UK and Europe by

John Wiley & Sons Ltd., Baffins Lane, Chichester, West Sussex, England.

Acknowledgments

IBM PC and PC-DOS are trademarks and IBM is a registered trademark of International Business Machines Corporation. PC1512 is a trademark of Amstrad Consumer Electronics PLC. BASIC 2 is a trademark of Locomotive Software Ltd.

Cover graphics and illustration by David Collins, Professional Graphics, Warrington.

Distributed by
John Wiley & Sons Ltd., Baffins Lane, Chichester, West Sussex, England.

Preface

A potential reader is standing in a bookshop with a copy of a possible purchase in his or her hand. Having looked at the front cover, and looked at the back cover, he or she now reads the Preface to determine whether or not the book should be purchased. The Preface, says the Theory, clinches the sale.

So much for theory. The real reason you should buy this book is because, for a book on computers, it is relatively cheap. It also contains working examples in BASIC for the IBM PC and close compatibles so you get some 'free' programs thrown in for your money. Actually though, the BASIC used is so basic that it could be pretty readily converted to most other computers if you don't happen to have a PC.

It tells you a moderate amount about Expert Systems, but, frankly, to disclose exactly what it does tell about Expert Systems would rather annihilate the reason for buying it. After all, you could just stand there, in the bookshop, reading the Preface and hang onto your money. But it will (just as a sort of appetiser) enable you to build your own expert system for medical diagnosis. Or an expert system to work out why your car won't start in the morning. Or it will enable you to build a learn-by-example expert system which can be taught expertise in a wide range of areas.

It will also teach you a fair amount about statistics and inferencing systems but, despite that, you should still shell out the necessary and buy a copy.

I know money is tight these days and you could usefully spend it on something else, like drink, which would give *you* greater pleasure but I have to make a living too you know and the cost of printer ribbons alone was pretty enormous when it came to bashing this lot out.

Well, after all that, maybe you've had the heart to fork out on a copy and you're actually planning to read the thing now. What you do is start at the beginning and carry on until you get to the Technical Overview. Then think of something you'd like to try out – such as a machine learning system or a bit of diagnosis – and dig out the relevant parts using the Contents pages, the Index, and the Technical Overview to tie it together.

Alternatively, you could have your computer switched on as you read the book and key in the examples as you go along, that way seeing how they work as an aid to understanding. If you do this it could take you ages to get to the end, of course.

The big point to note though is that this book is not arranged like a normal text book. The chapters are not isolated entities. One way or another you do have to churn right through from front to back to get the ideas in the proper sequence. A few people have commented that it reads more like a novel than a text book in the way it's arranged – which is a fair point, but it's probably as well to warn you that it's like that.

Prior to publication this book was read by Graham Beech, Phil Bradley, Bill Hudspith and Phil Manchester (in alphabetical order).

They all chipped in with comments of one sort or another and they each have caused some improvements to be made to the final version. Which was nice of them.

If anyone, having read the book, has any comments which might lead to useful alterations, then drop the publisher a line and let him know.

A Note on the Programs

All of the programs in this book have been written in Basic to run on the IBM PC and close compatibles.

They have been tested under IBM's Advanced Basic (Basica), GW Basic and Locomotive Basic 2 (as supplied with the Amstrad PC 1512).

However, they have all been written using a very simple sub-set of Basic which should enable the average Basic programmer to readily convert the programs to some other dialect to suit their particular machine or individual preferences.

Where examples of actual run-time output are given these were obtained using an IBM PC running Basica. Readers using other machines or other Basic interpreters can expect to obtain similar results at run-time to those shown but minor variations may arise. This is usually due to such things as the different methods used by other machine/interpreter combinations when rounding numeric variables and the differing behaviour of their random number generators and other built-in functions. Any variations in run-time performance due to these factors are usually of little practical consequence.

All of the program code shown in this book has been printed in upper case text except in the case of string constants where a combination of upper and lower case text is sometimes used. Depending on the Basic interpreter you use you may find that the program code displayed on your screen is not in the same combination of upper and lower case. For instance, users of the Amstrad PC 1512 running Locomotive Basic 2 will notice that their screen only displays Basic 2 key words in upper case whilst variable names are displayed in lower case. This is quite normal and is not a program fault.

Also, where a program line extends over more than one line on the printed page the line has been broken, indented, and continued in such a way as to try to make the overall program text as legible as possible to the reader. The result is that the lines as displayed on your screen may not be broken and indented in exactly the same way as shown in this book. For example, users of the IBM PC running Basica will notice that any lines extending over more than 80 characters are displayed on their screens in such a way as to continue on the next line without any indentation. Again, this is quite normal and is not a program fault.

In general, when entering programs into your machine try to maintain the sense of the code and do not try to make the physical spacing, layout or appearance exactly match that shown in the book.

Contents

Chapter 1

Why Expert Systems?

"An expert system is regarded as the embodiment within a computer of a knowledge-based component from an expert skill in such a form that the system can offer INTELLIGENT ADVICE or take an INTELLIGENT DECISION about a processing function. A desirable additional characteristic, which many would consider fundamental, is the capability of the system, on demand, to JUSTIFY ITS OWN LINE OF REASONING in a manner directly intelligible to the enquirer. The style adopted to attain these characteristics is RULE-BASED PROGRAMMING".

A formal definition of expert systems approved by the British Computer Society's committee of the specialist group on expert systems.

Once upon a time a long time ago when the Earth was still new and the Sun had a big smile on its face when it got up each morning, there was no such thing as Expert Systems. Yet suddenly, everyone seems to be talking about the things. Why is this?

Well, the answer is that Scientists Have Determined that there is an increasing quantity of Government Money around for computer applications and, further, they have also determined that there is scant chance of accessing this pile of money unless there is a goodish chunk of expensive and arcane research activity to be carried out on the application of computers. So, to this end, they invented Expert Systems which, because nobody in Government circles knows what they are, are liable to attract Government Money if only as an aid to identification.

Less mercenary scientists (whose names currently escape one) are not interested in Government Money *per se* and will, in fact, point to the notable absence of Government Money to date in this field. These altruists will simply state that they want to make computers more accessible to more people. They want to make computers *think* like people. They want computers to *replace* people. They want computers to be *user-friendly*. And, in the final analysis, they probably also want computers to take on the job of allocating Government Money.

1

All of this is fine – but the real problem lies in finding out enough about Expert Systems so that one can even begin to attract Government Money on one's own behalf. Beyond this point in the book the subject of Money will receive little attention but, hopefully, the book will enable you to get the hang of Expert Systems so that you can, at least, build your own – Government Funded or not.

The first part of the book relies on your total ignorance to build an Expert System – it is a *machine learning* system which can pick up skills in a wide range of subject areas. It *acquires* expertise.

Later, some knowledge of a specific area is assumed and we build an Expert System which is able to use this knowledge intelligently to offer *advice* after the fashion of a human expert.

A point which really must be made is this: that this book, as an aid to understanding and as a sop to sloth, gives all of its examples in BASIC. But it does not contain an overview of, or instructions on, how to program in BASIC. That is the one piece of expertise which the reader has to bring to the task for him or herself.

The program examples are all given in BASIC in a dialect which will run on the IBM PC and close compatibles including the Amstrad PC 1512. The programs have been tested in Advanced Basic (BASICA), GWBASIC and Locomotive Basic 2. No particularly advanced features of BASIC are used however which means that the programs should be readily modifiable onto most micros.

The final chapter in the book summarises the information given in previous pages so that, when you get that far, you'll be able to see exactly what it was that you were reading about earlier.

1.1 What do you want an expert system for?

There are two major faults possessed by most existing expert systems and these two faults are: that you, personally, don't understand how they work; and, that you, personally, haven't got one.

These faults can, in extreme cases, be quite serious.
You slink around avoiding other people's eyes. You avoid conversation with others. You hide behind COBOL manuals. You listen greedily to other's talk of 'knowledge bases', 'artificial intelligence' and 'real-world representations'. You are afraid to come clean and ask what it's all about for fear of social rebuff.

You become an outcast and a despised person in your own eyes.

All of which can become a bit irksome after the first five minutes or so. Particularly when you feel that the subject matter can't really be all that difficult as evidenced by the fact that those who do profess to understand it can't, surely, be any cleverer than you yourself are.

What is needed, to put matters right, is for you to have your Very Own Expert System. Tailor made to A Little Known Design it will enable you to lean confidently on any bar counter and pontificate on the subject of expert systems. Instead of hiding your head and keeping your own counsel you will be able to raise a slight sneer in the direction of those who don't really understand how their own expert system works. And at those who actually don't have an expert system of any kind (one doesn't even begin to know how such people manage to get by) you will be able to raise a deeply quizzical eyebrow.

For you (the tall, confident one standing near the centre of the bar and holding forth to a crowd of admirers, many of whom are young and nubile) are about to Build Your Own Expert System.

No special knowledge is required although it would be handy if you had access to a computer; otherwise much of what is to follow may come to seem, somehow, well, Academic.

1.2 What do other people want an expert system for?

There are two main uses for expert systems and these correspond to the sociological concepts of manifest and latent functions.

The manifest function of an expert system is to provide, on a computer, human expertise. For instance, they can diagnose illness, deduce chemical structures, suggest sites for digging up precious metals or carry out a host of similar tasks. They are user-friendly to some degree – embodying human knowledge in a form vaguely similar to the form in which a human expert might hold knowledge. They often have some ability to explain their actions and opinions in much the same way that a human expert might. And, like a human expert, they might even be able to teach their expertise to someone.

The other function of expert systems – hinted at earlier – is their latent function which is, one suspects, to baffle the ignorant with arcane explanations of how they were built. Typically, expert systems use large computers, of the sort you have not got, and employ exotic-ish languages, such as LISP and PROLOG, which you have not got either. This tends to have the advantage of somewhat sewing up the market for supplying expert systems because, if demand can be stimulated by a description of an expert system's manifest functions, this demand – surely? – can't be met simply by someone possessed of a micro and a BASIC interpreter. Which doubtless affects the price.

The way out of this problem is to provide a micro-orientated guide to building expert systems. Not a complete guide which gives the last word on the subject necessarily – but enough to break down some of the mystique and get the average person started.

Up to now the real problem in understanding expert systems has been simply that there was no simple place to go for an introduction to the subject. Unless you were prepared to put some pretty hard thought into the matter, all of the currently available writings on the subject just seemed to emphasise the difficulty of ever understanding any aspect of the subject – which tends to inspire one to give up and leave it to the experts! It's all rather reminiscent of trying to climb a mountain (well, hill maybe) on which there is just no first toehold to be found. If you could only get started you'd feel a lot more optimistic about what might be done and you'd even be able to work out a lot of the subsequent steps for yourself without the aid of a book. And after all, that's what the human experts on expert systems are doing: working it out for themselves.

The trick lies in getting yourself into the same way of thinking as the current leaders in the field. To realise that there is something concrete and accessible to think about with real toeholds to hang onto. To think that there are some interesting problems here and that these problems, with a bit of thought, are perfectly soluble and that the solutions as they appear are perfectly amenable to being explained in plain language. That the subject of expert systems is not in fact a mystic art but, like all computer subjects, is something as practical and down-to-earth as carpentry.

1.3 What is an expert system?

Before you climb into your overalls and rush to your workbench it's as well to just pause for a moment and ask: what, actually, is an expert system? For, if you think about it, you'll realise that the answer to this question might well have a profound effect on the finished object. Actually, the answer won't affect the object much – as we shall see – but, certainly, you'd think it should.

It all started many years ago, back in the empty vastnesses of time when computers were about as powerful as a pocket calculator and transistors were spoken of in awed tones. In between being struck speechless by the power and complexity of the monsters with which they worked, computer scientists found words to express their deepest desires.

"Wouldn't it be nice," they used to say to each other, "if we could get this thing to do something other than payroll calculations."

"Yes," they used to agree, "we've got literally hundreds of words of memory and it now works faster than the chief accountant yet, for all that, it is like working with an idiot."

"Certainly he is an idiot," another would concede, "but our computer is little better than him."

And they would drink beer long into the night and attempt to hatch schemes whereby the full power of their Frankensteinian monster could be unleashed.

Well, they are still there, drinking beer and plotting against the chief accountant and the computer is still doing the payroll. The progress has not been dramatic in the direction of getting the computer to do something more, but the motivation is still the same. For, like Frankenstein, they wanted to dream up a way of breathing a little life into their subject. They didn't just want a glorified adding machine – they wanted an actual thinking machine.

That, of course, is how the whole field of artificial intelligence started up, and the field of expert systems was just a part of it.

People noticed that the chief accountant, say, wasn't just a glorified adding machine (despite the rumours) but that he was something of an expert in his own field. He could cook the books, for instance, in a way quite beyond the abilities of any computer.

And it wasn't just the accountants that could beat computers. In every field there were human experts who had special skills and knowledge which made them both indispensable and expensive. Everytime a group of computer scientists talked to someone who was an expert in some field they would listen to him for, maybe,

4

a couple of hours. Then they would start to long for the day when he could be replaced by a computer so that they could switch him off and, then, forget to pay him.

The dream was an alluring one. So alluring that, in time, it took sufficient hold for people to think that there must be some way of realising that dream. The problem was: how?

It's easy to see that, if one did solve the problem, one could call the result an 'expert system'. It would have the expertise previously found in human experts yet it could be switched off at night. But the problem as to how this was to be done not only proved hard to solve – it has hardly been solved yet.

Ask anyone how a human expert works and, apart from comments like 'slowly', you'll find that nobody knows. Or, at least, they don't know to the extent that you could write a computer program to do it. Any explanation will be fuddled with words like 'judgement' and 'experience' which simply don't occur in the world of formal languages.

But the basic ideas are simple enough.

People, it's said, are general purpose thinking machines. Give them any problem and a bit of experience and they can use their judgement to think out a satisfactory solution to the problem. All that people consist of is a collection of brain cells, wired together somehow, and all that computers consist of is a collection of memory cells, also wired together somehow. So, write a program which will solve problems (in general) and you have a system which will replace people. With the added advantages of not breaking down, forgetting, going wrong, wanting to be paid, and so on. The problem is that this general purpose problem solver has been pretty elusive.

Less elusive have been specific problem solvers. For example, you might have a calculation to perform. Well, you could easily write a program to do that for you. In fact if you've used a computer you already have done that. Give your machine an arithmetic expression and it can work out the answer for you. That sounds pretty obvious, but in evaluating an arithmetic expression the computer has done everything which a human mathematician would have done. It hasn't just added a few numbers together, it's taken a string of symbols and manipulated them to put them into a sensible form. After that, any arithmetic would have been really trivial.

And if you should think that this is beside the point, consider a problem which your current computer maybe can't immediately handle. Take the problem of integrating a mathematical expression. Integrating expressions can be notoriously difficult to do with some functions – so you might reasonably think that it would be a suitable topic for an expert system. But now suppose that you had written such a system. What would it actually look like?

It would look, probably, just like your current computer with its BASIC interpreter. The only difference would be that it had a few more expressions in the language. In fact, if you look around at some pocket calculators, you'll find that they've got 'integrate' keys which will carry out numerical integration for you on any function. So there's really nothing remarkable about that anymore.

And this serves to illustrate a point: that once we know how to do something and can write a program for it, then it ceases to appear at all remarkable. Only a short while ago, if you didn't happen to be a maths graduate yourself, you'd have had to call one in to perform integration. In other words, you'd have sent for an expert. With the calculators and programs available today that isn't necessary because the task has ceased (virtually) to be one which needs an expert. And, as a consequence, we'd hardly call the 'integrate' key on a pocket calculator an expert system.

To take a more everyday example, there once were people who were payroll experts. In fact, some of the most agile minds in the British Empire could have been found in the Army Pay Corps. Adept at finding loopholes, special cases, hitherto unknown allowances, these human experts (some would say 'superhuman') held sway for years. It was simply the payroll program which sent pay clerks the way of the dinosaur. The payroll program can easily be seen as an example of an expert system – it embodies the total sum of human expertise on the subject of payrolls. But nobody thinks of it like that anymore.

It's simply another case of a problem seeming to be trivial once someone has solved it.

And that's really the case with expert systems today. Previous advances are dismissed as scarcely being advances at all for the very simple reason that, like the early computer scientists, we're all sitting around wishing that we could get the computer to do something 'special'. Something more than it's doing already. But, if it did, we'd still be looking for that something extra which, as yet, we have not got.

Each advance brings with it another computer program – no more and no less than that. But there just doesn't seem to be that one, final, Big Advance which brings the ultimate program. The one that finally breathes life into the monster.

And, just to make matters worse, if there were such a system, the next thing that would happen is that there would appear a new breed of experts. Human experts, they would be expert in the workings of of the ultimate systems. They would know more about it than did anyone else – and they would be well-paid for their expertise. And, if you don't immediately believe that, ask yourself how it was that computer programmers ever appeared on the scene in the first place.

Suppose, for instance, that you devise an expert system which is able to carry out medical diagnosis. This has of course been done already. What do you think would happen next? Well, learned papers would appear in academic journals describing the system and saying what it could do. And others, noting what it couldn't do, would set about building a better expert system. This of course, has already happened. It is past history. You might sum it up by saying that: a computer program was written which was then criticised and improved by human experts who then wrote a better computer program. And so on. ...

Inevitably then, any expert system is only going to be a temporary palliative. Something to stave off the pangs of deprivation for a while. The trick is to find a good palliative rather than a bad one. Something that makes you think 'That's clever!'– even if you don't always continue to think it's clever. A computer program, in short, which will do something that you hadn't realised could be done by a computer at all. A computer program which does something which you'd have thought really needed the services of a human expert to achieve.

But still, in the end, a computer program.

1.4 What do you want your expert system to do?

Having defined an expert system as a computer program, no more, no less, we could just sit around content in the knowledge that we knew what an expert system was and we already had one. This is the easy way out.

The hard way out is to take the functional approach and ask: what do you want your expert system to do?

This is a dangerous question to ask because the answers can involve you in having to do some work, something which is generally considered distasteful. But that's computers for you. Generally speaking, people don't define computer programs except by virtue of what they do. So, if expert systems are computer programs, what do they do?

At this point the onus goes over, temporarily, to you. Because the question is not "what does one, in general, want an expert system to do?" It's "What do you, in particular *you*, want your very own expert system to do?" After all, it's you who's going to build it. You might as well have some say in the matter if you can.

Well that question is, of course. easy. Settling into your armchair you switch on your computer, close your eyes and dream. The room swims before your eyes, a warm glow passes through your very being. A relaxed confident smile plays on your lips as you idly key in the question: *How can I become a Millionaire?* and a few simple, well-chosen, phrases appear on the screen by way of answer.

"Of course!" you exclaim. "Yes, certainly. Yes. That would obviously make me a millionaire. If only I'd built my own expert system sooner."

And you make a note of the answer and proceed to interrogate that machine on the previously-vexed question of how you can stop your hair going grey, followed by a session on how to stop dandelions growing in your lawn.

It all works like a dream and, in fact, it is a dream.

Which is a bit of a pity, really. But Life's like that and no amount of programming is really going to help that much.

The problem is that some things are impossible to program, expert system or no expert system, and if you want to program an impossible thing then you will encounter difficulties of implementation.

Returning from dreams of great things to the real world, in which you're sitting there with a computer in front of you, needn't be too much of a letdown though.

Having said that some things are impossible to program doesn't mean that all things are impossible to program. But why, you might ask, talk about programming when what you really want is to get on with building your very own expert system? Well, it's really just a matter of making sure that 'expert system' doesn't get mistaken for the phrase 'universal panacea'. Take an analogous case which has been around a bit longer: databases.

Databases can be pretty complex things. They can take a lot of working out and a lot of understanding. This can lead to paralysis of the intellectual kind on the part of those who encounter databases for the first time. Yet, if you have a few files (and who doesn't) then you have a database (of sorts). So where's the problem?

To be honest, there isn't a problem. You just ease into the subject kind of gradual and you soon get the hang of it.

It's much the same with expert systems. There's nothing much to them, really. Which is a good thing, seeing as how you're planning to build one.

There is one idea which is worth having in mind though: that's the idea of an expert system as being a system which has 'judgement'. Now, all computer programs tend to have some measure of judgement. As soon as you write code to compare one value with another and take specific action depending on the outcome you have judgement.

It's just that expert systems tend to place judgement rather centrally in their design. Judgement, rather than calculation, tends to typify expert systems. But, as the judgement usually comes as a result of calculation, the difference tends to be conceptual rather than actually, as it were, real.

So, think of something you'd like an expert system to do and ask yourself if it can be reduced to a series of judgements. If it can, you have a good chance of building an expert system to do it. And that allows an awfully wide range of possibilities.

To start you off, here are some possibilities:

Diagnosis of common illnesses.
Fault finding in simple circuits, or maybe a TV.
Diagnosing plant diseases.
Electrocardiogram analysis.
Classifying animals, birds or plants according to species.

But, you are certain to have your own ideas.

1.5 Expert systems: some untrue things

On the subject of expert systems, people say a wide range of things and not all of them are factually true.

The common error, strangely enough, is not to overstate what an expert system could, in principle, do. It is to understate the possibilities.

Typically, you might hear that "an expert system can only do ... " followed by a list of what it can do with the implication being that it can't do anything else. This is nonsense. If you can think of a way of doing something then you can build an expert system to do it.

Someone else's expert system may only be able to do such-and-such. But yours! That's another matter. Your expert system is under no such constraints. Yours is going to be bigger and better than anyone else's (if that's how you build it, that is). It is presumptuous of anyone to tell you what your expert system can't do.

Take for instance:

An Expert System can only be expert on one thing. Patently untrue. All you've got to do is to build one that's expert on two things and you've proved the critics wrong.

An Expert System can only do what a human expert could do (at best). Also untrue. Suppose you chose to build a system for which there aren't any human experts? If it ever works at all you've proved this statement false. More typically, there are plenty of fields in which human expertise is less than complete. In such a case, all your expert system has to do is be a little bit better than normal human judgement.

Expert Systems will never replace man. Of course they will. There'd be no point in building them if they couldn't.

Human nature being what it is, it's always possible to find someone who will disagree with this book's description of expert systems. You may even disagree with it yourself. So, let's note the following points:

To some people, a special characteristic of expert systems is that they are 'adaptive'–meaning that the behaviour of the program changes (usually for the better) over a period of time. They can do this by holding their knowledge in rules which can very readily be altered by the user, or by building up their knowledge from their own analysis of the inputs with little intervention on the part of the user. In both these senses the systems described in this book are adaptive.

An aim of many of today's expert systems is to make them generally expert in a wide range of tasks simply by drawing a distinction between the knowledge they use and the mechanisms which manipulate that knowledge. By changing the nature of the specific knowledge they use, the expert system then becomes able to exercise it's manipulative ability to become expert in a new field. For instance, an expert system designed to carry out medical diagnosis might, by removing the medical knowledge and substituting knowledge pertaining to structural engineering, become expert in structural engineering instead. The programs described in this book are organised in this way.

It is often said that a special characteristic of expert systems is the rule-based organisation of their instructions. Unlike conventional computer programs which proceed in a line-by-line system of execution, expert systems consist of a collection of rules which are not executed sequentially but which 'fire' only as and when appropriate conditions are met. In the literal sense this description is rather misleading because, apart from some very rare machines, all computers step through their code in much the same way. Conceptually, however, the point is a reasonable one to make – but only in the sense that expert systems often behave as if every line of code began with the word IF... . And that, indirectly maybe, is how the programs given in this book work.

Chapter 2

A Statistical Scheme

2.1 Setting up a matrix

But enough, you may well exclaim, of preliminaries. Having been promised an expert system, where is it? How, in short, do you build your own expert system?

Well, it's easy.

First of all define a two dimensional array and think of it as a rectangular matrix. Think of the question you want to ask your expert system and label the columns of the matrix with all of the possible answers. Then think of all the pieces of information which the expert might need in order to arrive at these answers and label the rows of the matrix with these pieces of information.

Take a concrete example, to make it clearer.

Suppose that you'd like your own expert system to tell you if it's going to rain tomorrow. The idea is that you want to be able to sidle up to your computer and ask: Is it going to rain tomorrow? And the computer will pause for thought and reply: Yes or No. To avoid confusion it won't reply: Yes and No.

So, there are two possible answers. Therefore, we want a matrix with two columns. We don't at this stage know how many pieces of information the expert will need in order to answer the question but let's allow, say, ten rows in the matrix. So, in BASIC, DIM E(10,2). In case you hadn't guessed, E stands for Expert.

Graphically, we have Figure 2.1, where, down the left hand side, we've listed the pieces of information available to the system to make a decision about the weather. These are the numbers, say, 1 to 10 and might correspond to questions such as: Is it raining today? Is it cold today? And so on. The letters $a, b, \ldots s, t$ in the array are items which, as yet, we do not have but they will represent the possibility of each outcome being true. They will later be filled out with information relating to the weather. The task for the expert system is to decide which of the two columns, Rain or No Rain Tomorrow, it should select given the answers to the questions 1 to 10.

Fig 2.1 An expert's matrix

Observation	Rain tomorrow	No rain tomorrow
1	a	b
2	c	d
.	.	.
.	.	.
.	.	.
10	s	t

For example, observation 1 may occur when the answer is YES to the question "Is it cold today?"
From numerous observations (by experts) of cold days, there is a 60% chance that it will rain tomorrow. So, *a* will be 60, or 0.6 if you like decimals. In a like manner, we would obtain values of *b, c* and so on, ensuring that we could get a sensible sort of answer based on the observations we make.

Now, as it stands, things might be looking a bit more concrete than they were but, despite that, have we really done anything useful? Well, yes. We've established a *Knowledge Base* and a *Domain of Enquiry* both of which are good phrases to remember next time you feel like waxing eloquent in a local hostelry.

Take the Domain of Enquiry. Well that's what it's all about. Literally. It's the subject matter of the expert system. If something falls within the Domain of Enquiry you can ask your expert system about it and, if it doesn't, you can't. 'Simple as that, really. In this case the Domain of Enquiry is the weather (or, Rain, if you want to restrict things a bit). There's absolutely no point in your asking this expert how you can become a millionaire because such a question would be outside its Domain of Enquiry. There may be other reasons why you can't ask that question but one will do for the moment.

Now consider the Knowledge Base. In this case, it is the array E(10,2). It contains all of the knowledge the expert has on the subject and, in this case, significantly, it's empty. It doesn't know a thing about the weather. Which means that, so far, there's absolutely no point in your asking this expert about the weather either.

As this is so crucial to our main theme, take a look at Figure 2.2

The Domain of Enquiry is the 'field' in which the Expert System is intended to be expert. In this example we have a weather-predicting expert so the Domain of Enquiry is The Weather.

To be expert in this field, the expert system needs a Knowledge Base. That is the information which we give it about the subject of weather. In an ideal world (which, in our case, we do not have) the Knowledge Base would encompass the whole of the Domain of Enquiry i.e. it would know everything there was to know about the subject in hand (the Weather). In practice, it's unlikely to know everything – it will just know a portion. We can represent this by showing the Knowledge Base as being smaller than, but existing within, the Domain of Enquiry.

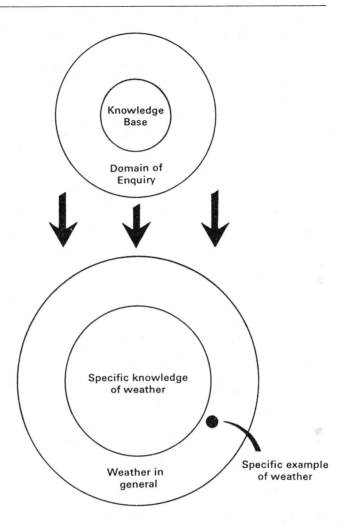

Fig 2.2 Knowledge Base and Domain of Enquiry

When a specific question arises, if asked with any hope of an answer, it must fall within the Domain of Enquiry. However, it may or may not fall exactly within the Knowledge Base on our diagram. Exactly where we place a specific example depends on the extent to which the Knowledge Base within the Expert System encompasses the specific example we produce.

Consider a human expert to whom you turn with a thrusting question concerning the likelihood of rain tomorrow. Most people would be willing to hazard some kind of guess on the matter. But, they have an advantage over the computer to date:

they know what weather is and they can look out of the window to see what today's weather is like – which might give them a clue about tomorrow's weather. Obviously, we want our expert system to do a similar kind of thing.

So, let's distinguish two different kinds of information in the problem. We could call them a number of different things, but let's try Fixed Information and Variable Information.

Fixed Information is what would go in the Knowledge Base. It contains invariable data which, in this case, would be about the weather in general.

Variable information is what wouldn't go in the Knowledge Base. This is specific information relating to the problem in hand. In this case it would be the specific information which would enable the expert to say if it would rain tomorrow or not given that we are asking the question today and not just asking the question about any day in general.

In a way, these two sets of information are like the difference between programs and data. The fixed information is part of the program and the variable information is the data for this specific problem. But, just to make sure that the subject doesn't become too clear-cut, it's worth making it woolly again by pointing out that we might want to alter the fixed information quite often (so it's not really fixed after all) and it might even be as variable as the variable information at times.

This is because most experts change their methods of working as time progresses and we wouldn't want to prevent our expert system from learning as time goes on, would we? In fact, this is often a feature of expert systems.

Anyway, back to the expert on weather. We've just asked if it's going to rain tomorrow and received a reply to the effect that it hasn't a clue. What next?

Well, give it something to work on. Tell it something about the weather. For instance: if it rains today it's more likely to rain tomorrow. This is because rain tends to go in spells. We have wet spells which implies that it will rain tomorrow. That, incidentally, is more or less true. So what we're doing is embodying a bit of human expertise in our expert system.

Suppose we reasoned that, if it's raining today there's a 60 per cent chance of it raining tomorrow. Therefore, by an amazing feat of arithmetic we see that there's a 40 per cent chance of it being dry tomorrow. Further suppose that if it's dry today there's a 55 per cent chance of it being dry tomorrow. By the same feat of calculation there's a 45 per cent chance of it's being wet. Now re-draw our original array with these gems of knowledge built in:

	Rain tomorrow	No rain tomorrow
1. Wet	60	40
2. Dry	45	55

At this point it becomes quite obvious what we should do. The expert system has to print out the statement Rain Tomorrow or the statement No Rain Tomorrow. To decide which, it asks if it is wet today. If it is, it prints out Rain Tomorrow because that's the most likely outcome. If it isn't wet today it can do one of two things depending on how you want to program it.

specifically: –

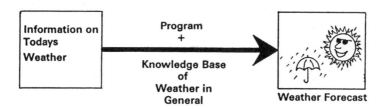

Fig 2.3 Weather forecasting

It can either print out No Rain Tomorrow on the grounds that if it isn't raining it must be dry and, therefore, it's most likely to be dry tomorrow. Or it can specifically ask if it's dry today and, on receiving the answer Yes, proceed from there.

Now, all of this might be concrete but, is it useful?

After all, you can always listen to a weather forecast or, failing that, just wait and see what the weather does. It's not really that important, you might feel.

And, what's more, you probably haven't got much faith in those numbers we put in the matrix (sorry, Knowledge Base) in the first place.

Well, it's fair enough to have some reservations. But consider some aspects of what we've done.

Take those numbers we dreamed up. They are, certainly, a bit *ad hoc*. But suppose they hadn't been. Suppose that they had been precisely determined numbers – what then? Well, it would have made some difference in some circumstances. Say, one of the numbers had been 100 per cent and another 0 per cent. Then our expert could have made a certain decision, not just a likely guess. Further, suppose that we didn't know that rain typically precedes rain or that weather goes in spells. If our expert system could have worked that out for us, then it would have known more than we did originally and might have been better at weather prediction than we are.

Now consider the actual question asked: Is it going to rain tomorrow? Probably rather trivial for the super-smooth expert system with which we intend to impress the world. But it could have been labelled differently providing different variables, different outcomes, and a different field of expertise.

We might have asked: Is Greyhound X going to win in this race? Or: Does my headache denote a hangover?.

Providing that we can contrive to specify some variables, some outcomes, and some method of linking the two, we can tackle a wide variety of problems with our expert system. The trick is simply to have some method, like this, for getting the system organised around the problem to start with.

2.2 Probabilities

In the previous example we thought of an event as being, say, 55 per cent likely to occur; 45 percent likely to occur; 100 per cent likely to occur. There's no particular reason why we shouldn't continue to do that but the use of probabilities has some advantages.

Probabilities are very precise things. They are represented by numbers which range between 0 and 1.

If an event is absolutely certain to occur, then it has a probability of occurrence equal to 1. If an event has no chance whatever of occurring then it has a probability of occurrence equal to 0.

If an event has a fifty:fifty chance of occurring then it has a probability of occurrence equal to 0.5.

All other cases fall somewhere in between.

Consider the cases of 0 and 1. There is a difference between a probability of exactly 1 and a probability which is approximately 1 – so close to 1 that we may as well write it down as 1. If an event has a probability of exactly 1 then it *must* occur. It simply cannot not occur. It may have a probability number associated with it but there is no element of chance involved with it at all. It almost has the force of a causal statement. Consider: Suppose that you happen to have a glass in your hand and that you then leave go of your glass when there's nothing underneath it. In this case it will fall to the ground. That is a certain event and has probability 1 associated with it. It's also a causal statement inasmuch as the falling glass is caused by the releasing of your grasp.

But consider: when you eventually leave that bar in which you had a glass you'll find that everyone else leaves as well. You all, in short, walk out of the public house at the same time with probability 1 – it is a certain event. But this isn't a strictly causal event. It isn't the fact that you, personally, are leaving that causes everyone else to decide that the hostelry holds no further pleasures for them. It is the fact that the barman is closing down for the night and is throwing you all out that is the causal item.

So, if two or more events occur together with probability 1 the relationship between them need not be strictly casual – they might just happen to always go together. But they still always happen together and there's no if or maybe about that.

Now go back into the bar and drop that glass again.

We said it was going to fall to the ground – but we didn't say it was going to actually break. It probably will and, maybe, it will break with probability 0.999999. In fact, to save writing out all those 9's we could say that it will break with probability approximately 1. But this isn't the same as saying it will break with probability exactly 1. If the probability had been exactly 1 then the glass would have broken – and no two ways about it. But as long as this magic figure of 1 is not exactly achieved there will always be some, albeit small, probability that the event won't occur – and the difference could well be an unbroken glass.

The same arguments go for probability 0. A probability 0 event *can't* occur. But an event which has probability of approximately 0 can certainly occur even though it's very rare.

By now, it may have dawned on you that there's no particular reason why we shouldn't have used percentages. 100 per cent likely to occur means that you're quite certain about something. For less certainty, you might be 99.99 per cent certain and so on.

You can use any scale you choose really. You could have a scale from minus five to plus five if you wanted. Or anything. But the reason for labouring the point is to make clear that it's possible to talk about probabilities in a very precise fashion. For our purpose a completely causal event can be described by probability numbers if we want to describe it like that. And the reason for using the usual 0,1 range of probabilities is really to remind ourselves that what we are doing is precise.

Take our statement that "if it rains today then there's a 60 per cent chance of it raining tomorrow." We mean, of course, a probability of occurrence of 0.6 for the event. Now, from this we can deduce that if we watched an infinite number of rainy days we would find that 0.6 of them were followed by another rainy day. There is no if, but, or maybe. In this case, of course, our figure is almost certainly inaccurate but that doesn't render the statement in which it was used meaningless. The meaning was very precise.

Only the figure was wrong. And, if we'd got the figure right, it would not only have been meaningful, it would have been true!

That's the reason for stressing the point.

Imagine yourself holding forth about your own expert system. "It decided," you announce, "that there was a 0.75 probability of World War Three starting on any one day of next week."

"Oh," responds a bored audience. "It isn't sure about it then?"

And they start talking about something more certain. Like the weather, for instance.

It could be absolutely infuriating to have an expert system which could work out something like that and then have it dismissed so lightly. Really sends the blood pressure up, that sort of thing.

So listen to what you said.

You were using a probability measure so, if there's a 0.75 probability of World War Version 3 starting on any one day of next week then the probability of World War 3 not starting on any one day of next week is 1-0.75=0.25. And, for War to hold off right through the week, not occurring on each and every one of its seven days, we have a probability of 0.25 raised to the power of 7 (i.e. 0.25^7). So the probability of a Peaceful Week is 0.000061035.

The probability of not having a Peaceful Week is, therefore, $1-0.25^7 = 0.999938965$. Which is the probability of World War Three breaking out on some day day next week.

This all assumes, of course, that when World War 3 does break out it does so quite independently of anything which might have occurred on previous days but, as it's all computer-controlled nowadays, this doesn't seem to be an unreasonable assumption to make – after all, chips do tend to go faulty in a statistically-independent fashion!

You haven't specified which day of the week it's all going to happen but there would be less than 6 chances in 100,000 that it wouldn't happen at all. So, all in all, everyone could reasonably go out and buy tin helmets on the strength of the information you've just given them.

But the important thing to remember is that you needn't look down on probabilities. You can calculate a lot of exact things with them and make some very exact statements, some of which just might be true.

And, on a more practical note, if you're going to build your own expert system then you won't be inspired to get very far with it if you think that anything with a probability in it is only a vague 'chance' and not really worth considering seriously at all.

More Probabilities

Now, it could be that probabilities are, as it were, an open book to you.

On the other hand, it might be worthwhile, just in case they aren't, mentioning a few basic points about what happens when you have more than one probability.

Some notation might help.

We'll try:

P(A), P(A&B), P(A:B) and define them this way:

P(A) is the probability of event A occurring.
P(A&B) is the probability of both event A and event B occurring.
P(A:B) is the probability of event A occurring given that event B has occurred.

Respectively, we say that:

P(A) is the probability of A
P(A&B) is the joint probability of A and B
P(A:B) is the conditional probability of A given B
They are not different ways of saying the same thing.

Going back to our weather example, we had the matrix (using probabilities, rather than percentages):

	Rain tomorrow	No Rain Tomorrow
1. Wet	0.6	0.4
2. Dry	0.45	0.55

These are *conditional* probabilities. They are the probabilities of particular weather tomorrow *given* today's weather. For instance, there is probability 0.6 of rain tomorrow if there's rain today. That is not the same as either the probability of rain tomorrow, or the *joint* probability of rain tomorrow and rain today. At a first reading it might sound as if they are much the same thing. But they aren't and it's worth sorting the matter out fairly early on otherwise all that stuff about probabilities being precise, exact things tends to be wasted.

First, what's the probability of rain tomorrow?

Note that we haven't said anything about today's weather. It's a single item in isolation of the previous day's weather. Just, in general, will it rain tomorrow? The information we have is that if, on any day, it's wet then the probability of rain tomorrow is 0.6. On the other hand, if it's dry, the probability of rain tomorrow is 0.45. What should we do to get the overall probability of rain tomorrow? Add them up (1.05)? Average them (0.525)?

Take P(R) as the probability of rain tomorrow and use W and D to mean Wet and Dry today respectively. We want to find P(R) and our table gives us P(R:W) and P(R:D) in the first column.

At this stage we introduce a formula:

P(A&B)=P(A:B)P(B)
In words, this says that the probability of both A and B occurring is equal to the probability of A given B, multiplied by the probability of B.

If you think about it you'll find it's fairly reasonable. We want to know about A and B occurring. If B definitely occurs then there is a probability P(A:B) that A also occurs. But B only occurs with probability P(B) so we have to allow for that to get the

19

figure for both A and B occurring. Hence we multiply P(A:B) times P(B) which, as P(B) is no greater than 1, tends to make the answer smaller, allowing for the chance of B not occurring.

So, the probability that it will rain tomorrow and that it rains today is:
$P(R\&W) = P(R:W)P(W)$

i.e. the probability that it will rain tomorrow and today is equal to the probability of rain tomorrow given rain today, times the probability of rain today.

Or: $P(R\&W) = 0.6 \ P(W)$

And, for a dry day today:
$P(R\&D) = P(R:D)P(D)$

Or: $P(R\&D) = 0.45 \ P(D)$

But we wanted P(R), the probability of rain tomorrow. Well, the probability of rain tomorrow is obviously equal to the probability of rain tomorrow and rain today plus the probability of rain tomorrow and a dry day today. So:
$$P(R) = P(R\&W) + P(R\&D)$$
$$= P(R:W)P(W) + P(R:D)P(D)$$
$$= 0.6 \ P(W) + 0.45 \ P(D)$$

At this point we recall that today is either a wet day or a dry day.
So: $P(W) + P(D) = 1$, as it must be one or the other with probability 1.

And we get :

$$P(R) = 0.6 \ P(W) + 0.45 \ (1 - P(W))$$
$$= 0.6 \ P(W) + 0.45 - 0.45 \ P(W)$$
$$= 0.15 \ P(W) + 0.45$$

So, in order to answer the question: what is the probability of rain tomorrow? we need to know the probability of a wet day today.

It is, of course, a question that we can answer easily because we reckon that the probability of rain tomorrow is the same as rain on any other day which means that it's the same as the probability of a wet day today.

That is: $P(R) = P(W)$

So $P(R) = 0.15 \ P(R) + 0.45$
$0.85 \ P(R) = 0.45$
$P(R) = 0.45 \div 0.85$
$= 0.53$ approximately.

Or, more likely than not, it will rain tomorrow as it has done today and will do until the world ends. That's our weather for you.

Note that we couldn't have got this result if P(R) hadn't been the same as P(W). If P(W) had been, say, mist today this wouldn't have been the same as rain tomorrow. Then we'd have had to go to some other source to find out a value for P(W).

The important point to note is that the probability of rain tomorrow isn't sitting in that original table staring at you. Those are *conditional* probabilities, not probabilities of isolated events, and they aren't the same thing at all.

In the course of working all that out we also obtained some *joint* probabilities, P(R&W) and P(R&D), which were 0.6 P(W) and 0.45 P(D), respectively. Now, we know that P(R) = P(W) and that P(D) = 1 − P(W) = 1 − P(R).

So: P(R&W) = 0.6 P(R) = 0.3176 approximately and
    P(R&D) = 0.45 (1 − P(R)) = 0.2117 approximately.

These probabilities are much lower, because we're asking what the probability of rain tomorrow and rain today is (ie. two wet days in succession) and what is the probability of rain tomorrow and a dry day today (ie. two days of alternating weather). This joint probability makes a more exact request for a specific situation. Less is assumed and the chances of getting just what we ask for are so much less.

In all probability, you're fed up with probabilities by now. Certainly they don't make particularly interesting reading owing to a pretty complete absence of plot, corpses and jokes.

There is one more thing to be done in this section though. After that we'll get back to the expert system proper.

On July 16, 1917 no less than 4.65 inches of rain fell in 2.5 hours at Kensington. No less than 8 inches fell in 5 hours near Bridgewater on August 18, 1924. On June 28, 1917, 9.56 inches of rain fell during one day at Bruton, Somerset.

Moving to other parts of the Empire:

In Gibralter on October 25, 1836, 30.11 inches of rain fell in a single day.

In Bagnio in the Philippines on the four days July 14 to 17, 1911 the rainfall was: 35 inches, 29 inches, 17 inches and 8 inches.

All of which goes to show something we haven't built into our expert system yet: the knowledge that sometimes it never rains, it pours.

2.4 More variables

It is a typical day again. It is cold, wet, windy and foggy. You turn up the collar of your threadbare jacket against the elements and light a soggy cigarette to warm yourself about its glow. A raindrop of more than usual size extinguishes the cigarette for you.

Will it, you ask yourself, be like this tomorrow?

Well, of course, it probably will. Anyone could tell you that, for this is England, the land where anything is possible as long as it involves getting rain down the back of one's neck.

But just to indulge a wild fantasy, it has to be admitted that a dry day might occur. So, will it rain tomorrow?

Switch on the expert system to find out. Before switching on, check for any rain water inside the casing. Remember matrix E(10,2)? Well, fill it in as follows:

	1. Rain tomorrow	2. No rain tomorrow
1.Cold	P(Rain:Cold)	P(Dry:Cold)
2.Wet	P(Rain:Wet)	P(Dry:Wet)
3.Windy	P(Rain:Windy)	P(Dry:Windy)
4.Foggy	P(Rain:Fog)	P(Dry:Fog)

Say that you know the conditional probabilities in the matrix and can find them easily. Now if, say, it was Cold today and *not* Wet, Windy or Foggy then you'd be laughing (in a manner of speaking, that is). Because all you'd have to do is to look at the table and see whether the conditional probability of Rain given Cold was greater than the conditional probability of No Rain given Cold and choose whichever was the most likely outcome. Go for the biggest probability.

The question that really arises though is what to do when more than one variable occurs. In this case we have four variables. How will your expert system work out if it will be wet or dry tomorrow?

It may sound a trivial question. After all, if it really is cold, wet, windy and foggy then it sounds as if any idiot could predict rain with a fair degree of certainty. It sounds like a bad spell of weather with more to come. And that, really, is just the point.

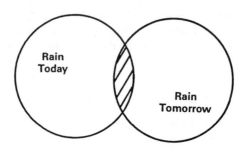

Fig 2.4 Two correlated variables

Figure 2.4 represents two variables. Rain Today and Rain Tomorrow, and the shaded area shows that these two variables are correlated. If we know whether or not we have Rain Today we can judge the probability of Rain Tomorrow by looking at the extent to which these two variables 'overlap'.

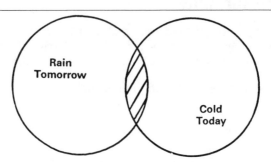

Fig 2.5 Similarly, we can do the same if one of our variables is Cold Today, instead.

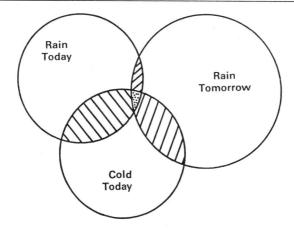

Fig 2.6 The 3 variable case: If we have information on both Rain Today and Cold Today simultaneously the problem becomes much more difficult because the size of the overlap into Rain Tomorrow depends on the overlap that exists between Rain Today and Cold Today i.e. the extent to which these two variables are correlated. This is shown in Figure 2.6

If even an idiot can make a decent guess on the basis of that information then surely your expert system ought to be able to make at least as good a guess.

First, let's think of the variables we have:

It's cold. That sounds like bad weather—but does it mean rain? Actually, it often doesn't. In cold weather the atmosphere can't contain so much water vapour as in warm weather so, if it did rain, there wouldn't be so much water in the sky to come down. In defence of this point you could look at monthly rainfall figures for Great Britain. You'll find that it doesn't rain much more in winter months than it does in summer months—which can be a bit of a surprise if you have strong memories of getting drenched in winter. Probably, you just don't notice warm rain so much as cold rain.

It's wet. Well, weather tends to go in spells, so a wet day could well precede a wet day. Unless, of course, there wasn't any left up there to come down tomorrow. (This latter suggestion is known as Optimism.)

It's windy. This often precedes rain. Warm, moist air being blown into a cold area will rise, cool, and pour water down onto our heads. And movements of air, like this, are just another way of describing a windy day.

It's foggy. Well, if it's foggy it's not likely to be windy, is it? Fog usually arises from still, damp air. It may or may not turn to rain.

So: taking our four variables, what do we have? Nothing, at this stage, very certain. Some, but not all, of the variables point to rain. Certainly, it would be handy if they did all indicate rain with a probability greater than 0.5 because, if they did, we'd have no hesitation in getting our expert system to predict rain. But suppose that instead of Foggy we'd used the variable Sunny. And just suppose that the weather had been:

Cold, Wet, Windy, and Sunny. Now this would be what meteorologists call 'unsettled weather'– but, for our purposes, it's just a nuisance because Sunny tends to indicate a dry day tomorrow whereas all of the other variables tend to indicate rain.

In general, we have a set of pointers and we're alright as long as they all point in the same direction. But we've got problems if, as in Figure 2.7, they don't.

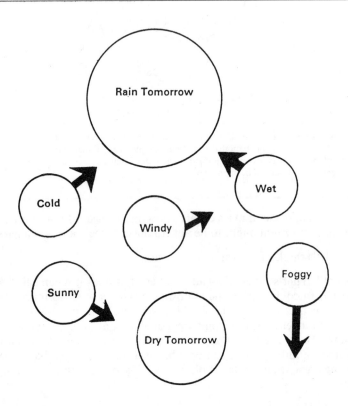

Fig 2.7 Pointers to the Weather

If we have several indicators, we can get our expert to judge the correct outcome easily if all the indicators point in the same direction If they all point in different directions problems arise because we don't know how much reliance to put on any one indicator.

So: what to do about it?

Back to our conditional probabilities and we started off with P(Rain:Rain today) – the probability of Rain given that it's raining today.

But what we've got is:

P(Rain:event X) where the event X is the event that today it is Cold, Wet, Windy and Foggy.

What we want to know is:

P(Rain:Cold & Wet & Windy & Foggy)

and, specifically, we want to know whether it's greater or smaller than:

P(No Rain:Cold & Wet & Windy & Foggy).

Going back to one of the formulae we had before:

P(Rain:event X) = P(Rain & event X)/P(event X)

or:

P(Rain:Cold & Wet & Windy & Foggy) =

$$\frac{\text{P(Rain tomorrow \& Cold today \& Wet today \& Windy today \& Foggy today)}}{\text{P(Cold \& Wet \& Windy \& Foggy)}}$$

Now, at this point, it should have become a little clearer why we spent some time talking about different kinds of probabilities earlier on. It was to make clear that there are different kinds of information which we can have about a situation and different kinds of questions we can ask.

For instance, we started off with statements like: P(Rain:Rain). Which isn't in exactly the same form as the question we've just asked. You can't, in general, take a lot of simple statements about conditional probabilities and turn them straight into one big statement about the probability of one event given the joint occurrence of a lot of other events.

In case you're not convinced, consider an example.

It's misty and it's foggy. The probability of rain the next day given mist today is 0.75, likewise the probability of rain given fog. As it's misty and it's foggy we add the two together and get a probability of rain tomorrow of 1.5 which is obviously wrong. Probabilities can't exceed 1.

But suppose we consider P(A&B), the probability of two events together. Let the first event be rain tomorrow given mist today. Let the second event be rain tomorrow given fog today. Suppose we could say the events are independent of each other then P(A&B) = P(A)P(B) which is equal, in this case, to 0.75 times 0.75 = 0.5625.

Well, that's worse. With both events pointing at rain we've calculated a probability of rain actually less than either pointer by itself!

The answer is, of course, that mist and fog are the same thing. They're both caused by water droplets in the air and the only difference is that fog has larger water droplets than does mist.

So fog and mist are just different words for the same thing and by including both statements we've said nothing extra about the situation at all.

Hence, the probability of rain tomorrow is 0.75 – the same as predicted by either statement.

And it only requires brief thought to see that, in our original table, there was absolutely nothing to indicate this. If we had Mist and Fog as entries on the left-hand side with conditional probabilities next to them we would, effectively, have had the same entry twice – but with nothing to indicate to the expert system that this might be so.

To some extent this problem is going to occur in lots of different ways for other variables because what we've found is a correlation amongst the variables. If they were all independent of each other then life would be easier but, in general, they won't be. Consider Wet & Windy. Now, these two variables certainly don't mean the same thing at all. But if it's wet it's often windy too – they aren't independent. If we had included Sunny then that wouldn't have been independent of Foggy either because when it's one it tends not to be the other.

Happily, there is a way of dealing with this problem. Unhappily, it tends to involve some labour. What you do is this:

1. Think of all the variables you have, say n.

2. Think of all the possible combinations of these variables.
This is the sum 'n pick x' for $x = 0$ to n

i.e.

$n!/((n-0)!0!) + n!/((n-1)!1!) + n!/((n-2)!2!) + ... +$ and so on

In the case of four variables on the weather, we have:

$4!/((4-0)!0!) + 4!/((4-1)!1!) + 4!/((4-2)!2!) + 4!/((4-3)!3!) + 4!/((4-4)!4!)$

which is:

$1 + 4 + 6 + 4 + 1 = 16$

i.e. there are 16 different combinations which could arise with our four Yes/No variables.

The exclamation marks mean 'factorial' as well as being rather like a cry of computational anguish.

3. Make out a new list of variables. This time you list all of those combinations of variables as well as the variables themselves.

4. Assign a probability for each outcome given the occurrence of each of the specific combinations of variables.

5. When you want to use the system you just look to see which combination of variables you have, find that combination in your extended table, and read off the probability for each of the possible outcomes.

6. Having contemplated this you raise an eyebrow, purse your lips, furrow your brow and exclaim: "You must be joking!" (Exclamation mark, not factorial).

Well, yes, sorry about that. But that's how you do it. It is a bit time consuming one does admit...

It would be much easier, of course, if you didn't have so many variables. It's really your own fault for thinking you can just sling anything at a computer simply because it's got a lot of memory.

2.5 Bayes' Theorem

If, however, you do try to make a go of this method you could always confuse yourself further by introducing Bayes' Theorem in your calculation. The Reverend Bayes, as you can guess from his title, devoted his life to the study of things eternal like, for instance, problems in statistics. And his theorem states that:

P(R:X) = P(X:R)P(R)/(P(X:R)P(R) + P(X:not R)P(not R))

In other words, consider R to be the event Rain Tomorrow and X to be a particular combination of events describing today's weather (say: Wet, Windy, Cold and Horrid).

Then, the probability of Rain tomorrow given X today is equal to the probability of X today given that it's going to rain tomorrow times the probability of rain tomorrow, divided by the total probability of X occurring anyway.

If you're not happy about why this should be true consider:

P(R:X) = P(R&X)/P(X) This is a standard result we gave earlier.

So, also P(X:R) = P(X&R)/P(R)

So, P(X&R) = P(X:R)P(R) = P(R:X)P(X)

So, P(R:X) = P(X:R)P(R)/P(X)
           = P(X:R)P(R)/(P(X:R)P(R) + P(X:not R)P(not R))

Now, if you knew P(R:X) you could just enter it in at the start – no trouble. But you might find it easier to find P(X:R) – it depends to some extent on the nature of the question as to which is easier. For the one question you have to provide the probability of rain tomorrow given X today. For the other you have to provide the probability of X today given that you know it's going to rain tomorrow (or, more realistically, the probability of X yesterday for each day that it rained today). You also (just so that you don't feel you're getting on top of the problem) have to give P(X:not R) the probability of X given that it's going to be a dry day today. And you might well feel that this method is even worse than any previous methods.

Which isn't quite true. It's certainly pretty bad if all the events are correlated with each other so that you have to provide probability values for each and every possible combination. But if they are independent then you can calculate an overall P(R:X).

Suppose, for instance, that X is the pair of events Y and Z.

Then: P(X:R) = P(Y&Z:R) = P(Y:R)P(Z:R) a simple multiplication.

But: P(R:X) = P(R:Y&Z) does not equal P(R:Y)P(R:Z). If you don't believe this, figure the two calculations out separately and see what sort of different results you get.

Later (much later, in the second half of this book) there's a program given which uses this method to build an expert system. It works by assuming that all events are, in fact, independent of each other – if they weren't it would run badly. Often, systems are designed which assume independence of the variables just to make life easier. Certainly it eases the problem of that vast number of combinations which must otherwise be considered but often the assumptions of independence are only roughly true. And if there is a lot of intercorrelation among the variables the problem really becomes immense.

If ever you get to the end of this book maybe you ought to come back to this section and think about it all again when you've seen how a system might be implemented using this particular method of working. Or, maybe, when you get to the end you could just sell the book and spend the proceeds on drink. That way you become less likely to care whether or not it's going to rain tomorrow.

Chapter 3

Avoiding Probabilities

By this time a strange unease should have filled your very being. You thought that building an expert system would be easy. In fact, you were more or less promised that it was. You have a computer – why can't that do some of the work for you? What, you ask, is all this talk of probabilities? Why, for instance, do you have to tell the expert the probability of every little outcome in order to get a decision out of it?

Frankly, if you've got to do all this work then you hardly need a computer. You might as well save a bit of time and do it yourself.

And, apart from anything else, if you knew the probabilities associated with each possible set of events you wouldn't need a mechanical expert. The reason you want an expert system is to do things for you which you can't do for yourself. To tell you things which you didn't previously know.

All of which are fair comments, one feels. But, your very own expert system is different to most existing systems in this way:

Most expert systems to date rely on fairly intensive research which, roughly speaking, involves picking the brains of an expert to find out the odds on each and every possible outcome to each and every possible event. The (human) expert knows these odds. People that pick his brains and write the expert system then know the odds too. They then write them into the expert system so that after due programming it knows all the odds too. They then give the expert system to someone who *doesn't* know all of the odds and that person is then duly impressed.

Some expert systems work slightly differently in that the computer picks the expert's brains – but in almost every case the presence of a (human) expert in the subject is assumed.

But consider your case as you build your very own expert system. If you knew everything about the problem you wouldn't need an expert system to tell you about it.

Typically, you don't know all there is to know. And, as you don't know it, you can't program it. And, if you went to all the trouble of finding out everything about the subject in which you required expertise it would then almost seem like a lot of additional trouble to write it into a program instead of just making a mental note about it.

In short, your requirements for an expert system are very different to the requirements of those who have built such systems to date.

You want something that's fairly quick and easy to build, gives good results, and doesn't involve you in taking up a lifetime's study of the subject in which expertise is needed.

So that's what we'll do. As outlined above. Right at the beginning we said that your expert system would be better than anyone else's – or, at least, different. This is largely where the differences start to appear.

3.1 How to make the computer do the hard work

The system now changes. You don't give the machine probabilities anymore – although you do know enough about probabilities to appreciate what it's got to do. You'll just give the machine enough information so that it can work out what to do by itself. It's not only going to have to be an expert system. It's also going to have to be a learning system because it's the machine that's going to have to do the learning, not you. That is what is called Delegation. It's also what is called *Machine Learning* which is another good phrase to remember next time you're down at the local hostelry and feel like impressing the populace.

Anyway, it's also about time that you had a program which you can put on the computer so that you feel that you're getting somewhere.

So what we'll do is this: we'll set up the expert system so that it can have a training session during which it can learn to make a decision on the basis of experience. After it's been trained we let it loose and allow it to make real decisions using its expert judgement. Unless you examine the program carefully, you won't need to know how it came to it's decisions at all. Certainly, you won't have to tell it explicitly, which is what you would have done previously.

Hopefully, this will make you feel a bit more optimistic about the whole business.

3.2 The learning system

The program that we will use is listed in Fig. 3.1 and a flowchart for it is shown in Fig. 3.2.

If you enter this program and run it, what it appears to do is this:

It asks how many variables you have and DIMensions three arrays. One, array RULES, is to hold a judgement rule which it will develop all by itself. Another, array VALUE, is to hold the value of the variables present in a specific case. And array VAR$ is simply to hold the variable's names. It asks for the names of the variables so that it can talk to you sensibly about them. It asks for the names of the two possible outcomes, OUTCOME1$ and OUTCOME2$. It then goes into a loop in which it asks you for the details of specific instances (is this variable the case—Yes or No). Having collected all the details of one example it makes a guess about what the outcome should be and makes a suggestion. If you agree with its opinion you reply Y for Yes and it goes on to another example. If you disagree it modifies its judgement rule slightly and then goes on to another case.

Fig 3.1 A simple learning program

```
10 CLS
20 INPUT "How many variables have you ";VAR
30 DIM VALUE(VAR),RULES(VAR),VAR$(VAR)
40 FOR I=1 TO VAR
50 VALUE(I)=0
60 RULES(I)=0
70 NEXT
80 PRINT "Please name these variables"
90 FOR I=1 TO VAR
100 INPUT "Variable name";VAR$(I)
110 NEXT
120 PRINT "Please name the outcomes"
130 INPUT "Outcome 1 ";OUTCOME1$
140 INPUT "Outcome 2 ";OUTCOME2$
150 PRINT
160 FOR I=1 TO VAR
170 VALUE(I)=0
180 PRINT "Variable ";VAR$(I)
190 INPUT "Is this variable the case [y/n] ";A$
200 IF A$="Y" OR A$="y" THEN: VALUE(I)=1
210 NEXT
220 DECISION=0
230 FOR I=1 TO VAR
240 DECISION=DECISION+VALUE(I)*RULES(I)
250 NEXT
260 PRINT"Outcome is ";:IF DECISION>0 THEN PRINT OUTCOME1$
    ELSE PRINT OUTCOME2$
270 INPUT "Is this right [y/n] ";A$
280 IF A$="Y" OR A$="y" THEN: GOTO 150
290 IF DECISION>0 THEN: FOR I=1 TO VAR:RULES(I)=RULES(I)-VALUE(I): NEXT
    ELSE FOR I=1 TO VAR:RULES(I)=RULES(I)+VALUE(I):NEXT
300 GOTO 150
```

What you should notice is that, gradually, the machine gets better at guessing the correct outcome although how much better it gets depends rather on what you give it to work on.

If, for instance, you're still worrying about the weather and the outcomes are Rain/No Rain then it's hard to see how you could tell if the machine was right or not—unless you're willing to wait until tomorrow to find out! And one entry a day isn't very fast as far as learning speed goes.

A better scheme would be to work from a collection of weather records so that you actually knew what the outcome should be.

On the other hand, you don't have to have that kind of problem. You could invent something rather stricter—like classifying objects, for instance. Suppose you think of an object—it has to belong to to one of two classes. Think of a number of variables which could be associated with it and enter those. The program has to be able to learn which class of object you're thinking of.

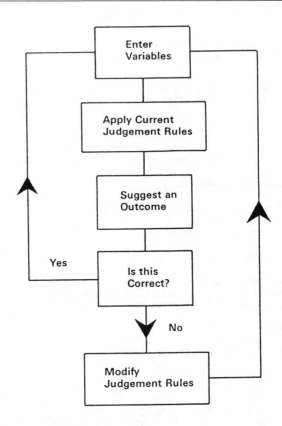

Fig 3.2 A learning process for developing a set of judgement rules.

You may, for instance, want the expert to tell you whether you're thinking of a Bird or a Plane (a typical workaday problem). Your variable list then might contain items such as: Wings, Tail, Beak, Engine, Feathers, Undercarriage, and so on. Now, obviously, everyone knows that as soon as you've specified that it's got an Undercarriage it's pretty likely it's a Plane rather than a Bird and, as you've got to specify all of the variables every time, there's no way of avoiding the Undercarriage question. So the answer is quite certain and the task is to see if the expert system can be as certain about it as you are.

If we choose a Bird or a Plane and run the program, we find that the first time, with you thinking of a Bird, the system guesses that it's a Plane. We tell it that this is wrong. The next time it gets it right. Then we think of a Plane and see if it can get that right. If it can't we tell it what the correct answer is and, eventually, it reaches a stage where it never makes a single mistake. It's become expert in judging between a Bird and a Plane.

Which is fine. It makes us feel as if we're getting somewhere at last. But, before we go out and celebrate, it's worth spending some time checking out just what happened and why it happened. Because what we really want to know is whether or not this program is a universal solution to all of our expert system problems.

First, we outline the variables which are set to "1" whenever they are true:

	Yes?
Wings	1
Tail	1
Beak	1
Engine	0
Feathers	1
Undercarriage	0

In other words, the variable array VALUE, is built up of noughts and ones according as to whether or not the current example (object under examination, call it what you like) has that particular property or not.

In the case of a Bird, VALUE is the array (1,1,1,0,1,0).

In the case of a Plane, VALUE is the array (1,1,0,1,0,1).

Now look into the program and find array RULES which is the rule the expert system has developed for judging between the two possibilities.

By the time the system has stopped making mistakes, we find that the rule array RULES is $(0,0,1,-1,1,-1)$.

We form the variable DECISION by multiplying arrays VALUE and RULES so that:

DECISION=DECISION+VALUE(I)*RULES(I)
for all the values of I (i.e. 1 to 6).

So, if we take VALUE for a Bird, we get $DECISION=0+0+1+0+1+0=2$

Taking VALUE for a Plane we get $DECISION=0+0+0-1+0-1=-2$

So the expert can say it's a Bird if DECISION is positive (greater than nought) and a Plane if DECISION is negative (less than nought).

As this is all we can say about Birds and Planes with these variables it's obvious that the expert system has learned correctly and can't make a mistake any more.

Looking at the rule array again we see that there's nought on the first two variables, Wings and Tail, so these aren't taken into account in making a decision. DECISION starts off with the value 0 and the variables do nothing to change that fact. Which is pretty reasonable because if it's got Wings and a Tail it could be either a Bird or a Plane. That knowledge doesn't tell us anything.

On the other hand, Beak and Feathers each have the value $+1$ and Engine and Undercarriage each have the value -1.

So it seems that the behaviour of the system looks reasonable, at least in this example.

But, at this stage, it might look as if we've done something very different from when we talked of probabilities. Have we?

It's fairly easy to check. We can write out the table again and fill in the conditional probabilities as before:

	Bird		Plane
P(Bird:Wings)	0.5	P(Plane:Wings)	0.5
P(Bird:Tail)	0.5	P(Plane:Tail)	0.5
P(Bird:Beak)	1.0	P(Plane:Beak)	0.0
P(Bird:Engine)	0.0	P(Plane:Engine)	1.0
P(Bird:Feathers)	1.0	P(Plane:Feathers)	0.0
P(Bird:Undercarriage)	0.0	P(Plane:Undercarriage)	1.0

If it's got Wings or a Tail the table tells us nothing about whether or not it's a Bird or a Plane – the odds are equal both ways – but it has to be one or the other. The other four variables tell us that it's either a Bird or a Plane, but not both, and the probabilities associated with that are 1 and 0 to denote certain events. In terms of a diagram, take a look at Figure 3.3.

In this example, if it's got a Beak then it must have Feathers and it can't have Engine or Undercarriage. So it's a Bird with probability 1. If it's got an Engine then it must have an Undercarriage and it can't have a Beak or Feathers. So it must be a Plane with probability 1. There is no possibility of making a mistake once we know these variables.

And that is just what our expert system has done – i.e. it has developed a rule so that there is no possibility of making a mistake. Which is in line with events which occur with probability 1.

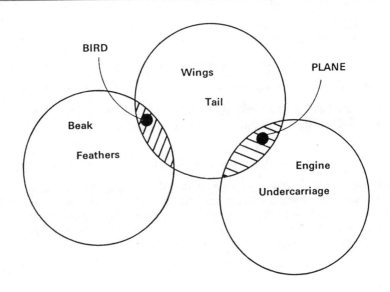

Fig 3.3 A Bird has Wings, Tail, Beak and Feathers. A Plane has Wings, Tail, Engine and Undercarriage.

3.3 Other types of data

In the previous section we concentrated on cases in which the expert system worked on a simple yes/no dichotomy. It just wanted to know if a given feature was present or absent and scored either 1 or 0 accordingly.

But note: it used 1 and 0 – not the words Yes and No. So, as it's using numbers, could it use any numbers? The answer is Yes. It would make no difference at all to its working.

Which is Good News. Consider the weather again. When we started off, we simply considered whether or not it was Cold, Wet, Windy or Foggy.

Now, if you glance at a weather report for yesterday you'll see that you could have had the temperature (maximum and minimum) measured in degrees, the rainfall measured in millimetres, the average wind speed measured in miles per hour, and the visibility measured in miles (well, millimetres in England). All of these items would surely give us much more information about the weather than simple yes/no indicators. We would instinctively tend to feel that we were losing something if we disregarded all of this potentially useful data.

So we don't disregard it. Instead of having the expert ask if a given variable has occurred we could have it print the name of each variable and take in a numeric value by way of response. So we could give the temperature in degrees, the rainfall in millimetres, the visibility in miles, and so on.

And, if we wanted to include a simple yes/no item – such as Thunderstorms Yes/No – we can continue to do so by replying, say, 1 for the presence of that feature and 0 for its absence.

The program will then proceed as before but might, hopefully, give better results because we're giving it better information.

However, to make it clearer as to what's happening most of the examples that follow will use discrete, dichotomous (Yes/No), data – but remember, you could have continuous variables just as easily, and in some cases they might be better.

On the other hand, we can't do this with the outcomes.

It can only choose between different categories of outcome. It can't produce an answer which says exactly how much rainfall it thinks there will be tomorrow – it can only say whether or not it thinks there will be rainfall.

This doesn't mean that we can't make a rough attempt at getting it to be more specific. We could decide that there will be rainfall falling, as it were, into five categories:

Rainfall Categories:

No rain	Less than 0.5″	0.5″ to 1″	1″ to 1.5″	Over 1.5″
1	2	3	4	5
Dry	Wet	Wetter	Really Wet	Horrid

In this case our expert system could, with five outcomes, say something a bit more sensible about the likely weather. And shortly we'll be seeing how to devise a system with this number of outcomes.

This doesn't mean that a system could not be devised to try to give exact numeric answers rather than simple categories. If we wanted to we could try, say, developing a multiple regression equation for rainfall based on a large number of input variables. This would give an exact estimate (exact estimates are not necessarily correct predictions) of tomorrow's rainfall.

The problem is that, although this system might work for predicting rainfall, it couldn't easily be modified to be expert in any other field. How, for instance, would it work out if that was a Bird or a Plane? (or, for that matter, a Glider?)

The object of building your own expert system is to produce something which can become reasonably expert in a number of different fields. A sort of general-purpose device which you could apply to something that interests you. And, that being the case, there's no point in enabling you to predict the weather if what you really want to do is diagnose your own medical symptoms so that you can be a successful brain surgeon, or some such.

3.4 The judgement rule

Maybe you've now set up the learning system and found that it does seem to, more or less, work. Fine, you say. But, exactly, why does it work? What's it doing and can it be made to do it any better?

Well, consider the idea of *Description Space* for, not only is it a useful thing to consider, it's also pretty impressive to be able to talk knowledgeably about other kinds of space than the boring old three-dimensional kind that you see before you.

To make it easy though, we'll start off by assuming that you're sitting at your desk which, conveniently, has a two dimensional top spread out before you in normal common-or-garden space.

Also, you have two sets of objects – pencils and paperclips say – which we can use to illustrate some points.

Now suppose that you want to get your heap of pencils and paperclips and divide them into two heaps – one containing only pencils and the other containing only paperclips. This is easy. Even the simplest amongst our midst can achieve this task – all you have to do is take each object in turn, look at it, say "Is this a pencil or a paperclip?" and place it in one or other of the heaps according to the answer you give yourself. It is as easy in fact as looking at an object and wondering if it's a Bird or a Plane – and categorising it depending on which it is. The point is that the problem of classifying the object is trivial if the description of that object coincides neatly with the criteria by which we want to carry out the classification.

But suppose that, for some reason, when you looked at the object you couldn't immediately tell if it was a Bird or a Plane, or a pencil or a paperclip? Then the problem is definitely non-trivial and you have to think of some other method of passing judgement. And this is exactly the position that the computer is in – it can't see the big difference, even if it's obvious to you, so it has to get a little more subtle.

So, now get the pencils and the paperclips and spread them out on the desk. Place the pencils on the left and the paperclips on the right. Now, ignoring the fact that you can identify pencils and paperclips at a glance, how would you decide which was which?

Well it's easy. All you have to do is to draw a line down the middle of the desk so that all of the pencils are on the left of the line and all of the paperclips are on the right. Now you can classify the two sets of objects simply by measuring their position along the desk.

And that, roughly is what the computer is doing. Except that it's got to work a little harder than you because the objects haven't been laid out neatly in real space. They've been laid out in a particular description space—which isn't really very different.

Go back to the Bird/Plane example now and suppose that two items of information are available. Does the object Fly? And, does the object have Feathers?

Now clear your desk and write 'Flies' along the length of the desk top and 'Feathers' along the depth of the desk top as in Fig.3.4. If an object can fly then it's placed to the right of the desk, and to the left if it can't. If an object has Feathers it's placed at the back of the desk, and to the front if it can't.

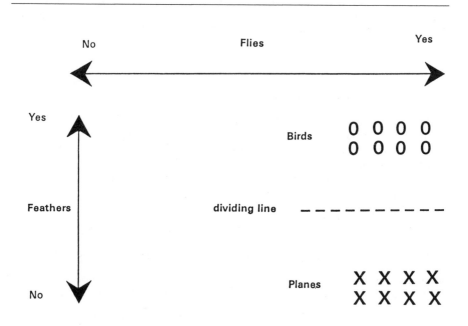

Fig 3.4   A Description space that consists of Two Dimensions specified as 'Flies' and 'Feathers'. Planes can Fly but have no Feathers. Birds can Fly and do have Feathers.

Obviously, if you had a Bird in your hand (!) you would place it at the back and to the right. If it were a Plane, then you'd place it at the front and to the right. And, if you wanted to know whether an object was a Bird or a Plane—without being specifically told what it was—you could answer accurately every time simply by looking to see which quarter of the desk it was on.

You could make a judgement simply by drawing a line between the two heaps of objects and seeing which side of the line any object fell.

And it wouldn't have to be simply Yes/No items such as Feathers/No Feathers. You could, if you wanted, consider a bit of weather forecasting and put a scale along the desk top to denote rainfall figures, say.

If you throw away the desk, you simply have any number and type of objects hanging there in Description Space. It isn't a space defined by the desk anymore. And, really, it isn't anything to do with normal three dimensional space anymore. It's a brand new type of space which is defined solely by the variables you're using – one axis to each variable. And the values on these variables that any object possesses uniquely define its position in this description space. Unfortunately, we can't draw a picture for you!

Just to illustrate the idea in three dimensions, suppose you were out walking in the garden one fine summer's evening (we do get fine summer evenings occasionally). Suppose that you see two clouds of midges buzzing around in the sunlight. One cloud of midges is made up of Big Midges and the other of Little Midges and you decide, perversely, to try to separate the two. One way which might work would be to get the biggest sheet of paper in the world and place it between the two clouds of midges.

This might work but, before you try it, the only reason for giving this example is to show that you can have two groups of objects which are defined by reference to three dimensions (the physical position of each midge) and that you could, in theory, separate them by placing a surface between them.

In fact, once you've moved into description space, the objects can be defined in terms of any number of dimensions. If you have one dimension for each measured variable then a set of objects defined in terms of ten variables exist in ten-dimensional description space. But the idea about placing a surface between them is just the same – you can have a ten dimensional surface for your ten variables and each object can be classified according to which side of the surface it falls.

Incidentally, the equation of a surface in n dimensions is $y = b_1 x_1 + b_2 x_2 + ... + b_n x_n$ where the x_i represent 'position' measurements on the n axes and the b_i are constants.

So the desk top would have the equation, in two dimensions, $y = b_1 x_1 + b_2 x_2$

By specifying the x_i for a new object we can calculate y for that object and we could use the value of y to say on which half of the surface the object occurred.

And that is what the learning program does. It takes all of the x_i we can give it by way of examples and calculates some values for the b_i so that, once it's working properly, it gets a value of y which uniquely determines which group an object should belong to.

The way you can think of it is as a process of trial and error. You present the program with an object and values for its variables. Initially, the program has a surface which is lying around just anywhere and it looks to see which side of the surface your object falls and decides accordingly. It may, by chance, be right. But if it's wrong, it nudges the position of the surface around a bit in description space using the values you gave it. It then has another go with a new object, maybe doing a bit more nudging of the surface. Then again, a bit more nudging, again... And so on, until it has the surface positioned so that it will always come up with the right answers – if, in fact, it's possible to do so.

Having given this explanation you might well wonder if there's a 'best' way of using this particular method.

Would it, for instance, be better to adjust the position of the surface in some way when the computer guessed right as well as when it guessed wrong?

The simple answer is that it all depends on the type of problem you give it – but not in a simple way. If you have some data to present to your expert system then the following points are worth bearing in mind:

If there's only a finite number of possible examples that can occur you'll get the best results by giving the expert all of these possible values to learn from.

It may take a while to get the surface (the judgement rule) into the correct position – one showing of each example often won't do. So you may need to present all of the examples a number of times.

It's difficult to say beforehand exactly how many goes the system will need to get things right – so you should work pragmatically (which means you suck it and see). Give the expert a set of examples and let it have one go at them and count how many mistakes it makes. Then let it have another go and count the mistakes. Carry on like this until either it's not making any mistakes any more or until it's not improving any more.

If you want it to work on examples which you do not, as yet, have (like, for instance, predicting the weather at some future date) then try to make sure that the examples you give it to learn from are as much like the ones it will eventually get as is possible. This may sound obvious – but if you train it on one thing it may not necessarily be able to use the same rules on other, rather different, data.

There is one point you might be wondering about – if expert systems are to replace human experts by embodying human expertise, how is it that the system worked out a set of rules all by itself? It seems almost as if it didn't need any human help at all. The answer is that you did, maybe without realising it, give it quite a lot of very human knowledge. What you gave it was the initial knowledge of which object was which – it was only because you, the user, were able to judge the difference between a Bird a Plane that enabled the program to learn at all.

3.5 Building a rule

Once you've realised that all the learning system does is to find the equation of a surface in n-dimensional description space, such that this surface reasonably well separates two groups of objects, you might well think that it's possible to do something rather better.

After all, the learning system finds its surface in an apparently rough and ready way and needs, often, fairly lengthy training. Why not, therefore, calculate a really good set of values for a surface and give those values to the expert system from square one? That way there's no training needed and, in cases where it's rather hard to judge between objects, you would at least know that the best possible surface was being used.

Well, without wanting to put a damper on any enthusiasm it's only fair to point out that the subject of discrimination is a rather hard one. Incidentally, some people refer to the subject as 'discrimination' others as 'classification' but they mean the same thing. And, typically, in books on multivariate analysis (multivariate = lots of variables) you'll find a chapter or two on the problem.

Consider again the problem of the two clouds of midges which you want to separate – this is fine as long as the two clouds are reasonably far apart, but if they aren't not only is the learning system likely to make mistakes but almost any system will make mistakes because there may not be any position in which a surface could be placed to separate the two groups.

But what could be done is to calculate the exact centre of each group, draw a line between the two centres, and then classify each individual item according to which side of the line's centre point it fell. This, in fact, is the basis of most methods of discrimination. In many ways it's better to do this than to rely on the learning system because the learning system relies heavily on outlying values when deciding the final position of its surface. That is to say, it only alters its surface when it makes a mistake and, towards the end of the process, it only makes mistakes when it's nearly in the right position anyway. So, if you think of the two clouds of midges, the surface is being moved around at the whim of a very few midges right on the edge of the cloud – and these might not be very representative of the position of the midges as a whole. And it's just the same with the objects in description space. Outlying objects may not be representative and might give some unwanted results.

The situation that we have is a problem of classifying objects in an N-dimensional description space so we could represent the N dimensions by the variable VAR because each dimension will represent one variable. Then we start by reserving space for the VAR variables and then find the examples. Suppose we have N1 examples of the first kind and N2 of the second kind :

```
10 REM N1 examples of the first kind and N2 of the second kind :
20 INPUT "N1 = ";N1
30 INPUT "N2 = ";N2
40 INPUT "Number of variables = ";VAR
50 DIM MEAN1(VAR),MEAN2(VAR)
```

Then, we calculate the average or "mean" values of each of the VAR variables of the first kind and store them in the array MEAN1 :

```
60 REM Calculate average of N1 values :
70 FOR I=1 TO VAR
80 MEAN1(I)=0
90 NEXT
100 FOR I=1 TO N1
110 FOR J=1 TO VAR
120 INPUT "Variable = ";VALUE
130 MEAN1(J)=MEAN1(J)+VALUE/N1
140 NEXT: NEXT
```

where VALUE is the value of variable J for example I

Do the same for MEAN2 on the N2 examples of the second kind and you then have the average values or "means" for each of the two kinds in the two arrays MEAN1 and MEAN2.

```
150 REM Calculate average of N2 values :
160 FOR I=1 TO VAR
170 MEAN2(I)=0
180 NEXT
190 FOR I=1 TO N2
200 FOR J=1 TO VAR
210 INPUT "Variable = ";VALUE
220 MEAN2(J)=MEAN2(J)+VALUE/N2
230 NEXT: NEXT
```

Now, try to classify another object using these means. Suppose that you have the values of the variables of this object in array VALUE. Don't forget to DIM VALUE(VAR).

The 'distance' of the new object from the two means can now be calculated as DISTANCE1 and DISTANCE2:-

```
240 REM Calculate distance of VALUE(J) from MEAN1, MEAN2 :
250 DIM VALUE(VAR)
260 DISTANCE1=0:DISTANCE2=0
270 FOR J=1 TO VAR
280 INPUT VALUE(J)
290 DISTANCE1=DISTANCE1+VALUE(J)*MEAN1(J)
300 DISTANCE2=DISTANCE2+VALUE(J)*MEAN2(J)
310 NEXT
```

Alternatively, you could calculate the difference between the means and store them in a new array MID to denote the mid-point.

```
320 REM Alternative method of working :
330 DIM MID(VAR)
340 FOR J=1 TO VAR
350 MID(J)=0
360 NEXT
370 FOR J=1 TO VAR
380 MID(J)=MEAN1(J)-MEAN2(J)
390 NEXT
```

Then you could simply calculate DECISION from array MID (DIM'd as MID(VAR)) and array VALUE and classify the object depending on whether or not DECISION was greater than or less than zero.

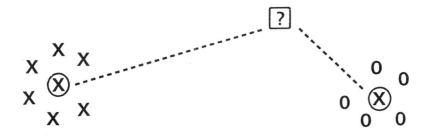

Fig 3.5 Measuring the distance to the nearest mean

```
400 DECISION=0
410 FOR I=1 TO VAR
420 DECISION=DECISION+VALUE(I)*MID(I)
430 NEXT
```

At which point it becomes fairly plain that this is, in terms of code, very similar to the method used by the learning system.

In fact it's possible to modify the learning system so that it turns into this 'nearest mean' method.

Instead of adjusting the decision rule only when a mistake is made, give the system an example and tell it which class the example belongs to. Then alter the decision rule so that it constantly holds the latest value for the difference between the two sets of mean values.

For instance, if there have been N1 examples from Class One so far and you then provide another Class One example,

```
440 REM Alternative method of working :
450 FOR J=1 TO VAR
460 MEAN1(J)=MEAN1(J)*N1+VALUE(J))/(N1+1)
470 NEXT
```

where the array VALUE holds the values for the new object.

This way MEAN1 is constantly updated with the latest estimates of the mean value for that group.

And, using the latest values in MEAN1 and MEAN2, it's possible to have the latest values for the decision rule, say

```
480 REM Establish a decision rule :
490 FOR J=1 TO VAR
500 RULES(J)=MEAN1(J)-MEAN2(J)
510 NEXT
```

and then to make subsequent decisions according as to whether DECISION is greater than or less than zero with:

```
520 REM Use this rule to form DECISION :
530 DECISION=0
540 FOR J=1 TO VAR
550 DECISION=DECISION+VALUE(J)*RULES(J)
560 NEXT
```

There are plenty of other ways of constructing decision rules which could be used but they all depend on a more intricate knowledge of the variables being used. In the meantime, if you want to know which of these two methods is best – the learning algorithm or the nearest mean approach – the best way is to try them and see. There isn't a general answer because so much depends on the exact nature of the variables which you, personally, choose to give the system.

3.6 Prior probabilities

But there is one refinement to the nearest mean approach which you might try. And this occurs in the case where you know for sure that one outcome is more likely than another, irrespective of the values of the variables. This is known as the prior probability of each outcome and if Outcome One was always three times more likely to occur than Outcome Two, then P(Outcome One)=0.75 and P(Outcome Two)=0.25. What you could do in this case is to make a decision which wasn't quite based on the nearest mean.

Consider: to make a decision based on the nearest mean with the array RULES holding the difference between the two means you would simply consider whether the calculated DECISION was greater than or less than zero. But maybe, if DECISION turned out to be approximately zero for some example and you knew that Class One, say, was much more likely than Class Two then you might decide to go for Class One even if the calculated value of DECISION tended to suggest the opposite.

In programming terms it simply amounts to testing for DECISION greater than some value C (say) and whereas, normally, C=0 it might improve matters a bit if C had some other value.

The difficulty lies in specifying a really good value for C other than zero. If you know enough about the data you're working with and are a competent mathematician it's possible to find a value which enables you to say some fairly definite things about how the system will behave. But if you don't and you aren't, then it's back to experimenting (which isn't a bad idea anyway) and the only real warning that needs to be given is that if you don't have enough typical examples to test the system on then you'll never really know how it's likely to work in practice at all and it would be better to avoid any complications.

3.7 Expanding your options

So, there you are, staring up at the sky. All around you people are crying out: "Is it a Bird? Is it a Plane?". You reach for your expert system and key in a few well-chosen variables and, in seconds, you make an authoritative pronouncement. "Wrong!" the people exclaim in tones of malicious glee. "It's a Glider".

It makes you feel every bit as bad as do your weather forecasts. Turning to your finely-wrought expert system it predicts Rain for you. Or, maybe, it predicts a dry day. But either way, as you grope your way around in an impenetrable fog the following day you feel kind of let down. Fog, you suppose, is kind of wet. But not completely wet like rain. And it's also kind of dry. What fog really is, you muse, is Fog. And nothing else.

And, somehow, you feel cheated that your expert system should have failed to allow for other outcomes.

In general, you want your expert system to be able to give any number of different outcomes. You might rest content with having to specify these outcomes in advance – but you still want more outcomes than just two, which is all we've had so far.

43

There are, of course, lots of ways of building an expert system so that you can have a variety of outcomes. But, for the time being, we'll just consider an extension of the system we've dealt with so far.

Recall that we had a rule for making decisions. It was one rule and the expert system made a decision – effectively, a Yes or No decision – on the basis of that one rule. What we'll do now is provide the system with a general number of rules so that it can pronounce on a general number of possible outcomes. To do this we draw up a two-dimensional array to keep the rules in, and this array will look very much like the rectangular matrix in which we first put our probabilities.

Call the array RULES(VAR,OUTCOMES) – the rules for VAR variables, with OUTCOMES outcomes.

And we will use the Bird/Plane example again:

	Bird	Plane
Wings	0	0
Tail	0	0
Beak	0	0
Engine	0	0
Feathers	0	0
Undercarriage	0	0

For the moment, we'll forget about Gliders and, with 6 variables, we have RULES(6,2), so OUTCOMES=2 outcomes.

The method of working is this:

Each column of the array RULES contains a rule which is used to indicate how strongly the expert system believes in the outcome corresponding to that column. The strength of the belief is measured by calculating DECISION, as before, using array VALUE which contains the values of the variables being considered at the moment.

So: for outcome J (J=1 or 2) we calculate DECISION as:

DECISION = DECISION + RULES(I,J)*VALUE(I) for I=1 to 6

You notice that, to start with, all RULES(I,J)=0 so, obviously, all DECISION=0. In other words both beliefs are equally strong (or weak) at this stage.

Now, depending on how you want to run things, you either tell the expert which group the array VALUE belongs to, or you let it guess and, if it's wrong, you let it take the following action:

If VALUE belongs to outcome Bird then we add the VALUE(I) values into the Bird column and subtract them from the Plane column. If VALUE belonged to Plane we would add the VALUE(I) values to Plane and subtract them from Bird. This is what it looks like after adding the 'Bird' values:

	VALUE(I) Bird	VALUE(I) Plane	RULES(I,1) Bird	RULES(I,2) Plane
Wings	1	1	1	− 1
Tail	1	1	1	− 1
Beak	1	0	1	− 1
Engine	0	1	0	0
Feathers	1	0	1	− 1
Undercarriage	0	1	0	0

So far, we've presented a VALUE for Bird to the array RULES. It couldn't make a decision because all of the DECISION were identical. So it added VALUE(I) to the Bird column and subtracted it from the Plane column. Now, if it gets a Bird again, it can make an accurate decision because DECISION will evaluate as +4 using RULES(I,1) and as −4 using RULES(I,2). So all the expert has to do is to select the column of rules which gives the biggest value to DECISION.

But, if we now give the expert a VALUE(I) for Plane we find it will still select Bird as the most likely outcome as, using RULES(I,1) gives DECISION a value of +2 and, using RULES(I,2) gives DECISION a value of −2.

So, our amazing expert system can't even tell the difference between a Bird and a Plane yet.

But add VALUE for Plane into the Plane column and subtract VALUE for Plane from the Bird column, and we get:

	RULES(I,1)	RULES(I,2)
	Bird	Plane
Wings	0	0
Tail	0	0
Beak	1	−1
Engine	−1	1
Feathers	1	−1
Undercarriage	−1	1

Now, if we present it with the VALUE(I) values for Plane, the Plane column gives DECISION a value of −2 and the Bird column gives DECISION a value of +2.

So, it will choose the outcome: Plane. Correctly.

And, if you re-check with VALUE(I) for Bird you'll find that this gives +2 on the Bird column and −2 on the Plane column.

So the expert system now works every bit as well as it did before.

In fact, if you check back, you'll find that it's doing just the same thing as it was doing before when we only had a one-dimensional rule array−so you might, rather cynically, think that this has been a lot of effort for nothing.

And if you just want to decide between a Bird and a Plane, it certainly was a lot of effort for nothing.

But, bring back that Glider and add another column to RULES(I,J) to allow for it. You'd proceed just as we have done with more than two options. You calculate the values of DECISION for each column and choose that column which gives the maximum value of DECISION. In the event of a mistake, or a tie, you tell the system which column it should have chosen. The system then adds the VALUE(I) values it's working with to the correct column and subtracts them from any other column which gave a value of DECISION greater than, or equal to, the column it should have chosen.

If you like, it gives a lift to the correct outcome's rule and pushes down the values of the other outcomes' rules to get them out of the way of the correct one.

45

Suppose we'd had a Glider. A Glider, of course, is like a Plane but it doesn't have an Engine or Undercarriage.

Now, on the first guess, given a Bird, all the RULES(I,J)=0 so it might have chosen Glider as well as the other two options. So the third, Glider, column is pushed down in the same way as the Plane column.

On the second try we gave it a Plane – and it guessed a Bird. So we added VALUE(I) for Plane to the second column and subtracted VALUE(I) for Plane from the first column. But now that we have a third, Glider, column which so far is equal to the Plane column we also have to subtract the VALUE(I) from the Glider column. This gives:

	RULES(I,1) Bird	RULES(I,2) Plane	RULES(I,3) Glider
Wings	0	0	−2
Tail	0	0	−2
Beak	1	−1	−1
Engine	−1	1	−1
Feathers	1	−1	−1
Undercarriage	−1	1	−1

Now, obviously, like this it's never going to select Glider because with every value in column 3 being negative there will always be one of the other rules which gives a bigger value of DECISION. But give it a Glider anyway.

	VALUE(I) Glider	RULES(I,3) Glider
Wings	1	−1
Tail	1	−1
Beak	0	−1
Engine	0	−1
Feathers	0	−1
Undercarriage	0	−1

We don't need to show the Bird and Plane columns anymore because everytime a Glider turns up and the expert fails to guess what it is the same values are subtracted from both Bird and Plane – minus one from the Wings and Tail rules. This won't affect the system's ability to guess between a Bird and a Plane at all. But, gradually, adding +1 to Wings and Tail in Glider will pull up the values there until when a Glider arrives RULES(I,3) will give the maximum value of DECISION and a correct choice will be made every time.

By that time RULES(I,J) will look like this:

	RULES(I,1) Bird	RULES(I,2) Plane	RULES(I,3) Glider
Wings	−1	−1	0
Tail	−1	−1	0
Beak	1	−1	−1
Engine	−1	1	−1
Feathers	1	−1	−1
Undercarriage	−1	1	−1

You can check for yourself that this will now choose correctly between the three alternatives. It's learned correctly and it won't make any more mistakes.

And, what's more, you could have had *millions* of different outcomes and *millions* of different variables and it would still have kept on churning the numbers around until it found something like a correct set of rules for choosing an outcome from a particular set of variables.

3.8 Can it make a mistake?

So far so good. But what are the odds on the thing going wrong – or never learning the correct outcomes adequately?

Well, the odds are pretty difficult to give in terms of exact probabilities because it depends so much on what type of problem you set the expert.

The method all depends on the concept of *Linear Separability* and this is another good phrase to remember.

"Of course," you pronounce as you lean casually against the bar of your choosing, "it works perfectly, does my Expert System, once it's built up its Knowledge Base." At this point you might try giving a thoughtful suck at your pipe, for effect, and add: "As long as it's working on a problem that's Linearly Separable, of course." At this point you might try a deprecating laugh and exclaim: "But show me a problem that isn't!"

This show of jargon should daunt all but your severest critics and will easily make up for the fact that your expert system doesn't always, as it were, work.

It's simply back to our clouds of midges. As long as you can draw a line or place a surface between the two groups this expert system will learn to distinguish between them. If you can't, it won't. It's a simple as that.

Consider, though, the example of the red and blue garden railings.

You have a garden with a line of railings down the side of it. They alternate: a red one, a blue one, a red one, a blue one (you'll soon get the hang of it). Are these railings linearly separable? Can you distinguish between the red ones and the blue ones by placing a surface between them?

Well, it depends. If you measure them (or describe them) in terms of distance down the garden, you can't. Suppose you did so describe them. You notice that ten feet down the garden is a red railing. Twelve feet down the garden is the next railing and it's blue. So you place a surface eleven feet down the garden between the two railings. Obviously, it distinguishes between those two railings – one red and one blue – but it fails to distinguish between all of the other railings both this side of the surface and the other side.

The railings, as you've described them, are not linearly separable.

If, however, you went down the garden and moved each red railing a little to the left and each blue railing a little to the right then you could easily place a surface between them simply by placing your surface along the original line of the railings. Then, they'd still be the same railings but they would, now, be linearly separable.

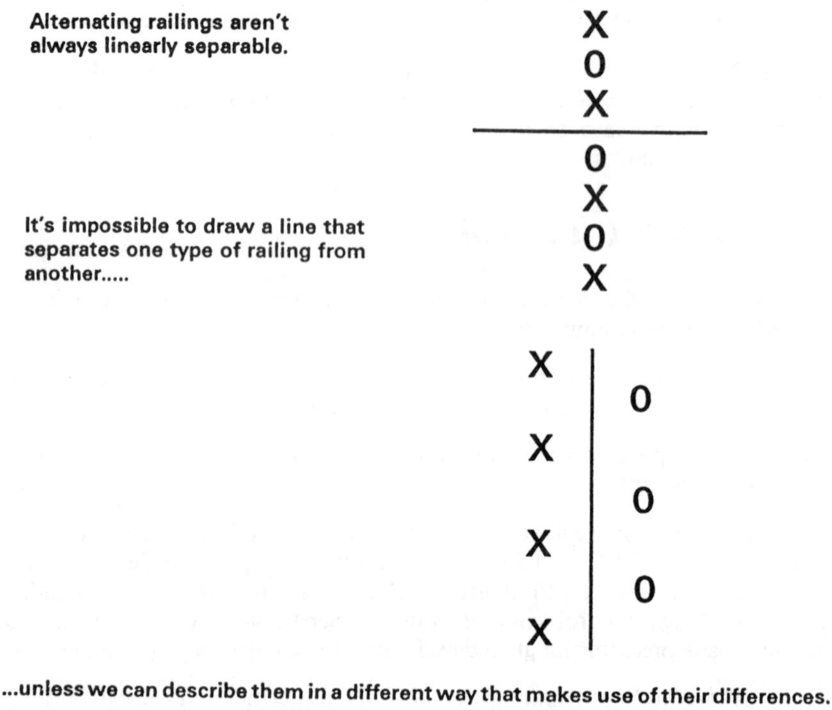

Alternating railings aren't
always linearly separable.

X
O
X
———————
O
X
O
X

It's impossible to draw a line that
separates one type of railing from
another.....

X | O
X | O
X | O
X | O

...unless we can describe them in a different way that makes use of their differences.

Fig 3.6   The alternate garden railings problem

Alternatively, you could stop describing them in terms of where they were in the garden and simply number them in order. As they alternate, first one and then the other, it's obvious that the even numbered railings will be one colour and the odd numbered railings another colour. So, if you described all of the railings in this way they would be linearly separable and our expert system could learn to tell which was a red railing and which was a blue railing.

The point is: that the railings haven't changed. You haven't even moved them about the garden. You've simply described them differently.

That's the essence of the matter. You must try to choose variables which look as if they're going to enable the expert system to distinguish between the various outcomes. Not a very subtle point to make, to be honest, because you'll naturally tend to do this anyway. After all, if you want your expert system to say whether or not it's going to rain tomorrow you're hardly likely to give it, say, the football results to work on. Giving a knowledge of today's football results won't help it predict tomorrow's weather so you aren't making the problem linearly separable by doing so.

(One might concede that the football results say something about today's weather, from which something might be deduced about tomorrow's weather, but one would hardly expect a clear-cut answer.)

Apart from the nature of the problem itself (are the cases linearly separable?) there is the matter of how long the expert system will take to learn a decent set of rules.

The best way is to give it all possible examples until it stops making mistakes if the number of possibilities is fairly small. If there's an enormous number of possibilities then you at least need to give it a couple of examples for each possible outcome and keep an eye in its operation until it seems to have settled a bit.

The program in Figure 3.7 works by using the methods we've described so far – but it's worth running through it just to make sure that nothing's wrong.

First, it wants to know how many variables are to be considered in the decision-making process and how many outcomes there can be.

These are the values VAR and OUTCOMES. Knowing these values the arrays can be DIMensioned. We have: VALUE(VAR) for holding the values of the current variables; VAR$(VAR) for holding the variable names; OUTCOMES$ (OUTCOMES) for holding the names of the outcomes: RULES(VAR,OUTCOMES) for holding the decision rules of the VAR variables for the OUTCOMES possible outcomes; and DECISION(OUTCOMES) for holding the values calculated for a given VALUE(I) using RULES(I,J) for the OUTCOMES possible outcomes.

The names of the variables and outcomes are entered so that they can be referred to by name.

At line 150 a training session begins. Values for VALUE(I) are entered and, using RULES(I,J), all of the OUTCOMES values of DECISION(J) are calculated.

Array DECISION is searched for its largest value and a guess is made that this largest DECISION(I)=DECISION(BEST) points to the correct outcome, OUTCOMES$(BEST).

If this is the correct outcome but the system isn't yet perfect the program returns to line 150 to continue training with another example.

If it isn't the correct outcome, all of the possible outcomes are displayed and you are asked to say which was the correct outcome. This is OUTCOMES$(CORRECT).

Using this knowledge the system readjusts RULES(I,J) accordingly, subtracting VALUE(J) from each rule that gave a value as big as or bigger than DECISION(BEST) and, finally, adding VALUE(J) to the rule CORRECT i.e. RULES(J,CORRECT).

Having adjusted array RULES the program then returns again to line 150 for another example.

As the training session proceeds the judgement of the system should improve and in some cases, such as the Bird/Plane/Glider example, will eventually get it right every time.

And there's a bit of inbuilt scoring so that the program can judge when it's perfect for itself.

Fig 3.7 The program so far

```
10 CLS
20 INPUT "How many variables have you ";VAR
30 DIM VALUE(VAR),VAR$(VAR)
40 PRINT "Please name these variables"
50 FOR I=1 TO VAR
60 PRINT "Variable ";I;"is ";:INPUT VAR$(I)
70 NEXT
80 INPUT "How many outcomes have you ";OUTCOMES
90 DIM OUTCOMES$(OUTCOMES),RULES(VAR,OUTCOMES),
   DECISION(OUTCOMES), SCORE(OUTCOMES)
100 PRINT "Please name these outcomes"
110 FOR I=1 TO OUTCOMES
120 SCORE(I)=0
130 PRINT "Outcome ";I;" is " ;: INPUT OUTCOMES$(I)
140 NEXT
150 CLS
160 PRINT "This is a training session"
170 PRINT "You must provide values of variables"
180 PRINT "I will guess an outcome"
190 PRINT "You must tell me if I am right or wrong"
200 DECISION=-10000
210 FOR I=1 TO OUTCOMES
220 DECISION(I)=0
230 NEXT
240 FOR I=1 TO VAR
250 PRINT "Variable ";I;" (";VAR$(I);") is";: INPUT VALUE(I)
260 NEXT
270 FOR I=1 TO VAR
280 FOR J=1 TO OUTCOMES
290 DECISION(J)=DECISION(J)+VALUE(I)*RULES(I,J)
300 NEXT
310 NEXT
320 FOR I=1 TO OUTCOMES
330 IF DECISION(I)>DECISION THEN DECISION=DECISION(I):BEST=I
340 NEXT
350 PRINT "Is it outcome ";BEST;" (";OUTCOMES$(BEST);") [y/n] ";:INPUT A$
360 IF A$="Y" OR A$="y" THEN SCORE(BEST)=1: SCORE=0:
    FOR I=1 TO OUTCOMES:SCORE=SCORE+SCORE(I): NEXT:
    IF SCORE=OUTCOMES THEN PRINT "I'm Perfect !": END ELSE GOTO 150
370 FOR I=1 TO OUTCOMES
380 PRINT I;" ";OUTCOMES$(I)
390 NEXT
400 INPUT "Which outcome is it ";CORRECT
410 FOR I=1 TO OUTCOMES
420 IF DECISION(I)>=DECISION AND I<>CORRECT THEN
    FOR J=1 TO VAR:RULES(J,I)=RULES(J,I)-VALUE(J):NEXT
430 NEXT
440 FOR J=1 TO VAR
450 RULES(J,CORRECT)=RULES(J,CORRECT)+VALUE(J)
460 NEXT
470 PRINT "I got ";SCORE;" right before I made a mistake !"
480 PRINT
490 PRINT "Press any key to continue"
500 X$="":WHILE X$="": X$=INKEY$:WEND
510 FOR I=1 TO OUTCOMES
520 SCORE(I)=0
530 NEXT
540 GOTO 150
```

Chapter 4

Improving your Expert

4.1 Parallel and sequential decisions

We've now reached the stage at which we actually have an expert system. After a suitable training period it should be making decisions for us on the subject of our own choosing and, unless we start examining the array RULES we won't even need to know exactly how it's doing it.

Which is enough, really, to make most people feel pretty pleased with themselves. Apart, of course, from the inevitable sceptics.

"If it was a real expert system," they whine, "it wouldn't work like this. It would work differently," they say.

And they would point to the fact that, every time they wanted an expert decision, they'd had to key in answers to a whole load of questions all at once before the expert deigned to do a stroke of work.

Real expert systems, they argue, ask you one question, then maybe another question, and then, depending on the outcome, either ask you more questions or tell you what their expert opinion is. They don't start off by asking you absolutely everything all at once.

What, in fact, is being said is that many systems use sequential decision procedures, not parallel ones.

What we have is a parallel decision procedure – it gets in all the information on a subject and then makes a decision.

The sequential procedure is always guided by the last piece of information it received. For instance, in our weather example, a sequential procedure might decide that the most important thing to know in passing opinion on tomorrow's weather was: Is it raining today? It would ask that question and either seek more information or pass judgement.

One of the difficulties with the weather example, though, is that we don't exactly know what will accurately predict rain tomorrow. Not so the Bird/Plane example – by definition we know the difference between Birds and Planes. So consider a sequential expert at work on this problem.

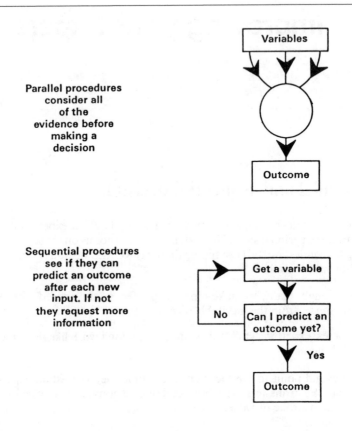

Parallel procedures consider all of the evidence before making a decision

Sequential procedures see if they can predict an outcome after each new input. If not they request more information

Fig 4.1 Parallel and sequential decisions

You state that you are thinking of either a Bird or a Plane and want the expert to say which it is.

"Does it," muses the expert as he sucks on his pipe, "have Feathers?"

"Actually, yes", you concede.

And at once the great thinker deduces that it's a Bird.

There was no need to consider all six variables at all.

Suppose, now, that you were thinking of an object and didn't specify that it could fly. The parallel and sequential approaches for this problem are shown in Fig. 4.2.

"Does it have Wings?" you get asked. You concede that it does and are instantly confronted with the previous question concerning Feathers. At once the expert has it. The sequential technique has won.

In general, sequential techniques ask less questions than do parallel techniques —which might make them seem, initially, more desirable. Or, at least, less garrulous.

But whereas the desirability of sequential procedures is obvious in the Bird/Plane example, it isn't so obvious in the weather example.

Because, even if you were a real expert and knew everything about the weather there is to know, you'd still never be absolutely certain if it was going to rain tomorrow or not. And, because of this, the wise expert would gather all possible evidence before him prior to making any judgement. And that's what parallel procedures do.

Knowing that one can't be absolutely certain, in general, about an outcome they gather all the information they can and then make the best guess they can. A sequential procedure smacks of leaping to conclusions – and our expert system doesn't do that.

If you think about it for a moment you'll realise that the best a sequential procedure can do is only as good as a parallel procedure. This is because as a parallel procedure uses all of the information to come to a conclusion then the parallel procedure comes to the most likely conclusion to be right. The sequential procedure can, by sequentially going through all of the available information, come to the same conclusion but, by doing so, it's effectively done just what the parallel procedure did but it did it by stages.

There isn't always much difference between the two methods. Suppose our expert had asked about the variables by clearing the screen in between each item. Then it might have looked like a sequential procedure – but, as it didn't decide anything until the end, it's really parallel.

We could obviously take some of the effort out of entering information if, when it had a crucial piece of information, the expert was instantly able to come to an opinion and skip the rest. But how would we write such a program?

Well, if we knew what the subject of our expert's inquiries was going to be we could write a tailor-made program for it. But, in our case, we wanted a general-purpose expert system.

Or, if we knew the exact probabilities for every outcome we could also write a program to do it. For instance, as the expert gathered pieces of information sequentially it could look through all the possible outcomes to find the most probable one. It could then check all other outcomes to see if they could ever, given the current information, become more probable than the one that was currently most probable. If they couldn't, then the expert could make a decision without going any further. If they could, then another piece of information would be needed.

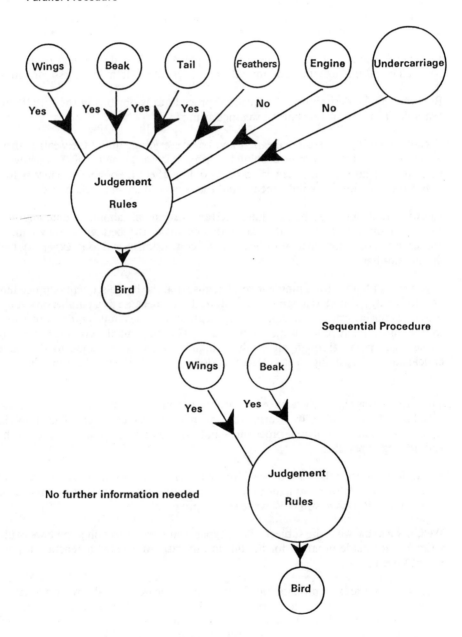

Fig 4.2 Parallel and sequential judgements.

Taking the Bird/Plane example, if we had entered the actual probabilities of the various outcomes instead of letting the expert learn for itself then we would have told the expert that if it had Feathers then it was Bird with probability 1 and it was Plane with probability 0. So, as soon as Feathers turned up (as it were) the expert could calculate that Bird was the only possible outcome and stop asking any more silly questions.

But we haven't proceeded in this way. Because of the examples we've given it the expert learns that only outcome Bird has variable Feathers. But it also knows a number of other things. For instance, it knows that outcome Bird has variable Beak as well. Does this mean that it's only a Bird if it's got both Feathers and a Beak? Or is it still a Bird if it's only got one of these? And, more to the point, does it mean that in the examples so far it happened by chance that Birds had Beaks and Feathers and that there might yet appear a Bird which had neither? In other words, is it a matter of absolute certainty, with probability 1 attached to it, or is it a very high probability, but not 1, which might not be the case later?

Now, as regards Birds and Planes, you could tell it what to expect. But what about the weather? In this case, nothing occurs with probability 1. It's all pretty uncertain and you aren't in a sufficiently knowledgeable position to explain anything further to the expert system. You don't know the answers yourself, except by waiting to see how the weather actually does turn out, so how can you explain it to the expert system?

In specific cases a sequential procedure can be devised which will save you time and trouble and which may give judgements which are just as good as a parallel procedure. But, in general, a parallel procedure will make decisions which are as good, and usually better, than a sequential procedure and the program using parallel procedures is much more general purpose because it makes fewer assumptions.

Having said that, let's consider how we might turn our expert system into a sequential device, as shown in Fig. 4.3.

Suppose that it displays the name of the first variable and asks for a VALUE for it which you then provide. It can then calculate all of the initial DECISION values for all of the OUTCOMES outcomes using just the value of this one variable.

Having done this it can then scan these values of DECISION, select the highest, and consider whether or not that might be the correct outcome. And the way it can do that is by scanning all of the rules in array RULES to see if any of them might increase any of the DECISION values by enough to exceed the currently-favoured outcome. But to do this involves guessing dummy values of VALUE(I) to work with. Now, if it really guesses it's introducing more uncertainty into the situation and there's enough uncertainty around already. If it's going to do it and be sure of itself it has to know the minimum and maximum values which VALUE(I) can take for each of the variables. If you can provide these values then the expert system may at least be able to discount some options and if it can discount all but one of the options it can make a decision.

But what if it makes an incorrect decision?

Well, if it's been given correct information about the minimum and maximum values of the variables then it can only make an incorrect decision if its array RULES is wrong. And it may be that RULES needs adjusting on all variables. So the program would have to revert to parallel mode to obtain all of the variable values from you and then adjust RULES as it did in the parallel processing case.

In terms of building your own expert system it may not always be really worth the effort to do all this. Especially if you don't like programming.

But in terms of making the system more interesting, or easier to use, it might be worth having a go. Whether it will make any difference to what the expert does depends on the minimum and maximum values you provide. They have to be wide enough apart

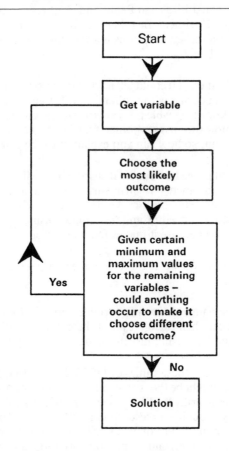

Fig. 4.3 A sequential expert algorithm

to be genuine limits on the input data – otherwise the expert will make mistakes. But if they're very far apart they won't help the expert to pin the decision down very much and so it will behave just like a parallel procedure again – but after a lot more programming effort on your part!

4.2 Adding some commonsense

As we've seen, if you can't tell the expert something more about the problem in hand the parallel procedures we've described give the best solution to date. But if, at the least, you could specify minimum and maximum values for the variables it would be possible for the system, under some circumstances, to skip a few items when asking for information.

Let's outline the method in BASIC, step by step. Suppose we DIMension the two arrays MINI(VAR) and MAXI(VAR) to hold the minimum and maximum values of each of the VAR variables. Minimum values in MINI(I), maximum values in MAXI(I). You can arrange to enter these at the start of the program training session either after each variable name is entered or as a separate block of information later on. You also need to DIMension VARFLAG(VAR) and POSSIBLE(VAR).

Then, as we go into a training session:

```
10 REM Values are needed for VAR and OUTCOMES :
20 VAR=6:OUTCOMES=3:REM ( for example )
30 DIM VARFLAG(VAR),POSSIBLE(VAR),MINI(VAR),MAXI(VAR),DECISION(OUTCOMES),
   VALUE(VAR),RULES(VAR,OUTCOMES)
40 REM Minimum and Maximum values must be provided into MINI(VAR) and MAXI(VAR).
50 REM Set up flag array VARFLAG to show which variables have been used
   so far in the decision process :
60 FOR I=1 TO VAR
70 VARFLAG(I)=1: REM a value of 1 means it hasn't been used yet.
80 NEXT
90 REM Clear array DECISION :
100 FOR J=1 TO OUTCOMES
110 DECISION(J)=0
120 NEXT
130 REM Input values for each element in array VALUE :
140 FOR I=1 TO VAR
150 INPUT VALUE(I)
160 VARFLAG(I)=0 : REM Flag set to zero once a value is obtained.
170 REM Now calculate/update array DECISION :
180 FOR J=1 TO OUTCOMES
190 X=VALUE(I)*RULES(I,J):DECISION(J)=DECISION(J)+X
200 NEXT
210 REM Find the maximum DECISION(J) and put it in DECISION
    so BEST will be the most likely decision to date :
220 DECISION=0
230 FOR J=1 TO OUTCOMES
240 IF DECISION(J)>DECISION THEN DECISION=DECISION(J):BEST=J
250 NEXT
260 REM Place the current values of array DECISION in array POSSIBLE :
270 FOR J=1 TO OUTCOMES
280 POSSIBLE(J)=DECISION(J)
290 NEXT
300 REM Now calculate the possible values which array POSSIBLE could take
    using the currently unknown variables :
310 FOR J=1 TO OUTCOMES
320 FOR K=1 TO VAR
330 IF VARFLAG(K) THEN IF RULES(K,J)>RULES(K,BEST) THEN
    POSSIBLE(J)=POSSIBLE(J)+(RULES(K,J)-RULES(K,BEST))*MAXI(K) ELSE
    POSSIBLE(J)=POSSIBLE(J)-(RULES(K,BEST)-RULES(K,J))*MINI(K)
340 NEXT:NEXT
```

What this does is to go through all of the variables that haven't been used yet. Using the known minimum and maximum values it alters POSSIBLE(J) in an attempt to find another outcome, BESTPOSS, whose value could exceed that of POSSIBLE(BEST). It does this by assuming that all the remaining variables will act against the current choice. As it only has to find out if the current choice can be displaced it can work with the difference RULES(K,J) − RULES(K,BEST) instead of RULES(K,J) and RULES(K,BEST) separately.

```
350 MAXPOSS=POSSIBLE(BEST)
360 FOR J=1 TO OUTCOMES
370 IF POSSIBLE(J)>=MAXPOSS THEN MAXPOSS=POSSIBLE(J):BESTPOSS=J
380 NEXT
390 IF BESTPOSS=BEST THEN STOP: REM All sources agree on the outcome.
400 REM There is no agreement as yet and another variable value is needed:
410 NEXT I
```

If, after all this, a wrong decision is still made array VARFLAG is checked to see which values of array VALUE have not been entered yet and these values are provided. The program then goes into its routine to alter array RULES.

Finding the values of array VALUE by working through them in order might not be the method which makes the most sense. For instance, if all values of array RULES were equal for a given variable then obtaining a value for that variable would tell the expert system nothing. It might as well skip it. In this case a few lines of code could check, before a variable was requested, if all RULES(I,J) are equal for that variable. If they are, the expert could jump to the next variable without requesting a value.

But what we really need is some general method for deciding which variable value the system should request next. For instance, some variables might be more crucial than others to the outcome. What we have so far is a method which divides the variables into two groups – those which might affect the outcome and those which won't affect the outcome. If we then write routines to try to first get values for those variables which seem likely to affect the outcome most we still have the possibility that, in the end, all of the variables which affect the outcome at all will still be required. So all we may have gained is a rearrangement of the order in which variable values are requested and not a reduction in the total number that have eventually to be considered.

One method which we might try is to look first at those variable values which have the biggest range of variation in terms of their minimum and maximum values (assuming we're able to provide such values). As these variables can vary the most it might be presumed that they contribute the most to the decision-making process. Obviously, in the Bird/Plane example the minimum and maximum values are 0 and 1 respectively corresponding to the presence or absence of a feature so this wouldn't help us much. However, using data relating to, say, weather conditions we could have variations in minima and maxima for various items. Cloud cover could be nought to ten, corresponding to nought to ten-tenths cloud; and rainfall could be nought to two, corresponding to nought to two inches of rainfall. So it would seem that cloud cover, with the greatest range, is the item we should check first. Unless, of course, we choose to measure rainfall in millimetres in which case the same rainfall is represented by nought to fifty (millimetres, not inches). And rainfall is the variable to check first.

All this rather serves to illustrate even further the point that, in general, the method of working the expert system uses can't be pinned down too closely—because if it's to be able to handle a wide range of different types of data we can't make it too specific in how it handles that data.

If you build your expert system to be fairly indifferent to the exact area in which it's supposed to acquire expertise then, in specific cases, it's likely to appear a little clumsy and laboured. If that happens then you may feel like customising the thing to a specific application by, say, getting it to ask about particular variables early on in the process and getting it to skip other variables according to some special knowledge of your own. But once you've done that you'll be likely to find that your expert system can't learn other problems quite so readily. It won't be a general-purpose expert system any more—even though it might be better for the purpose you built it.

It all really depends on what you want your expert system for. If you know what you want it for then you stand a good chance of being able to build a better one for that purpose than would be possible with any general method given by someone else.

Having said which, we might as well have a crack at getting the system to go for the 'best' variables first. We can do this by considering just how much variation they can cause in the decision rule.

If we DIM RULEVALUE(VAR) to hold an indicator of this variation (the 'Rule Values') for each of the VAR variables, we can write:

```
10 FOR I=1 TO VAR
20 FOR J=1 TO OUTCOMES
30 RULEVALUE(I)=RULEVALUE(I)+ABS((MINI(I)-MAXI(I))*RULES(I,J))
40 NEXT: NEXT
```

In this, we find the absolute difference between the minimum and maximum values of each variable and multiply this difference by the absolute values of the rules for that variable. Then we would search array RULEVALUE to find that variable with the greatest rule value. This is the variable that we suppose to be the most important so we input that value first. If the system calls for another variable it would call for the variable with the next highest value in RULEVALUE. And so on.

The success of this method, apart from the comments made already, depends on the accuracy with which we know the minimum and maximum values for the variables and the extent to which the rules developed by the system so far are good rules.

Obviously, when it's first starting and all RULES(I,J)=0 it won't have a clue which variables are important to the problem and which aren't. Whether experience will improve the system in this respect depends mainly on the problem it's given to work on.

There is another refinement that could be used when trying to decide which variable to ask about. You'll see that we've got a method of picking that variable with the maximum value in RULEVALUE. Now, suppose that this variable has already been entered, then VARFLAG(I)=0 to indicate that it's no longer needed.

The system then goes off to check if it can deduce an unequivocal outcome. It can't, so it goes looking for another variable, the one with the next largest RULEVALUE.

But, when it was checking for other possible outcomes there might only have been a small number of outcomes which remained possible contenders. By checking the possible decision values in array POSSIBLE some of them might have turned out to be less than the value of DECISION the system picked up for the most likely outcome so far. In this case, they aren't possible contenders under any circumstances and they can be ignored for all purposes.

Suppose we DIM OUTFLAG(OUTCOMES) for the OUTCOMES outcomes and use this array in exactly the same way as we used VARFLAG(VAR) for the VAR variables. Set all of the elements equal to 1 to start off with and set any OUTFLAG(J) to nought as soon as it becomes apparent that this outcome can never be chosen.

Then, whenever we are dealing with a set of values, we can quickly eliminate those which are 'dead'.

For instance :

```
10 FOR I=1 TO VAR
20 FOR J=1 TO OUTCOMES
30 RULEVALUE(I)=RULEVALUE(I)+ABS
   ((MINI(I)-MAXI(I))*RULES(I,J))*VARFLAG(I)*OUTFLAG(J)
40 NEXT: NEXT
```

Which has the effect of changing nothing if all of the variables and all of the outcomes are still active because VARFLAG(I) and OUTFLAG(J) are all equal to 1.

But, if any variable has been used, or if any outcome is no longer possible, then VARFLAG(I) or OUTFLAG(J) are equal to 0 and RULEVALUE(I) is unchanged by that variable or outcome. It simply means that we're only considering the reduced problem of what to do next given that some of the items are no longer active.

Incidentally, there isn't anything sacred about using the values of RULEVALUE as they're calculated here. You might, for instance, want to square RULES(I,J) instead of using the absolute values. It all depends on what you think might be useful. For instance, suppose that you wished to choose between two variables which had two outcomes and RULES(I,J) looked like this:

	Outcome 1	*Outcome 2*
Variable 1	2	2
Variable 2	1	3

Now, if both of these variables had the same maximum and minimum values they would both give the same values in RULEVALUE, because each of them adds up to 4. But you'd like variable 2 to be investigated first because it has the greatest effect on the outcomes (actually, it's the only one that has any effect, in this example). If you'd taken RULES(I,J) squared you'd have got :

RULEVALUE(1) $= 2^2 + 2^2 = 8$
RULEVALUE(2) $= 1^2 + 3^2 = 10$

which would have picked up variable 2 first.

Naturally, variable 1 would have been out of the running anyway because it had the same value for each outcome. But suppose you had a third variable:

	Outcome 1	Outcome 2
Variable 3	0	4

This would have made a contribution to RULEVALUE(3) of the order of 16 and would have been picked before variable 2 (or variable 1). Taking the absolute value of RULES(I,J) in RULEVALUE(I) wouldn't have picked up any differences between the three variables although you might have felt that they weren't all making an equal contribution to the problem.

Just as there wasn't anything sacred about the previous method, there's nothing sacred about this one either. Squaring RULES(I,J) accentuated any differences which might have existed. But taking a higher power would have accentuated them more. Taking an odd power (and not taking the absolute value) would have kept the positive or negative signs of the values intact which might be useful (one can't think why, actually); and, taking any other function could make it all behave in a pretty weird fashion which might suit someone's weird program.

Naturally, there's an even more complicated way of doing things which in some cases might actually be worthwhile.

And that is: to consider the sum of the squares about the mean of each variable's rule. To do this you calculate the average value of the rules for each variable and then calculate the squared deviation of the rules about these values. For instance:

```
10 FOR J=1 TO OUTCOMES
20 MEAN=MEAN+(RULES(I,J)/OUTCOMES)*VARFLAG(I)*OUTFLAG(J)
30 NEXT
40 FOR J=1 TO OUTCOMES
50 RULEVALUE(I)=RULEVALUE(I)+
   (RULES(I,J)-MEAN)^2*ABS(MINI(I)-MAXI(I))*VARFLAG(I)*OUTFLAG(J)
60 NEXT
```

This gives RULEVALUE(I) as the sum of the squares about the mean of RULES(I,J) for variable I over each of the possible outcomes.

You have to work this out for each variable and you should include VARFLAG(I) and OUTFLAG(J) as before when calculating both the means and the sum of squares if you want to allow for variables which have already been given and outcomes which are no longer being considered.

The point about this method is that you might have the following rules:

	Outcome 1	Outcome 2
Variable 1	1	2
Variable 2	1	−2

Intuitively, you feel that variable 2 is the most important because of the large difference it can create in the outcome. But ABS(RULES I,J)) wouldn't detect any difference between the two sets and neither would RULES(I,J) squared. Variable 2's rules vary most about an average value and it's this variation that we can try to measure in order to select the best variable for consideration.

The average value for variable 1 is 1.5 and that for variable 2 is -0.5 so we calculate respectively:

$$(1-1.5)^2 + (2-1.5)^2 = 0.5$$

and

$$(1-(-0.5))^2 + (-2-(-0.5))^2 = 4.5$$

This method picks variable 2. And, whether it's worth the trouble or not probably depends most on how many variables you have to deal with. If it's a lot you might be glad of any method which helps you get to the right ones first.

4.3 A trial run of our new expert

Suppose we modify our original program so that it will try to eliminate some variables by use of the maximum/minimum method from section 4.2. The modified listing is at the end of this section.

To see how well, or otherwise, the expert works we'll give it the Bird/Plane/Glider example. And, so that we don't get too bogged down, we'll give it three simple pieces of information to work on: Wings, Beak, Engine.

A Bird has Wings and a Beak, but no Engine. A Plane has Wings and an Engine but no Beak. A Glider has Wings but no Beak or Engine.

To start with, the array RULES contains zeros. We tell the expert system that the problem has 3 variables and 3 outcomes. We name the variables and the outcomes for it. We then provide minimum and maximum values for the 3 variables. Clearly, these are 0 and 1 corresponding to the presence or absence of the feature in question.

Variable	Minimum value	Maximum value
Wings	0	1
Beak	0	1
Engine	0	1

At such time as we enter a complete description for any one of the three outcomes the description would be held in VALUE(I) and would be:

Variable	Bird	Plane	Glider
Wings	1	1	1
Beak	1	0	0
Engine	0	1	0

The order of events is now up to the user (you) but we'll suppose that it happened like this...........

When we first run the expert it knows nothing – arrays RULES and RULEVALUE both contain zeroes – so it concludes that it's not worth its while asking any questions at all. Instead, it does the direct thing and asks you immediately which outcome you are thinking of.

We happen to be thinking of a Bird so we input VALUE(I) values to correspond to a Bird. The array RULES is adjusted because the expert, had it bothered to make a guess, would have made an incorrect guess:

RULES(I,J)	Bird	Plane	Glider
Wings	1	−1	−1
Beak	1	−1	−1
Engine	0	0	0

In other words, VALUE(I) for a Bird has been added to the outcome Bird rule and subtracted from the other rules.

The expert now enters another session. We think of a Bird again.

This time it thinks it might be able to get it right so it first asks for a value for Wings. We reply with 1.

The system then decides that it can't be a Plane or a Glider and asks if it can deduce outcome Bird. Which it can. We reply, Yes, and nothing is adjusted.

Now, obviously, we know that Wings aren't sufficient to indicate a Bird. It's really no evidence at all. But in the current state of knowledge of the expert it is enough. For with VALUE(I) = (1,x,x) the rules for Bird give a bigger value than the rules for any other outcome. And, considering the minimum and maximum information the system has, no values exist for the last two variables in VALUE(I) which could ever change this decision.

So, the expert has got the right answer on imperfect information, not by working incorrectly but because its set of rules are, so far, imperfect. We might show a little charity towards it at this stage – after all, it's only ever come across one Bird in its whole life so far.

Now another session. We think of a Plane.

It asks for a value for Wings. We reply with 1.

Again the system decides that it can't be a Plane or a Glider and asks if it can deduce outcome Bird. Which is a reasonable question to ask because, last time, it could. We reply that it can't.

The system asks which outcome it should have been. We reply Plane.

The system now asks for values for the rest of VALUE(I) so that it can readjust its rules. We give it the correct values for Beak and Engine so VALUE(I) = (1,0,1).

The rules are adjusted again.

Now another session. We think of a Plane again.

This time it first asks for a value for Beak. We reply with 0. It then asks about Engine. We reply with 1.

The system now decides that it can't be a Bird or a Glider and asks if it can deduce outcome Plane which it can.

Now this is quite promising. It didn't ask about Wings this time which is a good thing because it wouldn't have learned anything by the question.

Let's look at the array RULES as it now exists:

	Bird	Plane	Glider
Wings	0	0	−2
Beak	1	−1	−1
Engine	−1	1	−1

After the last mistake it made, the expert added the Plane variables to the Plane rule and subtracted them from the Bird and Glider rules.

Now: why did is ask about the Beak first?

It did it because this seemed like the most important variable of all. In each rule there is a 1 or −1 against Beak so, summing the products of the maximum variable values and the absolute values in RULES, the expert rates Beak as 3, Engine as 3, and Wings as 2 in order of importance. Beak comes before Engine in the list of variables so it asks about the Beak first.

From now on, if we just consider Birds and Planes, the expert will always be right. Every time it will ask about the object's Beak. If it's got one it will judge it to be a Bird. If it hasn't, it will ask about the Engine and, if it has one of those, it will judge it to be a Plane.

Now another session. This time we think of a Glider.

In response to a query about the object's Beak we reply with 0. It then asks about Engine – reply 0. And Wings – reply 1.

At this point it decides that it can't be a Glider and guesses that it's another Plane – which it isn't and we tell it so. We tell it that this is a Glider and it adjusts array RULES again.

Another session. This time we think of a Bird.

The expert asks about Wings and Beaks (reply 1 and 1), decides that it can't be a Glider, and asks about Engine. We reply 0 and it then decides, correctly, that it's a Bird.

Another session. We think of a Glider. It asks about Wings, Beak and Engine. We reply with 1,0,0. The expert guesses Glider – which is right.

Another session and this time we think of a Plane. It asks about Wings, Beak and Engine and we reply 1,0,1 and it deduces, correctly, that this is a Plane.

Another session, and this time we give it the Bird. It asks about Wings, Beak and Engine and we reply 1,1,0 – and it gets it right.

After this, it's perfect and makes no more mistakes. It can correctly identify a Bird, Plane or Glider, which is just what we want it to be able to do.

The set of rules at this stage is:

	Bird	Plane	Glider
Wings	−1	−1	−1
Beak	1	−1	−1
Engine	−1	1	−1

There are a few points to make about these rules at this stage.

First, it only guesses Glider correctly by, as it were, default.

That is: Glider has the variable values (1,0,0) – so any of the three outcomes gives a decision value of −1 and there is no reason for picking Glider against any other outcome. The reason it does pick Glider correctly is that, having found the object has Wings and no Beak, it searches for the maximum decision value. They are all equal so it comes to rest on Glider – the last value it looks at. When it then finds the object has no Engine it does the same thing – coming to rest on Glider as the last item in the list and finding that nothing can displace this judgement by being greater in value than this.

In an example like this a lot depends on whether rules are adjusted and decisions made on the basis of a conditional test of 'greater than' or 'greater than or equal to'. The more stringent test 'greater than or equal to' alters the rules more often and, initially, makes the most mistakes. But it often results in a slightly better rule set – one which asks fewer questions when it is possible to do so. A simple 'greater than' test alters the rules less often and works, in part, because of the natural order of the data in the list – which is something you should remember when you are trying to work out what your program has done with its rules.

A further point is that the expert often asks about Wings – and we know that this question has no bearing on the outcome at all. The reason it does this is because the values in array RULEVALUE are (3,3,3) for (Wings, Beak, Engine) – and it's this that makes us think that some other method of calculating the rule values might have been preferable. For instance, if we calculated the means for each variable ($-1,-\frac{1}{3},-\frac{1}{3}$) we could have calculated the sum of the squares about the mean of each variable (0,2.67,2.67) – which gives Beak and Engines as, clearly, the most important variables and leaves Wings right out, as it were, in the cold. (The sum of squares of a variable about its mean is, incidentally, the same as the variance of that variable but without dividing by n – see the Technical Overview at the back if you're not sure about this.)

Also, we'd have been quite likely to get a different set of rules if we'd trained the expert by giving it the problems in a different order.

But all that we require of a decent set of rules is that they should work – which these do.

Think about our talk about linear separability. We've got an expert system which has managed to draw lines between the three groups of objects – Birds, Planes and Gliders. It doesn't matter exactly where the lines are drawn as long as they serve to separate the three groups. The current set of rules does that but it wouldn't be hard to think of another set of rules which did it just as well.

This example is fairly neat – but don't suppose that every problem given to the expert will look as nice as this one does.

Suppose that we keep our three outcomes: Bird, Plane, Glider. Now give it six variables to work on: Wings, Tail, Beak, Feathers, Engine, Undercarriage. Commonsense tells us that most of these variables are redundant – they aren't needed to answer the basic question. But will the expert work that out?

The answer is: No.

As there are still only three outcomes we know that no more than two well-chosen questions will still settle the matter. However, after the expert had been sufficiently trained, it asked about the following items for each of the three outcomes:

Bird   Engine   – Reply 0
              Undercarriage – Reply 0
              Beak   – Reply 1   Deduction: Bird

Plane   Engine   – Reply 1
              Undercarriage – Reply 1   Deduction: Plane

Glider   Engine   – Reply 0
              Undercarriage – Reply 0
              Beak   – Reply 0
              Feathers   – Reply 0   Deduction: Glider

Now this isn't bad. It gets it right every time and it doesn't ask about all of the variables. For instance, it never asks about Wings and Tail which is good, because these variables don't tell it anything. However, from our point of view, it's rather dense in asking about the Undercarriage straight after asking about the Engine every time. But that's because we know that, in these examples, the two always go together. Likewise, it often asks about Feathers straight after asking about the Beak – another two items which we know always go together.

The point is, of course, that the expert system doesn't know that these things always go together. Having asked about the Engine, a question it thinks is important, it finds that it can't be sure of the outcome and so it has to ask another question. The Undercarriage seems important to it so it asks about that. It didn't realise that it could have deduced Undercarriage from Engine. For all the expert knew, Engine and Undercarriage might have just occurred together by chance so far. In the problem it was working on at that particular moment Engine and Undercarriage might not have occurred together and that would have changed its view of the possible outcome. It simply needed to keep on asking questions until, given the state of its rules and the minimum and maximum values assigned to each variable, there was absolutely no possibility whatsoever of its getting fresh information on any variable which would cause it to change its mind about the likely outcome.

Knowing that the object had an Engine wasn't enough for it to be absolutely sure of the outcome. Suppose (you can imagine it thinking to itself) I had an object with an Engine and then it suddenly turned out to have no Undercarriage. Would that cause me to think differently about what it was? Yes, it would. Better ask about the Undercarriage.

Precisely what sort of object the expert thought might have an Engine and no Undercarriage is a bit of a mystery. Maybe we should have included the outcome: Rocket. Just to keep the expert happy.

The following is a listing of the program used in this section. It uses the learning algorithm. Minimum and maximum values are used in order to try to come to a speedy conclusion. Questions are asked on the basis of their rule values – using the ABS function with the min/max values to try to assess their importance.
Outcomes which cannot achieve a high enough value to displace the current best guess are eliminated from further calculations.

Once you've run this try altering the code so that the values in RULEVALUE are calculated using the sum of squares about their means rather than the ABS function – it should influence the order of question-asking.

Fig 4.4   Minimum/maximum modified program

```
10 CLS
20 INPUT "How many variables have you ";VAR
30 DIM VALUE(VAR),VAR$(VAR),MINI(VAR),MAXI(VAR),VARFLAG(VAR),POSSIBLE(VAR),
   RULEVALUE(VAR)
40 PRINT "Please name these variables :"
50 FOR I=1 TO VAR
60 PRINT "Variable ";I;" is ";: INPUT VAR$(I)
70 INPUT"It has Minimum value = ";MINI(I)
80 INPUT"and Maximum value = ";MAXI(I)
90 NEXT
100 INPUT "How many outcomes have you ";OUTCOMES
110 DIM OUTCOMES$(OUTCOMES),RULES(VAR,OUTCOMES),DECISION(OUTCOMES),
    OUTFLAG(OUTCOMES)
120 PRINT "Please name these outcomes :"
130 FOR I=1 TO OUTCOMES
140 PRINT "Outcome ";I;" is ";: INPUT OUTCOMES$(I)
150 NEXT
160 REM Display details of variables :
170 PRINT "Variable","Min value Max value"
180 FOR I=1 TO VAR
190 PRINT VAR$(I),MINI(I),MAXI(I)
200 NEXT
210 PRINT "Press any key to continue "
220 X$="":WHILE X$="":X$=INKEY$:WEND
230 REM Start training here :
240 CLS
250 PRINT "This is a training session"
260 PRINT "You must provide values of the variables"
270 PRINT "I will guess an outcome"
280 PRINT "You must tell me if I am right or wrong"
290 REM Clear array VALUE and set flag array VARFLAG :
300 FOR I=1 TO VAR
310 VALUE(I)=0
320 VARFLAG(I)=1
330 NEXT
340 REM clear arrays DECISION, POSSIBLE and set flag array OUTFLAG :
350 FOR J=1 TO OUTCOMES
360 DECISION(J)=0
370 POSSIBLE(J)=0
380 OUTFLAG(J)=1
390 NEXT
400 REM Find most promising variable BESTVAR with rule value RV :
410 RV=0
420 BESTVAR=1
430 FOR I=1 TO VAR
440 RULEVALUE(I)=0
450 FOR J=1 TO OUTCOMES
460 RULEVALUE(I)=RULEVALUE(I)+
    ABS((MINI(I)-MAXI(I))*RULES(I,J))*VARFLAG(I)*OUTFLAG(J)
470 NEXT
480 IF RULEVALUE(I)>RV THEN BESTVAR=I:RV=RULEVALUE(I)
490 NEXT
500 IF RV=0 THEN GOTO 820: REM Most promising variable contributes nothing
```

```
510 PRINT "Variable ";BESTVAR;" (";VAR$(BESTVAR);") is ";:INPUT VALUE(BESTVAR)
520 VARFLAG(BESTVAR)=0: REM Set flag to zero once value is obtained
530 REM update array DECISION :
540 FOR J=1 TO OUTCOMES
550 X=VALUE(BESTVAR)*RULES(BESTVAR,J):DECISION(J)=DECISION(J)+X
560 NEXT
570 REM Find maximum DECISION ie DECISION(BEST) as current best guess :
580 DECISION=-10000
590 FOR J=1 TO OUTCOMES
600 IF DECISION(J)>=DECISION THEN DECISION=DECISION(J):BEST=J
610 NEXT
620 REM Update array POSSIBLE :
630 FOR J=1 TO OUTCOMES
640 POSSIBLE(J)=DECISION(J)
650 FOR I=1 TO VAR
660 IF VARFLAG(I) THEN IF RULES(I,J)>RULES(I,BEST)
    THEN POSSIBLE(J)=POSSIBLE(J)+(RULES(I,J)-RULES(I,BEST))*MAXI(I) ELSE
    POSSIBLE(J)=POSSIBLE(J)-(RULES(I,BEST)-RULES(I,J))*MINI(I)
670 NEXT: NEXT
680 REM Find maximum POSSIBLE ie POSSIBLE(BESTPOSS) as current best possible :
690 MAXPOSS=POSSIBLE(BEST)
700 BESTPOSS=BEST
710 FOR J=1 TO OUTCOMES
720 IF POSSIBLE(J)>=MAXPOSS THEN MAXPOSS=POSSIBLE(J):BESTPOSS=J
730 IF POSSIBLE(J)<POSSIBLE(BEST) THEN OUTFLAG(J)=0:
    PRINT "It can't be ";OUTCOMES=(J):
    REM This outcome is no longer likely
740 NEXT
750 IF BESTPOSS<>BEST THEN 400: REM There's still uncertainty so get another
    variable
760 PRINT "Is the outcome ";OUTCOMES$(BEST);" [y/n] ";:INPUT A$
770 IF A$<>"Y" AND A$<>"y" THEN 820
780 PRINT"WHOOPEE!"
790 PRINT "Press any key to continue "
800 X$="":WHILE X$="":X$=INKEY$:WEND
810 GOTO 230:REM Get another example
820 REM Ask for correct answer :
830 FOR I=1 TO OUTCOMES
840 PRINT I;" ";OUTCOMES=(I)
850 NEXT
860 INPUT "Which outcome is it ";CORRECT
870 REM Ask for any currently unknown variables :
880 FOR J=1 TO VAR
890 IF VARFLAG(J)=0 THEN 920
900 PRINT "What was the value of variable ";J;" (";VAR=(J);") ";: INPUT VALUE(J)
910 VARFLAG(J)=0
920 NEXT
930 REM Adjust array RULES :
940 FOR I=1 TO OUTCOMES
950 IF I=CORRECT OR DECISION(I)<DECISION(CORRECT) THEN 990
960 FOR J=1 TO VAR
970 RULES(J,I)=RULES(J,I)-VALUE(J)
980 NEXT
990 NEXT
1000 FOR J=1 TO VAR
1010 RULES(J,CORRECT)=RULES(J,CORRECT)+VALUE(J)
1020 NEXT
1030 REM Display current rule array :
1040 PRINT "The current rule array is :-"
1050 FOR J=1 TO OUTCOMES
1060 PRINT TAB(10+J*10);OUTCOMES$(J);
```

```
1070 NEXT
1080 PRINT
1090 FOR I=1 TO VAR
1100 PRINT VAR=(I);
1110 FOR J=1 TO OUTCOMES
1120 PRINT TAB(10+J*10);RULES(I,J);
1130 NEXT
1140 PRINT
1150 NEXT
1160 PRINT "Press any key to continue "
1170 X$="":WHILE X$="":X$=INKEY$:WEND
1180 GOTO 230: REM Carry on training
```

Chapter 5

A Real World Expert

5.1 The weather again

It's all very well to have an expert system which can answer contrived questions about Birds, Planes and Gliders. It makes a nice toy. But what happens if we give it a real problem such as the weather? What will it do if we ask it if it's going to rain tomorrow?

Well, it's certainly a real problem. We don't know how to answer that question ourselves so if the expert can work something out for us we might feel that we'd got something here.

So, forget contrived examples. We'll turn to the London Weather Centre for some real data.

Each month the London Weather Centre publishes figures showing the Rainfall, Temperature and Sunshine for each day. By looking at any given day we could provide data for the expert and train it by letting it know if it was raining on the following day or not.

As we progressed through the records we (might) find that our expert's guesses improve.

The figures shown in Table 5.1 are for March 1982 and give Minimum and Maximum Temperatures (in degrees Centigrade), Rainfall (in millimetres), and Sunshine (in hours). If the Rainfall is zero it's (would you believe) a dry day. Otherwise, we'll consider it to be raining.

We can provide some minimum and maximum values, although it wouldn't be too hard to find weather that fell outside these ranges.

Temperature:	minimum 0°C	maximum 20°C
Rainfall:	minimum 0 mm	maximum 25 mm
Sunshine:	minimum 0 hours	maximum 12 hours

Day of Month	Min. Temp.°C	Max. Temp.°C	Rainfall mm	Sunshine hours
1	9.4	11.0	17.5	3.2
2	4.2	12.5	4.1	6.2
3	7.6	11.2	7.7	1.1
4	5.7	10.5	1.8	4.3
5	3.0	12.0		9.5
6	4.4	9.6		3.5
7	4.8	9.4		10.1
8	1.8	9.2	5.5	7.8
9	2.4	10.2	4.8	4.1
10	5.5	12.7	4.2	3.8
11	3.7	10.9	4.4	9.2
12	5.9	10.0	4.8	7.1
13	3.0	11.9	0.2	8.3
14	5.4	12.1		1.8
15	8.8	9.1	8.8	
16	2.4	8.5	3.0	3.1
17	4.3	10.8	4.2	4.3
18	3.4	11.1		6.6
19	4.4	8.4	5.4	0.7
20	5.1	7.9	3.0	0.1
21	4.4	7.3	1.0	
22	5.6	14.0		6.8
23	5.7	14.0		8.8
24	2.9	13.9		9.5
25	5.8	16.4		10.3
26	3.9	17.0		9.9
27	3.8	18.3		8.3
28	5.8	15.4		7.0
29	6.7	8.8	6.4	4.2
30	4.5	9.6		8.8
31	4.6	9.6	3.2	4.2

Table 5.1

London weather summary for March 1982.

(A gap indicates zero)

Apart from the Minimum Rainfall and Minimum Sunshine figures these minimum and maximum values would have to be widened to allow for weather all the year round. Or, at least, they'd have to be widened in this our England.

Incidentally, it was the sunniest March since 1967 and the second sunniest March since records began in 1929 according to the Meteorological Office who are well-known optimists and who even extend their optimism to telling people that what we've just had was good weather.

Anyway, we set up the expert system with four variables: Minimum Temperature, Maximum Temperature, Rainfall and Sunshine.

Day of Month	Actual Weather next day	Weather Forecast by Expert	
1	Rain	Don't know	
2	Rain	Rain	
3	Rain	Rain	
4	Dry	Rain	– Error
5	Dry	Rain	– Error
6	Dry	Dry	
7	Rain	Dry	– Error
8	Rain	Rain	
9	Rain	Rain	
10	Rain	Rain	
11	Rain	Rain	
12	Rain	Rain	
13	Dry	Dry	
14	Rain	Rain	
15	Rain	Rain	
16	Rain	Rain	
17	Dry	Rain	– Error
18	Rain	Dry	– Error
19	Rain	Rain	
20	Rain	Rain	
21	Dry	Rain	– Error
22	Dry	Dry	
23	Dry	Dry	
24	Dry	Dry	
25	Dry	Dry	
26	Dry	Dry	
27	Dry	Dry	
28	Rain	Dry	– Error
29	Dry	Rain	– Error
30	Rain	Rain	
31	Rain	Rain	

Table 5.2
Actual & predicted weather for March 1982, London

We give it what we reckon are reasonable minimum and maximum values.

We give it two outcomes: Rain and No Rain.

The first item is: 1st March 1982. We enter the variables and let the expert know that there was Rain the following day.

Then it is the next day. We give it the values for the 2nd March and, if it guesses wrong about the next day's weather, we let it known that, once again, it rained the following day.

Then it is the next day and, yes, you are right. Excitement is not a feature of this process.

But if you glance at Table 5.2 you'll see that there are 18 wet days and 13 dry days in March 1982. Which suggests that there's a fifty-fifty (roughly) chance of getting the answer right just due to chance. How, then, does the expert get on – and is this any better than chance?

From Table 5.2 you can see that the expert predicted Rain, or its absence, correctly for 22 of the 30 days (the first day we don't count because the expert had no rules established until it knew the outcome of Day One). This is a 73 per cent success rate and actually sounds pretty good. Possibly much better than a human would have guessed. But let's go over the results in a bit more detail.

The first thing to do is to damp down a bit of the (possible) enthusiasm for the results. We do this by pointing out that there is a very simple rule which, with this data, would have made only ten mistakes over the whole month. This rule is: that the weather tomorrow will be the same (Rain or No Rain) as it is today. If we use this rule we'll only be wrong every time a dry day precedes a wet day or a wet day precedes a dry day. By and large, using this rule, we would expect to be right most of the time simply because we know that weather comes in runs – we tend to have a spell of dry days followed by a spell of wet days.

So, by this line of reasoning, if all the expert system did was to adjust its rules to predict for tomorrow what we had for today then it would have made only ten mistakes. In fact, it's done better than that with only eight mistakes – which shows that it hasn't been quite so simple. But, if you look at the results you'll see that it was when the weather actually did change that the expert was caught out. It wasn't always caught out by a change in the weather, as you can see on the 13th March, but it generally was.

What happens is that, after the first day, the expert makes predictions of, in this case, Rain. These are correct until (in case you hadn't guessed) they are wrong – due to a dry day occurring. This error causes the expert to adjust its rules and it eventually gets itself sufficiently sorted out to predict a dry day on the 6th March.

At this point the weather turns wet again and the expert makes a mistake. By this time it has adjusted its rules three times and these rules give it pretty good service until the 17th of the month when a dry day arrives unexpectedly. Some more adjustment occurs to the rules and, by the 22nd, the expert is running well enough to predict a dry spell. On the 28th and 29th more errors occur as rain returns.

In one way of thinking our expert has performed poorly because it does periodically make mistakes. It isn't perfect. And what will concern some people is the fact that, as it adjusts its rule base every time it makes a mistake, it isn't using the same set of rules throughout the performance – which might cause one to think that, in some sense, it's cheating. After all, you may say, what is it that we're judging here? With most games you aren't allowed to change the rules every time you lose.

It's this changing of the rules that makes our expert difficult to analyse except by trying it out to see what it does. If it had one set of rules which never changed then it would be possible to say more about them – but it doesn't, it just has a general method for supplying an answer.

In some ways, this makes the system more human. After all, if you were asked what you thought the weather would do tomorrow you'd probably take account of what the weather had been doing recently. By this, one doesn't mean solely what the weather has done today. If, by and large, the weather continues dry a light shower isn't going to cause you to change your mind about the chance of a dry day tomorrow. Or, at any rate, it's unlikely to. You'll approach the matter of weather prediction with a given mental 'set', or predisposition, to interpret today's clues in the context of generally recent weather.

Suppose, for instance, that you wanted to guess if it would snow tomorrow. Now, if it were the middle of January and there'd been a lot of snow recently and there were signs today of more snow to come then you'd be fairly happy to predict snow. But if it were the middle of July and there were signs which, in mid-January, would indicate snow then you'd by more reluctant to predict snow. The fact is: that you're using different rules yourself at different times.

And if, in mid-July, it actually did snow then you'd quickly adjust your internal weather prediction rules and be much more willing to reckon on the possibility of snow tomorrow if the same signs appeared again. And this is what our expert does. Having said which, its behaviour begins to look a lot more reasonable.

Also looking reasonable is its behaviour in asking for information. Recall that our expert is free to choose which variables it first enquires about and free to make a prediction without asking about all variables if it's sure of its outcome.

In this example it makes use of this freedom. Almost invariably the one question it asks first is: Rainfall?

Having got a figure for today's Rainfall it then, usually, makes a decision without checking any other items and, as we've seen, it's usually right.

What it appears to be doing is predicting Rain when today's Rainfall is high and predicting dry weather when today's Rainfall is low. Just how high is high and how low is low varies though. And, in between, there's a grey area in which it just can't make up its mind. In this grey area it will sometimes call on the other variables to add to the Rainfall information, typically asking about Temperatures and Sunshine. Very rarely does it want to know values for all the variables involved.

In all, its behaviour seems reasonable. Also reasonable is the set of rules which it has developed by the end of the month: The array RULES as of 31st March 1982:

	Rain Tomorrow	Dry Tomorrow
Minimum Temperature	−0.6999	0.6999
Maximum Temperature	−2.5	2.5
Rainfall	4.1	−4.1
Sunshine	4.6	−4.6

We can see that, for a prediction of rain tomorrow, the expert will look for high rainfall figures today with low temperatures. Strangely, it will also look for high Sunshine figures as a predictor of rain – but, maybe, this isn't so strange. Cold, wet and sunny weather is certainly 'unsettled' weather – so, maybe, that's what the expert is looking for. After all, by the end of March we might well expect some sunny April showers to be starting!

On the other hand, for a dry day tomorrow the expert is looking for warm, dry, overcast weather today – maybe this is the sort of still weather that doesn't presage rain. In all, these are not items which we would automatically use ourselves to predict the weather tomorrow – but maybe we should do. If our expert system can make a good prediction of the weather in this way it may well be that, by now, it genuinely does have some expertise which exceeds our own in some respects. Possibly, having initially learned from us, we can now learn from it.

But just how well has it done?

Actually, we can be a bit more precise about how well it's done by saying that, not only does it get things right 73 per cent of the time (for this example), but that the probability of this being due to chance is less than 0.025 – i.e. less than 25 chances in one thousand. And how, you may wonder, do we say such a thing as this?

Well, a bit of statistics comes in. We say that there have been 17 rainy days and 13 dry days in March and the expert has predicted 19 rainy days and 11 dry days. We can represent this as follows:

Expert prediction

		Rain	Dry		Total
Actual	Rain	14	3	=	17
Weather	Dry	5	8	=	13
	Total:	19	11	=	30

On 14 days Rain was predicted and there was Rain. On 8 days a dry day was predicted and it was dry. On $5+3=8$ days mistakes were made.

Using the totals we can calculate what those figures would have been by chance. These are the so-called 'expected values' and a description of how to calculate them is given at the end of this section:

Expected Values

		Rain	Dry		Total
Actual	Rain	10.77	6.23	=	17
Weather	Dry	8.23	4.77	=	13
	Total:	19	11	=	30

We can use these two tables in a statistical test called a chi-squared test.

A chi-squared test of significance says that this table built up from the actual predictions of the expert is different from the table based on chance and that it is so different that the probability that the expert is working by chance is less than 0.025.

The problem with that sort of statement is clearly this: that you may not know what a chi-square test is and you may not know whether to believe it or not.

Well, you can take it on trust if you like and believe it.

Or, if you actually want to know how it works...

The first table contains the Observed frequencies and the second table contains the Expected frequencies.

Chi-square is calculated by:

Chi = Chi + ((Observed − Expected)^2)/Expected

for each of the four cells in the table.
So:

Chi = ((14 − 10.77)^2)/10.77 + ((3 − 6.23)^2)/6.23 + ((5 − 8.23)^2)/8.23) +
((8 − 4.77)^2)/4.77 for this example.

So: Chi = 6.111196

Now you look up the value of chi-square in a table of statistics (sorry, you'll have to buy a table of statistics). Look against the values for 1 degree of freedom and you'll see that under the 0.025 (some call it 2.5 per cent) column, chi-square has a value of 5.02. Our value of chi-square is bigger than this so there is a probability of less than 0.025 that our results are due to chance. Or, if you want to look at it another way, you may find that value of 5.02 under a column headed 0.975 (97.5 per cent) which means that there is a probability greater than 0.975 that our results are not due to chance.

Some of you will find this all a bit tedious so you can always ignore it. But it does give you a way of judging the performance of your expert system in a fairly exact fashion. After all, you may have a different problem and may want to estimate how well your expert is at working on that.

You may also, if you're interested, wonder what degrees of freedom are and how we came by the expected values.

Degrees of freedom depend on the number of rows and columns in the table. We calculate:

DF = (ROWS − 1)*(COLS − 1), where DF = degrees of freedom.

In this case ROWS = 2 and COLS = 2 so DF = 1. But you might have had more outcomes and, so, a bigger table with more degrees of freedom.

Expected values are calculated for each cell by:

Looking to see what the row total is for that cell. (Observed).

Looking to see what the column total is for that cell. (Observed).

Multiplying these two together.

Dividing them by the overall total. (Observed).

Repeating this process for each cell.

Entering these values into the Expected Values table.

If you've done it right the Expected table should have the same row, column, and overall totals as the Observed table.

In our example, the first cell in the expected table was 10.77 because: 10.77 = 17*19/30.

Actually, it's an ideal subject for a computer program, if you're still interested and awake by now.

If you don't happen to have any statistical tables handy then you could just note that if chi-square equals nought then the results could certainly be due to chance. The bigger chi-squared, the better for our purposes.

5.2 A Chi-squared program.

If you feel interested in testing the expert's results in a formal way using chi-squared, but haven't come across the method before, then you might as well have a program to do it for you.

You could jot down your results, as before, into a table and then follow the logic of this program:

```
10 CLS
20 INPUT "How many rows have you ";ROWS
30 INPUT "How many columns have you ";COLS
40 DIM OBSERVED(ROWS+1,COLS+1),EXPECTED(ROWS,COLS)
50 FOR I=1 TO ROWS
60 FOR J=1 TO COLS
70 PRINT "Row ";I;" Column ";J;" = ";: INPUT OBSERVED(I,J)
80 NEXT: NEXT
90 FOR I=1 TO ROWS
100 FOR J=1 TO COLS
110 OBSERVED(ROWS+1,J)=OBSERVED(ROWS+1,J)+OBSERVED(I,J)
120 OBSERVED(I,COLS+1)=OBSERVED(I,COLS+1)+OBSERVED(I,J)
130 OBSERVED(ROWS+1,COLS+1)=OBSERVED(ROWS+1,COLS+1)+OBSERVED(I,J)
140 NEXT: NEXT
150 FOR I=1 TO COLS
160 FOR J=1 TO COLS
170 EXPECTED(I,J)=OBSERVED(I,COLS+1)*OBSERVED(ROWS+1,J)/OBSERVED(ROWS+1,COLS+1)
180 NEXT: NEXT
190 FOR I=1 TO ROWS
200 FOR J=1 TO COLS
210 CHI=CHI+((OBSERVED(I,J)-EXPECTED(I,J))^2)/EXPECTED(I,J)
220 NEXT: NEXT
230 DF=(ROWS-1)*(COLS-1)
240 PRINT "Chi Square = ";CHI;"Degrees of Freedom = ";DF
```

This prints the answers. And, sorry, but you still need those tables!

5.3 Exercising your expert

There is, at this stage, one little point which, in fairness, ought to be made about your expert system.

It's, in many ways, fine. There's nothing wrong with it. It will work. It will learn its expertise with little or no help from you. It only needs to be given a few examples to start with.

But how many examples does it need? At what point will it be making expert judgements of the very best quality?

Well...Considering the Bird/Plane/Glider example you might innocently suppose that three examples would do. One of each sort. After all, it will have seen everything once it's been shown all three. True, it will have seen everything. But not true that it will have developed adequate rules to recognise them again. It will take rather more than three attempts to shuffle its set of rules around until it's got a really decent method of working.

So, to be precise, just how many examples does it need to be given. In actual numbers.

Well (and at this point one sort of shuffles the feet a bit and attempts, as it were, to avoid the reader's eye) the theory actually depends on the expert having access to one example of each possible input actually, well, an infinite number of times, to be precise. That's what the theory says.

But the good news is that, if the outcomes are linearly separable, it will have developed a set of rules which will identify all the possible outcomes in finite time.

So with the Bird/Plane/Glider example you might be willing to give each of the three possibilities to the expert an infinite number of times but, if a good set of rules exists, it will find those rules in finite time. So: there's your answer. It wants 3*infinity examples!

At this point there are doubtless those amongst you who will have thrown aside this tract either on the grounds that it's inherently worthless or on the grounds that if you've got a nearly-infinite amount of data collection to do then you'd better get started now.

You are urged, however, to pause a moment. We'll trim the problem down a little.

First, there might, in theory, be an infinite range of different inputs you could provide. But, in practice, you won't have records of all of those possibilities (they'd take up so much room...).

In practice you'll have a nice, finite stack of data for it to start working on and in finite time the performance should become reasonably decent if you just keep on slinging all the examples you have at it.

So what the problem really comes down to is this: how to give the expert plenty of exercise at solving problems without spending the rest of your life at the keyboard and going to bed every night with bleeding fingers.

Fortunately, this all becomes pretty easy. It's just a matter of dull repetition – which is what computers were originally built to do. All you need is to take all of your N examples and put them in an array, say EXAMPLES(VAR + 1,N), and write a short routine to let the expert exercise itself in your absence.

The idea is that you set up EXAMPLES, get it working on them, and then retire to a local hostelry where you can tell the assembled crowds that your own expert system is currently doing all the work and there's nothing left, therefore, for you to do. That sort of comment always attracts a certain amount of respect amongst the audience because, largely, they won't know whether or not you're telling the truth but, if they think you might be, they will be consumed with powerful emotions.

So, suppressing the urge to retire to the hostelry prior to getting the expert working, we proceed:

First EXAMPLES(VAR +1,N). Obviously, the N is the number of examples you're going to give the expert. Equally obviously, the first dimension holds the VAR variables. The VAR +1 element is used to hold the outcome for that example.

At this point (ie. early on in the process) you could always cheat a bit and, instead of building up this data from scratch, you could fill in the array EXAMPLES at the same time as you input a few items to the expert system in a training session. It doesn't matter much though – it's up to you.

All you need to do now is to put a frequently-repeated loop into the routine so that it keeps on and on working over these examples and altering its rules as it goes. A possible method is to use the index on the loop, say I, to pick which example the expert should work next.

```
10 FOR I=1 TO N
20 FOR J=1 TO VAR
30 VALUE(J)=EXAMPLES(J,I)
40 NEXT: NEXT
```

This does have some disadvantages as the examples are always given in the same order. Maybe this wouldn't matter in some cases but suppose you had a set of rules which found a correct judgement on example I. Now, these rules might then give a correct judgement on example I + 1 so the rules wouldn't be changed. Now suppose we had an example I + 2 which the expert got wrong. The rules change and, maybe, example I + 3 will get the right response but, if example I had happened to be next again that might not have suited the current rules so well – there might have been a mistake and the rules could be altered as a result.

Clearly, to be as foolproof as possible, the expert should try out every possible order of picking the examples and it should work through them time and again. So, if you have N examples, there are N ways of picking the first example, N − 1 ways of picking the next example, N − 2 ways of picking the next example. In general, there are N! (N − factorial) ways of picking the examples. Where $N! = N(N-1)(N-2)...(2)(1)$.

Which is not only a lot, but it's rather hard to program in Basic.
And, what's more, it should be repeated a few times for good measure.

A more reasonable approach which gives easier code and works for any value of N is to pick the examples at random and just do it a lot of times. Suppose we do it 100 times:

```
10 FOR COUNT=1 TO 100
20 I=INT(RND*N+1)
30 NEXT
```

Doubtless, of course, you're happy about that piece of code – but RND and INT do vary a bit from one machine to another, so let's just define what it does on the IBM PC using Advanced Basic (BASICA).

The function RND gives a random number greater than or equal to nought and less than 1.

So, multiplying it by N gives a number greater than or equal to nought and less than N.

Adding one to this number gives a number greater than or equal to 1 and equal to N or just a bit more. Less than N + 1 actually.

The INT function gives an integer number which is just less than or equal to its variable – so we now have a number which is greater than or equal to 1 and less than or equal to N and which is an integer.

So we can use it for picking an example in the range 1 to N.

This way the expert just keeps on randomly bashing away at the homework you set it and, if you really want to give it a hard time, you could always put it into a continuous loop and leave it running until the cows come home.

From our previous in-depth studies the rest of the code is fairly easy, with VAR variables and OUTCOMES outcomes:

```
10 FOR COUNT=1 TO N
20 DECISION=0
30 FLAG=0
40 I=INT(RND*N+1)
50 REM CORRECT is the actual outcome with this data:
60 CORRECT=EXAMPLES(VAR+1,I)
70 REM Find the value of DECISION using CORRECT:
80 FOR J=1 TO VAR
90 DECISION=DECISION+EXAMPLES(J,I)*RULES(J,CORRECT)
100 NEXT
110 FOR K=1 TO OUTCOMES
120 WRONG=0
130 REM Find the WRONG value of the decision with the wrong outcomes:
140 IF K=CORRECT THEN 250
150 FOR J=1 TO VAR
160 WRONG=WRONG+EXAMPLES(J,I)*RULES(J,K)
170 NEXT
180 IF WRONG<DECISION THEN 250
190 REM Adjust RULES if the rules would have given the wrong answer :
200 FOR J=1 TO VAR
210 RULES(J,K)=RULES(J,K)-EXAMPLES(J,I)
220 NEXT
230 REM FLAG is a flag to indicate that CORRECT should be adjusted :
240 FLAG=1
250 NEXT K
260 IF FLAG THEN FOR J=1 TO VAR:
    RULES(J,CORRECT)=RULES(J,CORRECT)+EXAMPLES(J,I):NEXT
270 NEXT COUNT
```

Now, of course, you can retire to the hostelry of your choosing leaving the expert to do its homework. But take this tract with you (it creates a good impression to be seen able to read a book) for there is a bit more to be said.

Will the expert, when you return, have developed the same set of rules as if you had patiently hammered away at the keyboard for the rest of your life?

You would think so – but it might not. Because the data is being given to the expert in a different way.

Consider. It only alters its rules when it makes a mistake. And it only passed judgement when it was quite sure that no new variables could be entered which would cause it to change its mind, given the minimum and maximum values you so kindly provided.

So, at the keyboard, it might have decided that nothing could change its mind, made a judgement, and been right. Therefore, it would not have changed any rules. Now suppose that two rules, with a given example, gave the same decision value – a tie occurred. In our previous code it wouldn't have altered the rules unless the outcome it guessed at, from a tie, was the wrong outcome. If it could possibly get away without altering the rules, it did, because that saved you from the sweat of giving it any more information.

But, in this case, you aren't having to sweat away at the keyboard so the above code checks out all possibilities and alters the rules in the event of a tie until no further ties occur. So it will, in general, alter its rules more often.

An example:

Suppose you gave it a Bird. It checked its current rules and found that it could be a Bird but, equally, it could be a Glider. But a Bird was the first item it came to in the list and, as Glider only gives an equal result, it guesses Bird. Correct, you tell it. And the rules remain unchanged with Bird and Glider giving the same values when Bird is input. The system still works though.

But in the code we've just given it the expert won't put up with a set of rules in which Bird and Glider are the same. It will alter the rules until an absolute difference exists for each and every outcome.

This doesn't really mean that one set of rules is better than another – after all, if it gives the right answers who can argue with the way it does it?

If you wanted the same rules for both cases you'd have to make the code for exercising your expert a bit more complicated. For instance, you could change it so that the rules were only altered when:

WRONG>DECISION

instead of WRONG> =DECISION, which is what line 180 implicitly does when it skips the rule alteration code for WRONG<DECISION

or you could change it so that the rules were only altered when :

WRONG=DECISION AND K<ANSWER

which means that the rules are changed if a rule is found which gives an alternative, incorrect, outcome with an equal score to the correct outcome and this incorrect outcome occurs *before* the correct outcome. If it occurs after the correct outcome it won't cause any problems because, by then, the correct outcome will already have been picked up and another outcome which merely gives an equal score won't displace it.

It's a bit of a fine point but you will notice some practical effects when running your expert system. The most practical effect is simply that it may ask you for more information on the variables before it makes up its mind. This is because it keeps on asking for information until it's certain that nothing can occur to make it change its mind. By making more changes to the rules than before, the actual numbers in the elements of the array RULES may have got bigger or smaller. Because of this there will be greater possibilities for variation amongst the various values for the outcomes. So, when the expert is checking your minimum and maximum values on those variables you haven't entered yet, it will seem to the expert that there's more uncertainty than there was.

And it will go on asking questions of you to try to clear up this uncertainty.

The answer is, if you want to be a purist about it, to use exactly the same methods for exercising the expert as you use for running it normally. This would involve either writing out virtually the same code twice, or mixing in two possible sources of input – from the keyboard or from the array EXAMPLES(VAR + 1,N) – to the one stretch of code. Either way it's a bit more work and complication and, as it's you that's doing it, it's up to you whether or not you want to give it a try.

5.4 Direct estimation

What we've done so far is to pretend that our expert is going through a training session just as if we were sitting at the keyboard giving it examples one at a time. And there's no reason why we shouldn't continue to think like this. After all, it works.

But the whole gist of the technique is to find a set of rules which will give decent judgements and we might be able to do better than to leave the machine to bash away on a basis inspired mainly by a random number generator.

When we were considering the case of only two outcomes we pointed out that it would be possible to adjust the rules after every example whether the current rules gave the correct answer or not. And we could do the same with more than two outcomes.

In this case we'd ignore the random element and work through all of the examples we provided to the system as follows:

```
10 FOR K=1 TO N:REM assuming that we have N examples
20 FOR I=1 TO OUTCOMES:REM working through all of the possible outcomes
30 FOR J=1 TO VAR:REM working through all the variables
40 IF I=EXAMPLES(VAR+1,K) THEN RULES(J,I)=RULES(J,I)+EXAMPLES(J,K) ELSE
   RULES(J,I)=RULES(J,I)-EXAMPLES(J,K)
50 NEXT: NEXT: NEXT
```

What this does is to add the examples' values to the rule which gives the correct outcome and subtract the examples' values from all of the rules which belong to other outcomes. No reference is made to the question of whether or not the current rules would have worked or not.

At the end, after working through all of the examples in this way, we're left with a set of rules whose values (in theory) we know quite precisely.

Suppose, for instance, that we have three outcomes. Think of them as the corners of a triangle hanging somewhere in space as in Fig. 5.1. The rules consist of vectors – lines in particular directions – which each point to one corner of the triangle and away from the other two corners.

The corners of the triangle are, in fact, determined by the average values of the variables for each of the outcomes. Suppose that outcome 1 has average value x_1 for some variable or other and outcome 2 has average value of x_2 and outcome 3 has average value x_3. Then the rule vector for outcome 1 contains $x_1 - x_2 - x_3$.

Likewise, the rule vector for outcome 2 contains $x_2 - x_1 - x_3$, and so on.

Each rule vector tries to steer a course as much in the direction of its own average value as possible – but, by subtracting the average values of the other outcomes, it also tries to steer away from them as much as possible.

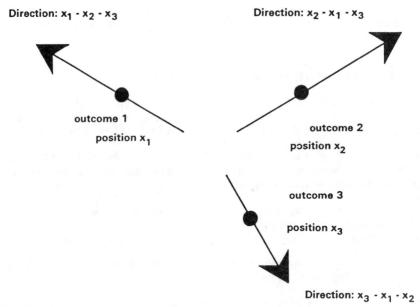

Direction: $x_1 - x_2 - x_3$

Direction: $x_2 - x_1 - x_3$

outcome 1

position x_1

outcome 2

position x_2

outcome 3

position x_3

Direction: $x_3 - x_1 - x_2$

Fig. 5.1 Direction vectors for 3 outcomes

You might have noticed that we haven't really used average values. Say there were n_1 examples of outcome 1. We haven't divided x_1 by n_1 to get the true average.

First consider what would happen if there were an equal number of examples of each outcome. Well, it wouldn't make any difference if we divided by the number of examples or not. Only their relative size is important so nothing would have been gained or lost.

Now suppose that there really are a different number of examples of each sort. Well, it could be that this is important. If you really give the expert a representative set of examples and that set of examples contains, say, one outcome which occurs twice as often as another outcome then this is useful information. The knowledge that one outcome is twice as likely as another and the fact that there are twice as many examples of it might cause you (or the expert) to think that twice as much faith (to use a scientific term!) should be placed in the outcome with the most examples. So we might, having got the mean values for that outcome, 'weight' them by multiplying them by two.

In general, if there are n_1 examples of x_1 we might multiply x_1 by n_1. And, if x_1 had been the average value of the n_1 examples we'd have been back where we started. Simply adding up all of the examples would have been quite adequate.

The snag is that things might not always be as simple as they seem. If we were still trying to predict the difference between a Bird and a Plane and we gave the expert one example of each it could then go away and work out a set of rules. But suppose, for some reason, that you give the expert two examples of the same thing. What would this mean?

The same set of rules would still separate the different possibilities quite nicely and there's no reason to think that one outcome is twice as likely as any other. In essence, what you gave it might not have been truly representative at all. And that would cause a bit of a problem. It's really up to you to judge what you should do here.

For a start, you could assume that the values you provide are fairly representative and work from the average for each outcome. After that, you could consider the question separately as to whether the actual number of examples in each outcome is important or not. If it is, you could weight the averages by the number of examples for each outcome and possibly gain some benefit. But if you feel that the actual number of examples you provide for each outcome isn't really a helpful guide – possibly because you just dreamed them up on the spur of the moment – then you could stick with the ordinary unweighted averages.

Clearly, though, to get the averages you need to keep count of how many examples you've got of each possible outcome. You could do this by splashing out on another array, DIM N(OUTCOMES) to keep track of it.

So:

```
10 FOR I=1 TO N
20 N(EXAMPLES(VAR+1,I))=N(EXAMPLES(VAR+1,I))+1
30 NEXT
```

And, then, divide the RULES(I,J) by the values in N(J) to give mean values.

The only snag with this method is that, in all honesty, it doesn't always work. Consider the following values in VALUE(I):

	Bird	Plane	Glider
Wings	1	1	1
Beak	1	0	0
Engine	0	1	0

So a Bird has Wings and a Beak, a Plane has Wings and an Engine, and a Glider has Wings and very little else. Now work out a set of rules for RULES(I,J) using average values and their differences:

	Bird	Plane	Glider
Wings	−1	−1	−1
Beak	1	−1	−1
Engine	−1	1	−1

Finally, give each of the sets of variables, in turn, to these rules to find the values for DECISION(J) with each VALUE(I) input to RULES(I,J):

Example values of DECISION(J) for each possible outcome:

Correct Outcome	Values in DECISION for each possible outcome		
	Bird	*Plane*	*Glider*
Bird	*0*	*−2*	*−2*
Plane	*−2*	*0*	*−2*
Glider	*−1*	*−1*	*−1*

Clearly, it hasn't got a clue about the Glider, even though it can guess the other outcomes with no trouble.

This problem wouldn't have arisen if Glider had been possessed of some other variables which uniquely identified it – like Towrope, for example. But as it is, it hasn't, and the method has broken down. It can easily be put right by counting Glider twice so that against Wings we have − 2 for Bird and Plane and 0 for Glider – but we didn't know that until we checked out the rules to see if they worked.

So, although it might seem useful to attempt a direct estimation of the rules, it's always a good idea to check them out afterwards. Maybe just by running the expert on a few examples. But while you're doing that the expert might just as well be building up its own rules in its own way – which rather takes us back to exercising the expert, just as we were doing before.

Chapter 6

Running for Real

6.1 Using your expert.

By now you've got, believe it or not, the makings of a general-purpose, fully-fledged, expert system with which you can amaze your friends and colleagues. You've been through all the important stages and, in case you hadn't realised it, they were these:

You've given the system the names of all the possible variables and you've told it what you think are the minimum and maximum values for each variable. The variables can be intrinsically numeric or just categories, like Yes/No data. Either way, it's treated as numeric input.

You've given the system the names of all the possible outcomes. As the expert is going to choose one of these outcomes every time it's asked for an opinion you'd better make sure that at least one outcome in the list will always be applicable. Ideally they should be mutually exclusive and the sum of the probabilities of each occurring should be one. Which means that only one outcome can occur but that there must always be one outcome which actually does occur.

You've given the system some examples (as many as possible) of likely inputs and told it what the outcome was for each input.

You've set up a training session in which the expert keeps on churning around the examples you've given it and modifies its set of rules until it's got a set of rules which always gives the right answers or, at least, until it's absolutely sick of trying.

But now, you actually want to use the expert for something. Obviously you can carry on just the same as you would do for a training session. Say you've set it up to predict the weather.

The day dawns, you go to your expert, key in a few variables, and it gives you a forecast. No trouble. And then, the next day, you do the same. And the next day. But suppose the forecast is wrong? Well, if it's running as a training session, the first thing the expert would want to know is whether its previous forecast was correct or not so that it could adjust its rules if it wasn't. Now, in this case, there's no particular hardship in satisfying its curiosity on the matter. You could let it know the outcome for the last set of data you gave it and then ask about a weather prediction for today.

But in your haste to pack umbrella, raincoat, wellington boots and all the usual equipment needed for an English summer you might either forget to let the expert know what happened to its last forecast or you might just want to forget.

Likewise, you might have set up the expert to carry out far-reaching medical diagnoses. You've had a training session and there you are, sitting in your consulting room with a queue of patients outside the door.

The first patient enters. You switch on the machine.

Typing his symptoms into the expert the screen flashes up the chosen outcome.

"Sorry, old chap," you observe sagely, "not your day, by the look of it. Only seven days to live. Next!"
And, at this point, you have to sit around with the next patient for a whole week before you can let the expert know if its predicted outcome was correct for the first patient. It's the sort of thing that loses you customers if you don't make provision for dealing with the situation in advance. And besides, you want people to get out of your consulting room as fast as possible if there's any chance that they may be carrying germs.

The point is that, overall, although it's a good idea to give the expert as much continuing feedback as possible there comes a time when you want to stop training and simply get on with the business of making expert judgements. And, in programming terms, all that this involves is going through the training routine but assuming that every response from the expert is correct. It doesn't ask you any more if it was right or not and it doesn't adjust its rules either.

In a nice clear-cut example, like the Bird/Plane/Glider problem, in which the expert can be quickly trained to be right every time it makes little difference if you stop giving it any feedback. But in the more usual cases – like weather forecasting – when you know, or are pretty sure, that mistakes will still occur from time to time the expert will lose out a bit by missing its feedback. You can largely get around this though by storing the details of the examples that occur and filling in the outcomes later when you feel like it – or when the outcomes become known.

That way you gradually build up an ever-bigger set of actual data which you can periodically use to exercise the expert to make sure that it isn't getting out of touch with its subject.

If, now, we go back to our weather example you'll see that we get different results when we run it for real to the results we got on a training session. During training, everytime a mistake was made the rules were adjusted. Now, we have a replay of March 1982 using the heavily-exercised rules without change throughout. The results are in Table 6.1

At first glance we might think that the results aren't wildly impressive – after all, it has made nine mistakes during March. But if we go on to apply the same rules, without any feedback, to April (Fig. 6.2) we find that we only get six errors in 29 days. So, over these two months we've got 15 errors in 60 days – a 75 per cent success rate. Which, again, isn't perfect but it's far better than chance. After all, that sort of success rate suggests that, if you were actually using the expert for real, it would only be wrong 1.75 days of the week!

And, as an added bonus, you could consider that it doesn't matter much if the expert predicts rain and the rain doesn't arrive. The worst that happens is that you walk around with an umbrella you don't need. The bad news is when the expert says it's going to be dry and it rains. And this happened on only four days in March and April 1982 – about every other week. So maybe the news isn't all bad.

Day of Month	Actual Weather next day	Weather Forecast by Expert	
1	Rain	Rain	
2	Rain	Rain	
3	Rain	Rain	
4	Dry	Rain	– Error
5	Dry	Rain	– Error
6	Dry	Rain	– Error
7	Rain	Rain	
8	Rain	Rain	
9	Rain	Rain	
10	Rain	Rain	
11	Rain	Rain	
12	Rain	Rain	
13	Dry	Rain	– Error
14	Rain	Dry	– Error
15	Rain	Rain	
16	Rain	Rain	
17	Dry	Rain	– Error
18	Rain	Rain	
19	Rain	Rain	
20	Rain	Rain	
21	Dry	Rain	– Error
22	Dry	Dry	
23	Dry	Dry	
24	Dry	Dry	
25	Dry	Dry	
26	Dry	Dry	
27	Dry	Dry	
28	Rain	Dry	– Error
29	Dry	Rain	– Error
30	Rain	Rain	
31	Rain	Rain	

Table 6.1 Weather forecasts for March 1982, London

Day of Month	Actual Weather next day	Weather Forecast by Expert	
1	Rain	Rain	
2	Dry	Dry	
3	Dry	Dry	
4	Rain	Dry	– Error
5	Rain	Rain	
6	Rain	Rain	
7	Rain	Rain	
8	Rain	Rain	
9	Dry	Rain	– Error
10	Dry	Dry	
11	Dry	Rain	– Error
12	Dry	Rain	– Error
13	Dry	Rain	– Error
14	Dry	Dry	
15	Dry	Dry	
16	Dry	Dry	
17	Dry	Dry	
18	Dry	Dry	
19	Dry	Dry	
20	Dry	Dry	
21	Dry	Dry	
22	Dry	Dry	
23	Dry	Dry	
24	Dry	Dry	
25	Dry	Dry	
26	Dry	Dry	
27	Dry	Dry	
28	Rain	Dry	– Error
29	Dry	Dry	

Table 6.2 Weather forecasts for April 1982, London

The interesting point to note about April's weather though is that it wasn't this weather on which the expert was trained. Suppose that weather prediction was a problem that really was linearly separable. It isn't, and that's why it's such a hard test for our expert system. But suppose it was and expert was trained on March's weather. Then, after due exercise, the expert could infallibly predict the weather for March. But that doesn't mean that it could predict the weather for April – which might have entirely different values. The fact that it has produced a fairly decent set of predictions is something of a bonus inasmuch as it suggests that there is something about weather forecasting in general which our expert system can do for us. It can take genuinely novel data and come up with something like a reasonable solution even though we don't know ourselves exactly how to predict tomorrow's weather and have only been able to give our expert system the most general of approaches to work with and a few examples to help get it going.

6.2 Reserved judgement

If, when attempting to make a decision, our expert system couldn't make up its mind what the outcome might be the best thing it could do would be to say so. Admit defeat rather than putting out a simple guess.

Unfortunately, this is a particularly difficult thing for it to do.

Suppose it was back with the Bird/Plane/Glider example and, early in its training, it found that all three outcomes gave identical values on a given input. As the expert is built so far it would make a guess as to the correct outcome if this happened and, if it was wrong, it would correct its rules. But, you say, if all the rules give identical answers it could reply: Don't Know. Rather than pretending it did know when it really didn't. Yes, fine. Of course you could program that in. A slight alteration to the code and, if there's more than one most likely outcome, print "Don't know" or, better, list the several possible outcomes. That would tell you a lot more about the judgement that had taken place and, so, you might as well include it in the program now.

But will it ever use this extra bit of code? Yes, sometimes. For instance with that Bird/Plane/Glider example it may well give a Don't Know – reserved judgement – answer while it's training. But once it's rules are established it won't reserve judgement at all because it will always get the answer right. Which is just as you'd want it to do.

But now turn your attention to the weather (again).

What do you think the odds are of a given set of inputs concerning the weather giving rise to two or more identical judgements on the basis of a given set of rules? It's hard to calculate an exact answer to that question: but, certainly, it's approximately nil.

The variable values you input are continuously variable. Real variables they can vary infinitely (within the limits of the machine) from any one value to any other. Take several of these variables and combine them with a given rule which is also made up of Real values. Take another, different, rule with Real variables and see if you get the same answer. In general you won't. Even if two answers are very similar it's going to be most unusual for them ever to be exactly the same.

Further, if you think back to the rules as a method of placing a surface between the different outcomes, you'll see that as long as the surface actually does separate the outcomes it doesn't matter exactly where it is. Likewise, it doesn't matter exactly what values are in the various rules as long as they work. So those values could be altered quite a bit, thereby altering any equalities which might have occurred, without upsetting the main working of the expert.

Naturally though, you'll say that you don't need the values to be exactly the same in order for the expert to reserve judgement – just similar. But how similar is similar? And to a machine? If you divide all of your variables by, say, 100 before applying the rules the difference between the values given by each rule will be reduced by a factor of 100. So: they're more alike. At least they give more similar answers and so, surely, the expert could reserve judgement more readily. Obviously this isn't right. But what would be a correct way of working?

As so far we've been thinking in terms of categories, we could introduce an extra outcome and call it: Don't know. But how would you train the expert on that outcome? The whole point of the training sessions is that you certainly do know the outcomes. If the expert asks you if Don't Know is the correct outcome, how would you know the answer? Perhaps you should give up and reply that you don't know either.

The problem, in essence, is not one of deciding whether or not the expert really does know the answer or not. It's the problem of deciding the extent to which it believes in each of the possible outcomes individually. Its final answer will be to suggest that outcome which it believes in the most. But, if this is very similar to the extent to which it believes in some other outcome, then you'd like it to reserve judgement, or at least tell you about it all.

And, with the expert system we've built, this isn't really possible. Our expert system is designed to accept any input on any problem and give the best answer. If you want to know how much confidence you can place in the answer there is only one way to proceed. That is to give it some data and see how often it gets it right.

For the Bird/Plane/Glider example we found that, after training, it got the right answer every time. So its opinion is expressed with probability 1. For the weather forecasts it was right 75 per cent of the time. So its answer is expressed with probability 0.75. But these are figures for the answers in general. They are not figures for isolated, specific, answers. One answer may be given with well-nigh absolute certainty and another with a great deal of uncertainty. But the problem is that we do not know which is which. Nor, for this general case, do we have any means of finding out.

6.3 The problem of distance

Now, surely, one might think that we could work as follows:
We have a decent set of rules in our expert, built up after a long-ish training session. We then give the expert another item to decide on. It could then list all of the possible outcomes and, against each, list the values which the rules gave for this outcome with the given input. The expert will pick that outcome with the highest value and, surely, this value, and the values for the non-chosen outcomes, will reflect the probabilities for each outcome being correct?

Sadly, no. They won't. The expert has been trained to pick the largest value but it has been told nothing about what these values actually mean in terms of probabilities. The biggest value denotes the most probable outcome – but how much more probable is, to the expert, a complete mystery.

It's all tied in with the problem of distance and distance measures – and that's what we'll look at now.

In the current, learning, system the expert has to place a boundary fence between several different outcomes. As long as the fence accurately separates the outcomes it doesn't matter exactly where it is. What matters is simply which side of the fence the variables fall – it doesn't matter at all how close to the fence they are. And in this sense, the concept of distance doesn't occur to it.

To help get these ideas straight let's imagine that we have before us a map of a strange country. As you can see, in Fig. 6.1, it has two axes (North – South and East – West) and it has two locations marked on it (X and Y, say) and it has contour markings to denote the height of the terrain. Locations X and Y are, we see from the contour markings, each situated on the top of a mountain.

So, we now have Mountain X and Mountain Y and, we see on the map, that point P is, more or less, on Mountain Y. Which means that anyone could look at the map and say which Mountain point P belonged to.

Having set up this map, we can now look at the various ways in which our expert could solve the problem.

Using the learning algorithm all the program does is to lay down a boundary fence between the two mountains and as long as point P is on the Mountain Y side of the fence then the boundary is in the right place because point P will be classified correctly. But that doesn't really tell us to what extent P belongs to Mountain Y– it could be right on the peak, at point Y itself, or right down in the foothills. At best, all it really tells us is that point P isn't part of Mountain X.

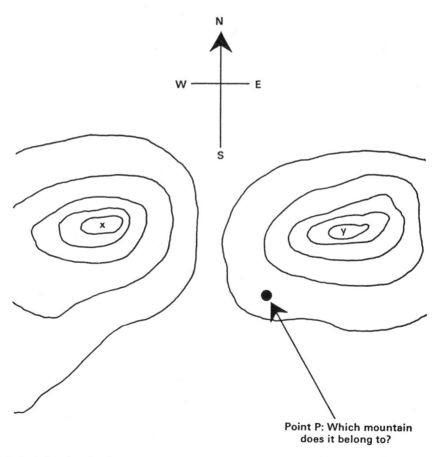

Point P: Which mountain does it belong to?

Fig 6.1 A physical analogy for distance measurements

So now to measuring distances.

The easiest way, and the one that would first occur to you, is to measure the distances from P to X and from P to Y – and classify P according to which is the least distance. That's not a bad method to use so we'll do it.

Unfortunately, it isn't just a question of getting out a ruler because what the computer has is not a map, as such, but a series of map references denoting measures along the two axes. So point X has co-ordinates in North – South and East – West as (NS_x, EW_x) and point Y is at (NS_y, EW_y) and P is at (NS_p, EW_p).

To calculate the distance of P from, say, X we calculate:

$$d^2 = (NS_x - NS_p)^2 + (EW_x - EW_p)^2$$

which is the Euclidean Distance measure (squared to keep everything positive) of P from X. We calculate the same thing for distance P to Y and we've then implemented a Minimum Euclidean Distance Classifier for point P.

The fact that the mountain example works in real space and our problems exist in an n-dimensional description space makes no difference to the way we now proceed. All we need to do is to work out the 'position' of each variable for each of the categories denoting an outcome. Taking the Bird/Plane example with two variables, Beak and Engine, we have, for a Bird, co-ordinates (1,0) – Beak and no Engine. And, for a Plane (0,1) – no Beak and an Engine. Now, given an object P which has co-ordinates (1,0) we can classify it as a Bird because this gives the minimum Euclidean Distance measure out of the two possibilities. In fact, if in array RULES we held the 'positions' of each outcome we could input a new object with VAR variables into array VALUE and calculate:

```
10 FOR I=TO VAR
20 DISTANCE=DISTANCE+(VALUE(I)-RULES(I,J))^2
30 NEXT
```

and choose that outcome J out of the entire set of OUTCOMES outcomes which gave the minimum value for DISTANCE. No trouble. Working like this would, in fact, be quicker than implementing the learning algorithm.

The point to be made now is this: that, maybe, without noticing it, we actually were very woolly about what we actually asked the expert to do. When we asked to which category point P belonged we didn't really define the categories at all well because we could have been asking either:
Which is the shortest distance, P-X or P-Y?
Or:
To which mountain, X or Y, does point P belong?
And, whereas the distinction doesn't really matter too much in the Bird/Plane example, it would matter a great deal, for instance, in weather forecasting.

Staying with the Bird/Plane example, all we did was to find the minimum of the two distances, P-X and P-Y, and we carried out our calculations more or less as the crow flies.

We were able to do this because the variables were point functions – they only exist at a single point and, if you like, the nature of the terrain between the points is quite immaterial.

If we'd been working with continuous variables, rainfall figures say, then we wouldn't have had point functions. We'd have had continuous variables and these would define an intervening terrain. What is more they would have needed a bit of calculation in order simply to ascertain where the mountain tops actually were.

In general, the position of the mountain tops is best calculated by finding the mean (or average) value of the variables for each outcome. If we have n observations for a given outcome then the mean, m, is:

$m = (x_1 + x_2 + x_3 + ... + x_n)/n$ which is fairly familiar.

So, whether we've got discrete or continuous variables, we could still proceed by calculating the mean values for each outcome, placing them in array RULES, and then implementing a Minimum Euclidean Distance Classifier.

The problem still remains though that we've calculated the distance to the mountain tops – we haven't fully attempted to answer the question of which mountain point P belongs to.

To see why this might matter, suppose that the mountains were of different sizes – one might be a proper mountain and the other much more like a molehill. Now suppose that point P is only three feet away from the centre of the molehill and five hundred feet away from the centre of the mountain. Now: does point P belong to the mountain or the molehill? Using the Minimum Euclidean Distance Classifier it certainly belongs, not to the mountain, but to the molehill. But is this right? After all, three feet away from a molehill is a long way – well clear of it. Whereas five hundred feet from the centre of the mountain might be half way up it. You see the problem.

That's where the contour lines come in. If we were looking at a real map we'd intuitively take the size of the mountains into account in answering the question – and that's what we must try to do with the problem of classifying objects now.

In terms of variables the contour lines represent the probability distribution function (pdf) of the variable – the normal pdf is just one example and, viewed from the 'side', it looks like this:

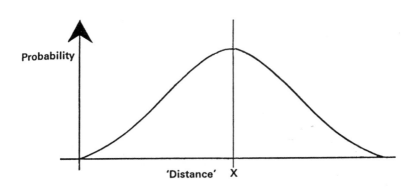

Fig 6.2 The normal probability distribution function

Point X is the mean value for variables with that pdf and, if it were measured in two dimensions and viewed from the 'top' it would look just like the picture of a mountain with contour lines.

Now, associated with every pdf is a 'standard deviation', sd, which is the square root of its variance. The standard deviation is:

$$sd = \sqrt{((x_1 - m)^2 + (x_2 - m)^2 + (x_3 - m)^2 + ... + (x_n - m)^2)/n}$$

So you calculate the mean, m, for the n observations on each variable and then calculate the sd.

The sd is a measure of the 'size' of our mountain – it measures the spread of each variable. So we can make all of the mountains the same size by dividing all of the measurements by the sd. This is called Scaling to Unit Variance.

Working from a sample set of data it's possible to calculate the means, calculate the sd, then calculate a new 'distance' measure as:

$$d^2 = ((x - m)/sd)^2$$

which gives a minimum distance classifier scaled to unit variance.

This will certainly help the expert in making decisions – but will it enable the expert to say with what probability its statements are true?

Well, the answer is: maybe.

Suppose that the variables were, actually, normally distributed (that is, they have the normal pdf). The measured $d = \sqrt{d^2}$ has been tabulated for the normal pdf and it is possible to look in the tables (or calculate your own tables on the computer – not a very easy task) to see just what the probability is that, with a given value of d, the new observation belongs to mountain X (or, in statistical terms, to see what is the probability that the given observation comes from a given population). Doing this for each outcome would enable the expert system to make statements with probabilities attached to them.

The problem that really arises though is that many variables aren't normally distributed and it can be quite difficult to determine exactly what their pdf is.

Returning to the Bird/Plane example with two variables, Beak and Engine, it is immediately obvious that these variables aren't normally distributed. As point functions they don't resemble mountains so much as lamp posts – with everything concentrated in one place. In fact, that makes life somewhat easier, in this instance, because we don't need to use tables – the probability is either 0 or 1 depending on which variables and which outcomes we have. So the system can make exact probability statements about its opinions. The 'distance' measure will always be either 0 or greater than 0 and the probability for each classification being correct will be 1 if the distance is 0 and 0 if the distance is greater than 0. Easy.

The real problem occurs when we simply don't know what the pdf is for a given variable – and this might be the case for, say, rainfall figures. We can be pretty certain that it isn't normally distributed because it isn't symmetrical about the mean value. And we know it isn't a point function because we have continuous variables. So: what is it? And, if we knew the answer and implemented it on our expert system we'd then have an expert system which was very good at weather forecasting but, probably, quite useless at anything else with a different pdf.

The concept of distance measures is a good one – but translating these distances into probability statements can be a very complex task, because distance and probability are not the same thing at all.

The problem of distance is really a very general one and shades into the problem of similarity.

---

a) For a nicely-behaved pdf, like the normal pdf, probabilities vary in a very regular fashion as the distance from the mean varies.

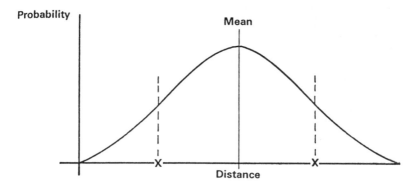

b) For less well-behaved functions the relationship can be much harder to define. In this "skew-left" example below-average readings can be much more likely than some above-average readings.

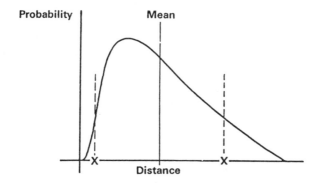

Fig 6.3 Symmetric and asymmetric probability distribution functions.

Suppose that we had a given set of variables and we wanted to decide an outcome. What we might do is to run through the set of values the expert was trained on to see how many of these items were exactly the same as the values we've just got. We could then get the expert to pass judgement by choosing that outcome which contained the largest number of examples with exactly the same variable values. And this isn't a bad way of working if the data suits it.

It has the merit, in its simplest form, of not relying on the distance measure – so we can use categories, or any other method of describing the data we like. For the Bird/Plane/Glider example it would work well.

But back to the weather. In this case, the chance of finding even one set of identical readings is very remote – so how do we measure the similarity? And it's back to the distance measure and all of its problems. It's a bit of a pity really because, if it worked, we could actually assign probabilities to the various outcomes based on the number of similar cases which fell into each category. Certainly, if you had a specific problem which suited this method of working you'd find it simple to use, easy to understand, and reasonably accurate. The sort of situation in which it would work might be the case in which your variables consist of a number of categories but these categories don't precisely define any particular outcome. In the Bird/Plane/Glider example the categories did exactly define the outcome. But if you had a list of medical symptoms which tended to indicate particular complaints, but did not point with absolute certainty to exactly which complaint, then this method would give as good results as any. It would, in fact, give as good results as our original method (which is one reason for sticking to that method) but it would also be able to indicate the extent to which it thought its judgement might be correct.

A variant on this technique is, obviously, to use the original method to make a judgement and then to search through past records to check for exact instances which might be identical so that an indication might be given of other judgements that might be considered.

6.4 Understanding your problem

The whole essence of this approach to building an expert system has been to produce a method which will work with a reasonable degree of reliability in any circumstances. It must produce a moderately decent outcome irrespective of the problem you give it and, more to the point, irrespective of whether or not you actually understand the problem.

Take weather forecasting. You may be working at the Meteorological Office, but you probably aren't and you probably don't know how to predict the weather. But you can still develop an expert system to help you do it.

The same goes for many other problems you might think of. You can use the same basic expert system to have a crack at a wide range of problems.

But if you really have a problem which you understand well then you'll stand a chance of getting much better, more precise, results if you make up a tailor-made program for it. The point is: if you really understand your problem you won't need anyone else to tell you how to do it. Will you?

Chapter 7

An Expert on Everything in the Entire Known World.

7.1 Nodes

Having got your expert system up to this stage there's one very special application for it. You can get it to become expert in Absolutely Everything in the Entire Known World. It sounds difficult, perhaps, but it isn't really. Just a bit time-consuming.

First, set up the system as before with seven variables and five outcomes. Say:

Variables:	*Outcomes:*
Wings	Bird
Beak	Plane
Engine	Glider
Min. Temp.	Rain Tomorrow
Max. Temp.	Dry Tomorrow
Rainfall	
Sunshine	

Now you start running a training session. First, teach it about the secrets of Birds, Planes and Gliders by providing examples of things with or without Wings, Beaks and Engines. If it asks about the other variables reply with a zero or something equally non-committal. When it seems to have got the hang of that, teach it about the weather and, if it asks about Wings, Beaks or Engines, give it zeroes again. Now let it run away and practice for a while.

Now, believe it or not, you will have an expert system that is simultaneously expert in predicting the weather and in identifying flying objects.

The extension of the situation to cover Every Field of Human Endeavour is obvious. You just keep on adding new variables and new outcomes and new training examples. And the expert will, finally, become expert in Everything in the Entire Known World. Subject, of course, to the limitations of your computer's memory size.

"But surely," you exclaim, "this is wonderful!"

Well, yes, it is, of course. One doesn't waste one's time designing trifling systems when there are the entire problems of the world to be solved. But you will, possibly, find this system a little slow. And you may, possibly, get irritated if it keeps on asking you about Beaks and Engines when you really only want a weather forecast. For one of the difficulties in this scheme is that, as it stands, the expert is not only capable of solving every problem in the Entire Known World. It will actually, really, try to solve every such problem every time you switch the wretched thing on. It's a noble attempt on its part, of course. But the admiration one feels for it can soon pall.

The answer, obviously, is to have two versions of the expert. One which is good with flying objects and one which is good at predicting rain. And further versions which are good at other things too, if you like. And you don't connect them to each other because there's no point in connecting them.

Which brings us to nodes.

For what we've designed is a node. There is one node for flying object identification and another node for weather forecasting. The two nodes aren't connected because they have no need to be. But each node has several inputs (variables) and several outputs (outcomes) and they could have been connected if we'd wanted to connect them.

For instance, suppose we had two expert weather forecasting nodes. We could have connected the output from one node to one of the inputs on the other node. And, then, we could have used the first node for predicting, say, this afternoon's weather and the second node for predicting tomorrow's weather.

Then, when the expert had formed a prediction for this afternoon it could use that prediction as an input to its long-range (tomorrow!) forecast.

However, going back to the one big node which was expert in absolutely everything, that big node was simply the ultimate example of a parallel process. You told it everything it wanted to know and it told you something in return. By splitting it up into two smaller nodes – weather forecasting and flying object identification – we changed it into two parallel processes.

As they won't be executed simultaneously, they are two parallel processes arranged sequentially. As they don't have anything to do with each other they aren't connected. But, if they had been connected, we would have had a kind of sequential process built up out of a series of nodes (two, in this case) with a tree structure, if you want to think of it like that.

Each node could be set up and trained individually so it would be just as good as if it was the only node in town.

And although in theory it's no better than one big parallel process, in practice it might help save you some time, as well as giving you a bit more information about what's going on.

Think, for another boring instance, about the weather again.

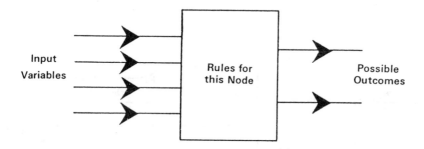

Fig. 7.1 A single node.

Currently, you have a node which will tell you if it's going to rain tomorrow or not. Fine. But it could have told you other things. Like, for instance, whether or not it was warm today. Now surely, one comments, any idiot can work that one out? True, but this is a computer so it's a bit more complicated than that.

Set up another node and start training it. Get it to say Warm Today if the temperature is over, say, ten degrees Centigrade. It should get the hang of that without too much trouble even if you, personally, have some doubts about ten degrees Centigrade being warm.

Now go back to your first node and give it five variables – Max. Temp., Min. Temp., Rainfall, Sunshine and Warm Today. The Warm Today is the output from the first node and is obviously 1 if the Max. Temp. is over ten degrees Centigrade and 0 if it's not. Train the second node to predict Rain or Dry Tomorrow. The process is shown in Fig. 7.2.

Now, you should notice that, for some strange reason, it behaves differently to the way it behaved before with only four variables.

It's almost as if it had some extra information – but all you've given it is a variation on the theme of the exact temperature which is something it already had.

But not quite for you actually have given it some extra information. That item about Warmth is extra to what it had before. Not very much extra, but a bit. The point is that Warmth, as we've just defined it, is a non-linear transformation of the Maximum Temperature. As the expert only works with linear transformations you've given it something it didn't have before and that it couldn't ever have worked out for itself.

One way of thinking about it, if you're not convinced, is to suppose the expert only had the four variables : Minimum Temperature, Maximum Temperature, Rainfall and Sunshine. From these it works out a set of rules for predicting the weather. You then ask for a forecast and, ignoring for the moment the other three variables, it picks out Maximum Temperature and multiplies that by a number in its set of rules. According to the answer it makes its prediction.

Now add in Warmth. This is 0 if the Maximum Temperature is below ten degrees Centigrade. So, below that temperature , everything is calculated as before.

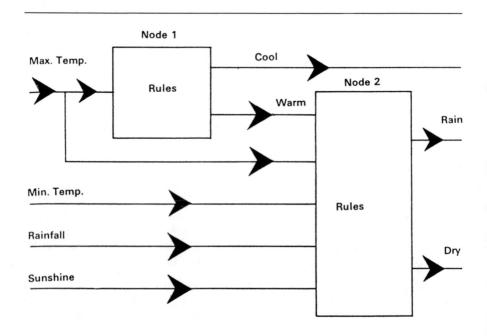

Several nodes can be combined together to form a network giving intermediate conclusions and inputs to other nodes.

Fig. 7.2 Adding an extra node.

But as soon as the Maximum Temperature goes above ten degrees Centigrade Warmth gets the value 1 and this is multiplied by some value in the new set of rules and added to the final results. So, suddenly, as the Maximum Temperature rises the decision process is given a boost, as it were. Mathematically, this is called a step function and it is a non-linear transformation of the data.

So now you have an extra variable, a real, new, extra variable and, obviously, you could just say that you've got five variables and every time the expert asks if it's Warm Today you could just look at the Maximum Temperature and give it 0 or 1 accordingly.

But you could also get the expert to do this for you by setting up a special node for it. This node only really needs one variable for input – Maximum Temperature – and you could go to that first, train it to recognise Warmth, and get the answer to that matter first. Then you could take the outcome – Warmth or not – and use it as the input to the next node, which is the one that predicts Rain.

It's a bit like messing around with the wiring on a hi-fi set. You take the output lead from one unit and plug it into another unit. And Maximum Temperature is an item with leads which go to both units. And, like a hi-fi set, you can keep on adding fresh leads and plugging bits in and unplugging them until you go blue in the face. Hopefully, it will start working before the strain destroys you.

It takes a bit of alteration to your program to do this – but not too much. Suppose you decide that your program has N nodes. Then, when you set up your variables and rules, you could write:
DIM VAR$(VAR,N),VALUE(VAR,N),OUTCOMES$(OUTCOMES,N),
    RULES(VAR,OUTCOMES,N)

In other words, just add another dimension to every variable – most of which are arrays anyway – and then reference each node in turn simply by specifying N.

And, say you've come to a node which makes a judgement OUTCOMES$(J,N1) – outcome J on node N1 – a short routine can search all the other variables to see if this outcome is an input variable for any other node anywhere else. If it is then VALUE(I,N2)=1 for variable I on node N2, assuming that VAR$(I,N2)=OUTCOMES$(J,N1).

It's a bit like automatically scanning around to see if any switches can be set in the system.

And, having set a switch, this is equivalent to providing the expert with another variable value. So, of it's own volition, it can now check around to see if it can draw any further conclusions. If it can, then that's another outcome it can work on for possible inputs to new nodes. And so on, and so forth, until it comes up with something you think is actually useful. Like the answer to the original problem you set it.

Of course, the real difference in the expert's behaviour with more than one node lies in the fact that, typically, at each node non-linear transformations of the data take place – it isn't the presence of nodes as such that make it act differently.

But there is an incidental advantage. The nodes give you an idea of what's going on in your expert's head. For each of these nodes provides an outcome which you might think of as an intermediate solution. Like:
Input: Maximum Temperature Today
Output: It's warm today!
Input: Minimum Temperature, Rainfall, Sunshine
Output: I bet it's going to rain tomorrow (gloom descends).

Exactly how your expert replies is up to your programming – but that's roughly what it can do and, put like that, the matter of whether or not today's weather is warm doesn't sound quite so trivial. After all, it might almost be people talking if, of course, people were actually in the habit of flashing their words up on a screen everytime the weather was mentioned.

Doubtless any application of your own will have lots of nodes and lots of variables and lots of outcomes and deal with something much more non-trivial like, for instance, DIY Brain Surgery. If this is the case, having the Expert show you a few intermediate conclusions before it finally advises you "Remove Patients Head" could help avoid much acrimony.

7.2 The variables so far.

By now, unless you've been concentrating hard and taking notes at the same time, you've probably got an amazing collection of unrelated statements lumped together under the heading Expert System. It really is quite surprising how these things can creep up on you. All you do is write a bit of code, add another bit, modify the first bit, add a bit more, think of something else, wander off to make coffee, have a bright idea and add that...

So what you really need is a bit of a sort out. So, here it is – a collection of all the main variables you might have used so far.

DIM VAR$(MAXVAR,N)

This is the list of all the variable names that you have in your expert system. There is one list for each node. The maximum number of variables you can have at any one node is MAXVAR and the number of nodes is N.

When you're first setting up the expert and want to start DIMensioning arrays the first thing you should get the system to ask is:

INPUT "How many nodes have you ";N

after which it can ask:

INPUT "What is the maximum number of variables at any one node ";MAXVAR – or words to that effect.

Obviously, you're going to waste array space doing things this way, unless all of the nodes happen to have the same number of variables going into them. But, although this can be avoided, it would make life complicated to do it any other way. A separate one-dimensional array for each node's variables would be economical but it's hard to see how you would DIMension them all in BASIC without knowing how many nodes the program was going to have in the first place.

This way you can have up to MAXVAR variables at each node.

DIM VALUE(MAXVAR,N)

This is the list of variable values at each of the N nodes corresponding to the variables names.

DIM VARFLAG(MAXVAR,N)

This is a sort of 'flag' array marking which variables have been input into the decision process and which haven't. It has values of 0 for elements which have been input and 1 for elements the system's still waiting for. The sequence is that you name the variables VAR$(x,y). The system asks for a value of some VAR$(x,y) for which VARFLAG(x,y)=1 and it puts this value in VALUE(x,y) and, then, sets VARFLAG(x,y)=0.

DIM RULEVALUE(MAXVAR,N)

This is the array which holds a 'rating' on each of the variables at each of the N nodes. The system uses this to judge which variable it wants a value for next. The VAR=(x,y) it asks for will, typically, be the one with the greatest corresponding RULEVALUE(x,y).

DIM MINI(MAXVAR,N),MAXI(MAXVAR,N)

These arrays hold the minimum and maximum values of the variables VAR$(x,y). So, the minimum value that VALUE(x,y) can have is given by MINI(x,y) and the maximum value it can have is given by MAXI(x,y). You, personally, have to provide these values – usually at the time you name the variables VAR$(x,y). They are used to help the expert assess the relative importance of each variable in coming to decisions and are needed to calculate RULEVALUE(x,y). If you don't know the minimum and maximum values the variable can take you could try guessing. After all, there must be a limit to them somewhere.

DIM VAR(N)

This holds the number of variables that occur at each of the N nodes. The system already knows the maximum number that can occur (MAXVAR). But it must know how many actually do occur. This is where it's held. In a single node situation – such as we've dealt with already, this problem was solved with the single variable VAR. So, for several nodes, you can get rid of VAR and use VAR(x). If you've written a single-node expert and decide to convert it to several nodes you can save a bit of sweat by still using the variable VAR in the main body of the code but, before you use it to any great extent, insert VAR=VAR(x), assuming that you're in a piece of code which is working on node x.

DIM OUTCOMES(N)

This holds the number of outcomes that can occur at each of the N nodes. It's much the same as for the comments on VAR(N). Similarly, you can carry on using the old variable OUTCOMES for the number of outcomes but you need to put OUTCOMES=OUTCOMES(x) when you're working on node x.

DIM OUTCOMES$(MAXOUT,N)

This is the list of all of the outcome names that the expert system uses, just like VAR$(MAXVAR,N) was the list of all the variable names.

Just as with the variable names, MAXOUT is the maximum number of outcomes at any one node and you should:

INPUT "What is the maximum number of outcomes at any one node ";MAXOUT

early on when setting up the system.

Much the same comments apply here as to VAR$(MAXVAR,N).

DIM RULES(MAXVAR,MAXOUT,N)

This is really the heart of the system, the array of rules the expert uses to make judgements. There are N sets of rules, one set for each node. Each set of rules has VAR(x) variables going to it and OUTCOMES(x) outcomes leading away from it. RULES(MAXVAR,MAXOUT,N) is set up by giving the system a whole list of examples and letting it work through them by itself.

DIM DECISION(MAXOUT)

This holds the values formed for each rule on each outcome at any one node. You could DIM DECISION(MAXOUT,N) for the N nodes so you always have everything to hand. It depends a bit on how you choose to search through the nodes as to whether this is necessary or not. If you get the expert to solve one node at a time then you don't really need the extra dimension and, anyway, you could always calculate DECISION(y) afresh every time the system went on to a new node.

DIM POSSIBLE(MAXOUT)

This holds the possible values for each outcome. Suppose, at a given node, only some of the variables have been entered. Then, for these variables, DECISION(y) can be calculated from VALUE(x,y) and RULES(x,y,node). For these variables DECISION(y) and POSSIBLE(y) are the same. But, for the currently unknown variables, POSSIBLE(y) can be 'guessed' by the system from the minimum and maximum values you placed in MINI(x,node) and MAXI(x,node). The idea is that a 'best' guess will be made by the system on the basis of the maximum value in DECISION(y) so far. POSSIBLE(y) will then be calculated assuming that all the rest of the variables will take either their minimum or maximum values in an overall attempt to discredit the current best guess. If the system can't discredit the current choice in this way an outcome can be chosen for the current node. If it's possible to discredit the current choice by finding a different outcome with a maximum in POSSIBLE(y) that exceeds the current maximum in DECISION(y) then, obviously, more values for other variables are still needed.

DIM EXAMPLES(MAXVAR+1,50,N)

This holds any examples you might want to give the expert to practice on. There is room for a set of up to 50 examples on each of the N nodes.

The system will want to know how many examples you have on each node so you might as well keep this number in EXS(N) and update it every time you add some more examples. If you're working a training session from the keyboard you could place every example you give the system in array EXAMPLES so that it can work over them later in the privacy of its own chips. This will save you wearing your fingers out entering the same examples twice. Obviously you might want a different number of examples to 50 and you might want to hold them permanently on disc rather than in an array in memory. It's largely up to you.

Suppose that you've built a single-node expert and want to convert it to a multi-node expert. First, contrive an example and run it as a single-node example. This will serve as a reference for the future behaviour of the system.

Next, go through the list of variables and convert the program to N nodes. Insert extra code to ask about N, MAXVAR, and MAXOUT. Place one big loop around the main code to step through the nodes:

FOR NODE=1 TO N
.
.
main body of code
.
.
.
NEXT NODE

Now run your single-node example again with N = 1. The results should be exactly the same as before. You should have made no noticeable progress. Actually, of course, the results won't be the same for the program will go wrong, thereby announcing that you have made a mistake. So, correct the mistakes. You've probably forgotten to convert some VAR or OUTCOMES to VAR(x) or OUTCOMES(y). This is what is known as debugging.

If, by some quirk of fate, you get the program working on one node then run it with two nodes – and put your previous example in the second node this time. As before, nothing should change. You'll be astonished and amazed at how much can change on these little occasions when nothing should have changed. It's quite an education, really.

Now run it again with two nodes. This time put your example in both nodes. What you should notice is – nothing should change. So correct the code until it doesn't.

Now comes the big moment when you start fastening these nodes together. Try it this way:

When you've found an outcome for node NODE:

```
10 FOR I=1 TO N
20 FOR J=1 TO VAR(I)
30 IF OUTCOMES$(OUTCOME,NODE)=VAR$(J,I) THEN VALUE(J,I)=1: VARFLAG(J,I)=0
40 FOR K=1 TO OUTCOMES(NODE)
50 IF VAR$(J,I)=OUTCOMES$(K,NODE) AND K<>OUTCOME THEN VARFLAG(J,I)=0
60 NEXT
70 NEXT:NEXT
```

What this does is to take the current outcome from node NODE and search through the entire list of variable names to see if it matches the variables being input to any other node. If it does then it sets that variable's value to 1 and sets the flag, VARFLAG(J,I), for that variable to 0. The value 1 is pretty arbitrary corresponding to Yes/No states. You could use some other value if you wanted to – for instance, the maximum value MAXI(J,I).

It also searches through all of the outcomes on node NODE which didn't occur. The idea being that all of the outcomes are mutually exclusive so, having got one outcome, it can't have the other outcomes and their values for VARFLAG(J,I) can then be set to zero so that the expert doesn't go asking for values for them.

Also, when you provide a variable value, say VALUE(BESTVAR,NODE), you could :

```
80 FOR I=1 TO N
90 FOR J=1 TO VAR(I)
100 IF VAR$(BESTVAR,NODE)=VAR$(J,I) THEN
    VALUE(J,I)=VALUE(BESTVAR,NODE):VARFLAG(J,I)=VARFLAG(BESTVAR,NODE)
110 NEXT:NEXT
```

so that if any given variable occurs as an input to more than one node its value won't be requested more than once.

The whole idea is to squeeze as much out of the information you're giving as possible. If you provide a variable value it has to work for its living by providing inputs to as many nodes as it can. If an outcome is chosen this should be fed into as many nodes as need that information as quickly as possible in the hope of determining further possible outcomes with the minimum intervention from your good self.

If you now set up the system again with two nodes and make each of the two nodes identical, so they both contain your previous example, you should find that, having solved the first node, the expert immediately gives the answer to the second node. The same answer with no more help from you – after all, it got all of the information for the second node when it solved the first node so it shouldn't have wanted any more information.

This should leave you with a basic multi-node system which is adequate for a number of problems.

Try setting it up with an example. Say, two nodes:

Node 1

Variables:	Outcomes:
Feathers	Animal
Metal	Machine
Beak	

Node 2

Variables:	Outcomes:
Animal	Bird
Machine	Plane
Beak	Glider
Engine	

The exact details of the example don't matter too much. The main points to note are that it should first decide whether or not it's being given an Animal or a Machine. It should then use this information to decide whether or not it's being given a Bird, Plane or Glider. It should not have to ask about Beak twice (you provide that information in node 1). And it should not have to ask about Animal or Machine at all (it should be able to work that out for itself in node 1).

7.3 Going through the nodes

Suppose that you decide to set up an expert system with more than one node in it. The expert would then have several points at which it became able to pass some kind of judgement and, depending on each judgement, it might then be able to go on to make more judgements.

The problem that you face when you're building a system like this is that the program has to pass from one node to another. You have to give it a method for deciding which node it should go to next, and the method you choose will influence how well, or how badly, the system works.

To make matters worse, there isn't really any ideal method for every situation. Depending on what you want to do with the expert system one method might be better than another.

It's exactly the same as the problem of tree-searching. Or graph searching. And, to really go into it in detail needs the best part of a book on the subject.

Fortunately, the way we've worked so far has left us with a pretty loose sort of problem so we might as well attack it in a pretty loose sort of way.

For a start, you could visit the various nodes in exactly the same way as you selected variables in the single node case.

Recall, that we had an array RULEVALUE(VAR) which held a value for each of the VAR variables. This value was calculated as being the maximum amount of variation that each variable could introduce into the problem. Take the minimum and maximum values for a variable, calculate the difference between them, and then go to the rule array and look at the values in the rule array for that variable. Multiply them together for each outcome and that gives some sort of measure of the likely importance of each variable. Take the most important variable and let the expert ask for a value for that variable first. If that doesn't enable it to make a judgement, then go and get the next most important variable. And so on.

There's no reason why we shouldn't use the same approach over a large number of nodes. There would be some differences in the programming because some variables might occur in more than one node—but, generally, that would make them seem rather more important to the expert and it would ask about these first. Which seems a reasonable approach. It simply consists of selecting for study those variables which provide the most information to as many nodes as possible.

Actually, what we're doing if we do this is to turn ordinary tree searching techniques on their head a bit. Normally, one would specify a method of searching a tree with reference to the structure of that tree. You know the sort of thing—search down one path until you get to a dead end, then search down the next path, and so on.

In this case we're not searching in that way at all. We have labels on each path corresponding to the names of the variables we've provided. What we're saying is: find the most important variable and then explore all the paths that use that variable. And there's something to be said for doing this. For, in general, we don't know the exact form of the problem you might set your expert to solve so we don't know the best searching method through that problem. We do, however, know that it must have variables in the problem so we ignore the structure and concentrate on the variables themselves. This approach is often called 'Forward Chaining'.

It's a method that will eventually produce answers, even if it means a value has to be provided for each and every variable before you get the specific answer you want. It's just that some people might feel uneasy about a method that seems to proceed with complete disregard for the network through which it's proceeding or the eventual goals you might wish to achieve. Not so much a method, it's rather more like some kind of primordial sludge which oozes through the network of nodes on the basis of: "This bit looks interesting, let's look at that next."

But, as the system ignores the particular way the nodes are organised it also leaves *you* free to ignore the way they're organised too. All you've got to do is to specify your nodes and then name variables and outcomes for each one, and the system will get somewhere in the end. It does have a number of practical disadvantages though.

One of the most practical disadvantages is the fact that all linkage between nodes is done by giving variables and outcomes specific names. This means that if you happen to forget exactly how you spelt some variable's name last time the required linkage won't be made. This is certainly a bit like saying that if you press the wrong keys on your computer you'll get the wrong answers. But if you have a large number of variables and you've had a tiring day it can be a real problem. There isn't much that can be done about it in principle but, in practice, it's a good idea to get the system to let you name variables by showing you a list (menu) and asking which variable you want, rather than by typing it in (sometimes incorrectly) each time.

More specific to this method of working is the fact that the expert might consider a certain variable to be important and, so, ask you for a value for that variable. You then realise that you don't really want to be asked about that variable at all. This might be because you don't have a value for it at the moment or because you know, even if the expert doesn't, that it just isn't useful to provide that information for this particular problem. You'd rather it had asked about something else.

This problem can be fairly easily overcome with several nodes. Suppose you have N nodes you can access them by placing them inside a loop. So the system considers node 1 first, node 2 next and, so, node N last.

At each node, the system could use the previous method for deciding which variables to ask about and, on finding an outcome, it could check all other nodes to see if that outcome was an input variable anywhere else. But, the exact order of passing from one node to the next could be rigidly specified at the time you set the system up. This way, if you know the problem you want to train the expert on, you could set it up to deal first with those things that you, personally, know should be handled first. And if you don't know the perfect order, or don't care, then nothing's really lost by it.

Roughly speaking, this problem is the problem of where to start the expert working on the task in hand and it's at its worst if *you* don't know where to start the task either. Not a trivial point. Consider: the system could look for the most important variables and ask for values on those, but what seems important to it might not seem important to you. Or you could specify some starting point by means of an orderly progression through the various nodes. But suppose you sometimes have one lot of variables and you sometimes have another lot. In general, you may not have values for all of the variables and, depending on what you do have, the expert should obviously start from different points and then pass to different points.

Ideally you just want to be able to go to the expert and give it what information you have and let it make what it can of it. This you can do by giving the expert a variable name and a value for that variable. The variable name then determines which node or nodes the system goes to first. And, because of the danger of miss-keying the variable name you should either select them from the menu or check that the input corresponds to an existing variable before it gets accepted into the system and clogs everything up.

If that was the problem of where the expert should start working, there's an equal problem of where the expert should finish up in the end.

It's fine to say that eventually it will have worked out everything it can so you'll always get an answer to your problem. In practice you don't always want to sit around entering data for various nodes which are really quite incidental to the main problem.

The method of working through the nodes in order allows you to control this to some extent inasmuch as node N could contain the final, overall, decisions and the aim then is to get to node N as quickly as possible. In general, what you can do is to always go to the node which is nearest to node N. And the problem is then to define 'nearest'.

The simplest way is to think of each node as either 'active' or 'dead'. If it's already produced an outcome it's dead – you don't need to go through it again. If it hasn't produced an outcome it's active – and you have to find an outcome for that node. You can then travel in order through the nodes, resolving the active ones to take you successively nearer to node N. At which point it's easy to observe that node N is the nearest node to node N – so why not try to resolve that one first? It would save so much time.

Well, if you could do that, you wouldn't have needed the other nodes in the first place. And, if you can't do that, where can you start in order to finish there? It's at about this point that you realise that searching through nodes isn't necessarily an easy subject to cover completely.

The most general method takes us back to you supplying details of what variables you have values for, entering those, and seeing what outcome turns up.

But, if you don't want to enter more details than you have to and you have specific ideas about which intermediate results you'd like to see the picture gets more complicated. Suppose, for instance, that you simply want the quickest route from some starting point to a final solution. Does that mean, by quickest, that the smallest number of nodes should be visited? Or the least number of questions asked? It's up to you what the answer is to that question – but it does show that there isn't just one, single, answer. Asking the smallest number of questions gives you the least amount of work to do. Visiting the smallest number of nodes gives you the smallest number of intermediate results. Maybe you'd like to get as many intermediate results as possible for the least effort. So you'd like to visit as many nodes as possible whilst the system asks you as few questions as possible. And, possibly, these aims are incompatible.

At the risk of increasing the programming effort you could keep track of the distance to node N, in terms of nodes and in terms of variables still unresolved, for each point in the network of nodes. But the increase in programming effort may be daunting. This is especially the case if there's more than one route to node N from some points in the program. You not only have to find out what the 'distance' is for one route but you also have to find out how many routes there are and how far they are from node N and, somehow, you have to keep track of all these routes so you can choose one which suits you best.

This isn't an impossible problem by any means. If you go through the literature on graphs and trees you'll find plenty of solutions. But it certainly isn't trivial.

In general, the programming effort will be much reduced, and the strain on the intellect lessened, if you proceed by one of the following methods:

1. Volunteer the information to the system. Specify on which variables you have information and let the expert proceed on all nodes that are applicable to that information to see what conclusions it can reach.

2. Let the system ask for information on those variables which seem most important to it. Assuming that you have all the information it's likely to want you can provide what's requested and let the system draw what conclusions it can until it either gets the answer you want or information has been provided on all variables.

3. Get the system to pass from node to node sequentially. This way it won't miss anything and will get to the end eventually. When you first set the system up you should try to establish the nodes in an order that seems sensible to you. You might as well let the system make what deductions it can, when it can, with this method though – because it might happen to get to the end by some route faster than you expected. And, if the system comes to a node which has, by this means, already produced an outcome it might as well skip it otherwise it's doing the same job twice.

It's worth mentioning that you could do exactly the same with a single-node system. Or a system which looks like a single node. If, say, you just have RULES(I,J) to represent one node, you could have a variety of possible outcomes some of which could be identical to some of the variables.

If the expert decided on some outcome and this happened to match up with an input variable this outcome could be used to switch on, as it were, that input variable. After which a flag would have to be set on that outcome so that its effects weren't counted in more than once.

You could then proceed by specifying the names of variables on which you intend to provide information, or letting the system pick its own variables on which it wants information, or proceeding sequentially through all variables in turn.

The problem with this approach – of having all the separate nodes effectively contained in one big node – is the scope it offers for getting confused. Suppose, for instance, the system was meant to predict the weather and, for a start, it judged that it was a warm day today. What's to stop it then making the comment that it was *not* a warm day today? After all, with a given set of rules the two most likely outcomes might be mutually exclusive but it might still give both of these outcomes before it gives any others.

Of course, you can easily devise a method for dealing with this problem. But avoiding confusion is one of the best ways of getting programs to work and a less than ideal method in some respects quickly becomes the best method in every respect if it happens to be the only one you can get working reliably.

7.4 Tailor made nodes

On the day when you're setting up your expert system for a particular problem you might be faced with the odd node which seems to be either too complicated or too simple for you to want to just let it learn by example.

For instance, suppose that you've decided to set up an amazing medical diagnosis system. One of the input variables is the patient's temperature. The first thing you want to do is to get the system to say whether the patient actually does have a high temperature or not. Now – that's easy. If it's over, say, 99 degrees Fahrenheit we want Outcome 1 at some node – Outcome 1 being High Temperature. Clearly, if you give the expert enough examples to train on it will eventually learn to give this information of its own accord. But it might seem like rather a lot of hard work. After all, you actually, in this case, know what the rules should be. Why mess around with a training session?

Quite. So, skip the training session and set up a tailor-made node to assess the patient's temperature. The problem is simply to find values for RULES(I,J) which will give the right answers. Here's a node that will do it:

	High Temperature	Low Temperature
Constant	0	99
Temperature	1	0

This uses a node of size RULES(2,2). Suppose, now, that you have an input VALUE(I). VALUE(0) contains the value 1, the constant, and VALUE(1) contains the patient's temperature. Multiplying by the first rule, High Temperature, the answer is always equal to VALUE(1). Multiplying by the second rule, Low Temperature, the answer is always equal to 99. Obviously, the first rule gives the highest value as soon as VALUE(1), the patient's temperature, is over 99 and the second rule gives the highest value at any time that VALUE(1) is less than 99 – and, so, the system will always get it right about the matter of High versus Low Temperature. Much easier than giving the thing a whole load of examples and waiting for it to sort out the answer on its own.

In general, the decision rule always gives an answer which depends on:

$$DECISION = b_1 + ... + b_n x_n$$

so, if you can put the decisions into this form, it's fairly straightforward.

If you can't think of a way of expressing the problem in this style then you can always give the system some examples and see if it can work something out for you. If what you want the system to do is particularly complicated then you've got problems – a comment which isn't particularly encouraging because there isn't, in general, any method for fitting everything you might want to do into this form.

Suppose, for instance, you had an input variable which could take values from 0 to 100. If it falls in the range 50 to 60 then this has some special significance for you and you want the expert system to detect this situation. It's not an unusual problem – it might be some measurements you're taking and 50 to 60 might be optimal values. Now, it isn't immediately apparent that a set of rules could be written to detect this particular band of values. But you could get around the problem in two ways. First, you could use two nodes to deal with it. The first node could detect if the value was over 50 – in just the same way as we set up a node to detect a high temperature. If it is over 50 the system could pass its result to another node which, in the same way, would detect if the value was under 60. If the system gets the right outcome from both of these nodes it can then deduce that the variable is in the range 50 to 60 and it's solved your problem. So it is possible to detect the required values using this framework.

On the other hand, it would seem to be so much simpler to put in a piece of code:

IF VALUE(I)> = 50 AND VALUE(I) < = 60 THEN OUTCOMES(J) = 1:
and so on, and so forth, rather than to force the problem into a rather alien framework.

But once you've started to do this sort of thing you've still got the remaining problem of how to fit odd items like this into the overall pattern. The simplest way is to place tailor-made pieces of code like this very early on in the program so that every time the program starts to work on a new node, say, the variables' values for the tailor-made items are checked to see if they've been provided yet. This means that the code is likely to get executed more often than is strictly necessary – but it has the important advantage of ensuring that the expert doesn't forget to execute them at all!

Suppose now, thinking back to our amazing medical diagnosis problem, that we want to decide if a patient has fever. We define a fever as a high temperature and flushed cheeks (or any other set of symptoms that you'd like to choose). The system has already decided about the patient's temperature so all that's left is to see if he has flushed cheeks as well. Given enough examples, the expert will work out a set of rules for this by itself. But equally, you can put in your own rules. And this is an example of logical connectives:
    IF (high temperature) AND (flushed cheeks) ...

Suppose that we had rather different medical views we might reckon that it was sufficient for the patient to have just one of those symptoms:
    IF (high temperature) OR (flushed cheeks) ...

The logical connectives 'AND' and 'OR' are so common that it's worth having some tailor-made rules for them:

	Outcome 1	Outcome 2
Constant	0	$n - \frac{1}{2}$
Variable 1	1	0
Variable 2	1	0
.	.	.
.	.	.
.	.	.
Variable n	1	0

Using the next set of rules Outcome 1 gives a maximum value of n, if all n variables have the value 1. Outcome 2 gives the same value irrespective of the variable values it gets and the value it gives is always $n - \frac{1}{2}$. So, Outcome 2 will always be chosen by the expert except in the special case when all n variables have the value 1. In other words, Outcome 1 will be chosen when we have:

(Variable 1) AND (Variable 2) AND (Variable 3) ... AND ... (Variable n)

Using this set of rules Outcome 2 always gives the value $\frac{1}{2}$. Outcome 1 will be less than this, with a value 0, as long as all of the variables have the value 0. As soon as any one variable produces a value of 1 Outcome 1 gives the highest value. So, Outcome 1 will be chosen by the expert when we have:

(Variable 1) OR (variable 2) OR ... OR (Variable n)

	Outcome 1	Outcome 2
Constant	0	½
Variable 1	1	0
Variable 2	1	0
.	.	.
.	.	.
.	.	.
Variable n	1	0

You can see that these two sets of rules are very similar to each other. In fact, if the constant on Outcome 2 has the value $(x - ½)$ the expert will reckon on Outcome 1 as soon as x or more of the input variables have the value 1 instead of 0. For the 'AND' connective $x = n$ while for the 'OR' connective $x = 1$. But you could have any other number if it suited your application.

The advantages of setting up your own rules like this are that you know exactly what the system's going to do at any moment (or, roughly, anyway). The advantages of letting the system learn it's own rules by example are that it provides a relatively easy way of entering rules into the system coupled with the bonus that you don't have to bother to sit down and work out in advance what those rules should be.

7.5 Specific code

Thinking about amazing systems for medical diagnoses, one ponders on the matter raised in the last section. The matter of fever. Suppose we reckoned a fever as a high temperature and flushed cheeks. Well, we saw how we could, either explicitly or by example, build this into our knowledge base in the form of rules and how a fever could then be diagnosed. But wouldn't it have been simpler just to write the BASIC line:

IF TEMPERATURE > 99 AND FEVER = 1 THEN PRINT "Fever"

where FEVER = 1 if the patient has flushed cheeks?

Well, yes, actually, it would be much easier. You could scarcely go wrong at all.

In fact, you could have a whole collection of statements like this and they'd give you a system to diagnose anything (as long as the 'anything' was covered by your programming). It would be quicker and easier to do things this way because BASIC is such a straightforward programming language. If you've had a bit of practice at programming, you can just sit down and write the code almost as quickly as it would take to set up a collection of rules in a more general purpose system. It might be a bit haphazard until you'd sorted out the exact program design – but the general purpose approach has to be a bit haphazard too just to make sure it covers all possible uses it might be put to.

It's all to do with a theoretical claim that's sometimes made about expert systems. It's said that, ideally, they're general purpose programs. They contain a method for making expert judgements in general. And it's suggested that, with an expert system, you add a knowledge base and get a different kind of expert for each new knowledge base. Now, that is something you can't do if you just sit down and write your own code for a specific problem. If you write a medical diagnosis system just by sitting down and writing it you'll never be able to readily alter it to solve another problem.

All of which is hardly a fair criticism if that's what you want to do. After all, most existing expert systems only really work on one specific problem – they aren't truly general purpose programs. The one you're building might be general purpose, able to do anything, but there aren't many others like it. And, as we've seen so far, it does have its limitations at times.

7.6 Saving your expert

Come the end of the day, you've been sitting at the keyboard training your expert to a high degree of skill and it's time to go to bed. Switch the machine off and – lo and behold! – the expertise vanishes like mist.

You knew this would happen, after all it was only data. But it's no use having an expert that has to be rebuilt from scratch every time you want to run it. You want it to get better, not worse, every day.

Obviously, the program itself can be SAVE'd onto disc but exactly how you save the data depends on how you want to go about it. You might, for instance, have found it better to use file-handling techniques rather than all those arrays so that everything was always accessed from disc rather than being held in memory (now he tells us!).

But the quickest and simplest way of saving everything is to write code to dump all of those arrays and their associated variables to disc and read them back in again. That way you can stay with the relatively quick and easy array handling techniques shown in this book but don't lose the results of a lengthy training session, for instance. If you do this then you'll be likely to find that ideas tend to keep springing to mind for ways in which you can make your expert system yet smoother still.

For instance, you could have the data for several different expert systems (their Knowledge Bases actually, if you remember the jargon) sitting on disc in different files and offer the user the choice of which one to load when he starts the system. And, when you create a new Knowledge Base you could write code to offer the option of storing this under a new filename. So, gradually, you finish up building a vast collection of expert systems all available to you at the flick of a disc.

The only danger if you start to go in for this sort of thing is that you might finish up with something that's genuinely usable and useful – and when that happens you really don't know where you'll finish up.

7.7 The multi-node code

To save anyone the inconvenience of having to do any thinking, here's a complete, menu-driven, multi-node, machine learning expert system which should enable anyone, after a few seconds practice, to achieve some reasonably modest aims. Like, for instance, World Domination (as long as you can think of some examples to give it).

116

Fig. 7.3 Menu-driven multi-node expert

```
10 MINI=-10000:FALSE%=0:TRUE%=NOT FALSE%
20 GOSUB 2750
30 PRINT: PRINT
40 PRINT "1. Initialise Expert"
50 PRINT "2. Input Examples"
60 PRINT "3. Exercise Expert"
70 PRINT "4. Training Session"
80 PRINT "5. Normal Running"
90 PRINT "6. Save Current Expert"
100 PRINT "7. Load Current Expert"
110 PRINT "8. Examine Rules and Examples"
120 PRINT "9. Quit"
130 PRINT : PRINT: INPUT "Choose an Option";OP
140 ON OP GOTO 160,1390,1580,490,490,1770,2010,2260,150:GOTO 130
150 END
160 REM Initialise Expert:
170 GOSUB 2750
180 PRINT "To set up an Expert System"
190 PRINT "Please answer the following :-"
200 PRINT: INPUT "How many Nodes have you ";N
210 PRINT: INPUT "What is the maximum number of Variables at any one Node ";
    MAXVAR
220 PRINT: INPUT "What is the maximum number of Outcomes at any one Node ";
    MAXOUT
230 GOSUB 2810
240 FOR NODE=1 TO N
250 GOSUB 2750
260 PRINT"Node";NODE
270 INPUT "How many Variables have you at this Node ";VAR(NODE)
280 PRINT: PRINT "Please name these Variables :-": PRINT
290 FOR I=1 TO VAR(NODE)
300 PRINT "Variable ";I;" is " ;:INPUT VAR=(I,NODE)
310 X$="N"
320 FOR J=1 TO NODE
330 FOR K=1 TO VAR(J)
340 IF VAR$(I,NODE)=VAR$(K,J) AND NODE<>J THEN
    PRINT "(";VAR$(I,NODE);") already occurs on Node";J:
    PRINT "with minimum value ";MINI(K,J);" and maximum value ";MAXI(K,J):
    INPUT "Is it the same here [y/n]";X$
350 IF X$="Y" OR X$="y" THEN
    MINI(I,NODE)=MINI(K,J):MAXI(I,NODE)=MAXI(K,J):K=VAR(J):J=NODE
360 NEXT K
370 NEXT J
380 IF X$="N" OR X$="n" THEN
    PRINT "It has minimum value = ";:INPUT MINI(I,NODE):
    PRINT "It has maximum value = ";:INPUT MAXI(I,NODE)
390 NEXT I
400 GOSUB 2750
410 PRINT "Node";NODE
420 INPUT "How many Outcomes have you at this node ";OUTCOMES(NODE)
430 PRINT: PRINT"Please name these Outcomes:-":PRINT
440 FOR I=1 TO OUTCOMES(NODE)
450 PRINT "Outcome ";I;" is ";:INPUT OUTCOMES=(I,NODE)
460 NEXT I
470 NEXT NODE
480 GOTO 20
490 REM Normal Running/Training Session:
500 IF OP=4 THEN TRAINING%=TRUE% ELSE TRAINING%=FALSE%
510 FOR NODE=1 TO N
```

```
520 FOR I=1 TO VAR(NODE)
530 VARFLAG(I,NODE)=1
540 VALUE(I,NODE)=0
550 NEXT I
560 FOR J=1 TO OUTCOMES(NODE)
570 OUTFLAG(J,NODE)=1
580 NEXT J
590 NEXT NODE
600 FOR NODE=1 TO N
610 REM Start on a new Node:
620 VAR=VAR(NODE):OUTCOMES=OUTCOMES(NODE)
630 GOSUB 2750
640 PRINT "Node ";NODE
650 IF TRAINING% THEN PRINT "Training Session" ELSE PRINT "Normal Running"
660 DECISION=MINI:MAXPOSS=MINI:BEST=1:BESTPOSS=1
670 REM Find Max DECISION and BEST:
680 FOR J=1 TO OUTCOMES
690 DECISION(J)=0
700 FOR K=1 TO VAR
710 IF VARFLAG(K,NODE)=0 THEN
    X=VALUE(K,NODE)*RULES(K,J,NODE):DECISION(J)=DECISION(J)+X
720 NEXT K
730 IF DECISION(J)>DECISION THEN BEST=J:DECISION=DECISION(J)
740 NEXT J
750 REM Find POSSIBLE and BESTPOSS:
760 FOR J=1 TO OUTCOMES
770 POSSIBLE(J)=DECISION(J)
780 FOR K=1 TO VAR
790 IF VARFLAG(K,NODE) AND OUTFLAG(J,NODE) THEN
    IF RULES(K,J,NODE)>RULES(K,BEST,NODE) THEN
    POSSIBLE(J)=POSSIBLE(J)+(RULES(K,J,NODE)-RULES-(K,BEST,NODE))*MAXI(K,NODE)
    ELSE
    POSSIBLE(J)=POSSIBLE(J)-(RULES(K,BEST,NODE)-RULES(K,J,NODE))*MINI(K,NODE)
800 NEXT K
810 IF POSSIBLE(J)<POSSIBLE(BEST) THEN OUTFLAG (J,NODE)=0:
    REM Eliminate impossible outcomes
820 IF POSSIBLE(J)>=MAXPOSS THEN MAXPOSS= POSSIBLE(J):BESTPOSS=J
830 NEXT J
840 IF BESTPOSS=BEST THEN 1080:REM No uncertainty left.
850 USEFUL%=FALSE%
860 RV=0:BESTVAR=0
870 FOR I=1 TO VAR
880 RULEVALUE(I,NODE)=0:MEAN=0:NUMBER=0
890 FOR J=1 TO OUTCOMES
900 MEAN=MEAN+RULES(I,J,NODE)*VARFLAG(I,NODE)*OUTFLAG(J,NODE)
910 NUMBER=NUMBER+OUTFLAG(J,NODE)
920 NEXT J
930 IF NUMBER THEN MEAN=MEAN/NUMBER
940 FOR J=1 TO OUTCOMES
950 RULEVALUE(I,NODE)=RULEVALUE(I,NODE)+
    ABS(MINI(I,NODE)-MAXI(I,NODE))*((RULES(I,J,NODE)-MEAN)^2)
    *VARFLAG(I,NODE)*OUTFLAG(J,NODE)
960 NEXT J
970 IF RULEVALUE(I,NODE)>RV THEN BESTVAR=I:RV=RULEVALUE(I,NODE)
980 NEXT I
990 IF RV=0 THEN 1150:REM No RULEVALUE>0 so no further questions
1000 VARFLAG(BESTVAR,NODE)=0
1010 FOR J=1 TO OUTCOMES-1
1020 FOR K=J+1 TO OUTCOMES
1030 IF RULES(BESTVAR,J,NODE)<>RULES(BESTVAR,K,NODE)
    AND OUTFLAG(J,NODE) AND OUTFLAG(K,NODE) THEN USEFUL%=TRUE%
```

118

```
1040 NEXT K
1050 NEXT J
1060 IF NOT USEFUL% THEN 860
1070 GOSUB 2560
1080 REM Match any outstanding VALUE's :
1090 FOR NN=1 TO N
1100 FOR I=1 TO VAR(NN)
1110 IF VAR$(I,NN)=VAR$(BESTVAR,NODE) THEN
     VALUE(I,NN)=VALUE(BESTVAR,NODE):VARFLAG(I,NN)=0
1120 NEXT I
1130 NEXT NN
1140 IF BESTPOSS<>BEST THEN 660
1150 IF NOT TRAINING% THEN
     PRINT "I suggest ";OUTCOMES$(BEST,NODE);" as likely":
     CORRECT=BEST:GOTO 1270
     ELSE
     PRINT "Can I deduce Outcome : ";OUTCOMES=(BEST,NODE);" [y/n]";:
     INPUT A$: IF A$="Y" OR A$="y" THEN CORRECT=BEST ELSE GOSUB 2610
1160 REM Get any outstanding VALUE's:
1170 FOR BESTVAR=1 TO VAR
1180 IF VARFLAG(BESTVAR,NODE) THEN GOSUB 2560
1190 NEXT BESTVAR
1200 GOSUB 2680
1210 INPUT "Do you wish to keep this Example [y/n]";E$:
     IF E$="N" OR E$="n" THEN 1270
1220 EXS(NODE)=EXS(NODE)+1
1230 FOR I=1 TO VAR
1240 EXAMPLES(I,EXS(NODE),NODE)=VALUE(I,NODE)
1250 NEXT I
1260 EXAMPLES(MAXVAR+1,EXS(NODE),NODE)=CORRECT
1270 REM Match any outstanding OUTCOMES:
1280 FOR NN=1 TO N
1290 FOR I=1 TO VAR(NN)
1300 IF VAR$(I,NN)=OUTCOMES$(CORRECT,NODE) THEN
     VALUE(I,NN)=MAXI(I,NN): VARFLAG(I,NN)=0
1310 FOR J=1 TO OUTCOMES
1320 IF VAR$(I,NN)=OUTCOMES$(J,NODE) AND J<>CORRECT THEN
     VALUE(I,NN)=MINI(I,NN):VARFLAG(I,NN)=0
1330 NEXT J
1340 NEXT I
1350 NEXT NN
1360 NEXT NODE
1370 PRINT "Do you wish to continue ";:
     IF TRAINING% THEN INPUT "Training [y/n]";B$
     ELSE INPUT "Normal Running [y/n]";B$
1380 IF B$="Y" OR B$="y" THEN 510 ELSE GOTO 20
1390 REM Input Examples:
1400 FOR NODE=1 TO N
1410 GOSUB 2750
1420 PRINT "Node ";NODE: PRINT
1430 PRINT "Input some Examples"
1440 PRINT : INPUT "How many Examples have you at this Node";NUMBER
1450 FOR I=1 TO NUMBER
1460 GOSUB 2750
1470 PRINT "Example No. ";I;" on Node ";NODE;:PRINT: PRINT
1480 FOR BESTVAR=1 TO VAR(NODE)
1490 GOSUB 2560
1500 EXAMPLES(BESTVAR,I+EXS(NODE),NODE)=VALUE(BESTVAR,NODE)
1510 NEXT BESTVAR
1520 GOSUB 2610
1530 EXAMPLES(MAXVAR+1,I+EXS(NODE),NODE)=CORRECT
```

```
1540 NEXT I
1550 EXS(NODE)=EXS(NODE)+NUMBER
1560 NEXT NODE
1570 GOTO 20
1580 REM Exercise Expert:
1590 GOSUB 2750
1600 PRINT "Expert is working on it''
1610 FOR NODE=1 TO N
1620 FOR P=1 TO EXS(NODE)*10
1630 EXAMPLE=INT(RND*EXS(NODE)+1)
1640 CORRECT=EXAMPLES(MAXVAR+1,EXAMPLE,NODE)
1650 VAR=VAR(NODE):OUTCOMES=OUTCOMES(NODE)
1660 FOR I=1 TO OUTCOMES
1670 DECISION(I)=0
1680 FOR J=1 TO VAR
1690 VALUE(J,NODE)=EXAMPLES(J,EXAMPLE,NODE)
1700 DECISION(I)=DECISION(I)+VALUE(J,NODE)*RULES(J,I,NODE)
1710 NEXT J
1720 NEXT I
1730 GOSUB 2680
1740 NEXT P
1750 NEXT NODE
1760 GOTO 20
1770 REM Save Current Expert:
1780 OPEN "EXPERT.DAT" FOR OUTPUT AS #3
1790 PRINT #3,N;MAXVAR;MAXOUT
1800 FOR NODE=1 TO N
1810 PRINT #3,VAR(NODE);OUTCOMES(NODE);EXS(NODE)
1820 FOR I=1 TO MAXVAR
1830 PRINT #3,CHR$(34);VAR$(I,NODE);CHR$(34);",";MINI(I,NODE);MAXI(I,NODE)
1840 NEXT
1850 FOR I=1 TO MAXOUT
1860 PRINT #3,CHR$(34);OUTCOMES$(I,NODE);CHR$(34)
1870 NEXT
1880 FOR I=1 TO MAXVAR+1
1890 FOR J=1 TO EXS(NODE)
1900 PRINT #3,EXAMPLES(I,J,NODE)
1910 NEXT
1920 NEXT
1930 FOR I=1 TO MAXVAR
1940 FOR J=1 TO MAXOUT
1950 PRINT #3,RULES(I,J,NODE)
1960 NEXT
1970 NEXT
1980 NEXT NODE
1990 CLOSE
2000 GOTO 20
2010 REM Load Current Expert:
2020 OPEN "EXPERT.DAT" FOR INPUT AS #3
2030 INPUT #3,N,MAXVAR,MAXOUT
2040 GOSUB 2810
2050 FOR NODE=1 TO N
2060 INPUT #3,VAR(NODE),OUTCOMES(NODE),EXS(NODE)
2070 FOR I=1 TO MAXVAR
2080 INPUT #3,VAR$(I,NODE),MINI(I,NODE),MAXI(I,NODE)
2090 NEXT
2100 FOR I=1 TO MAXOUT
2110 INPUT #3,OUTCOMES$(I,NODE)
2120 NEXT
2130 FOR I=1 TO MAXVAR+1
2140 FOR J=1 TO EXS(NODE)
```

```
2150 INPUT #3,EXAMPLES(I,J,NODE)
2160 NEXT
2170 NEXT
2180 FOR I=1 TO MAXVAR
2190 FOR J=1 TO MAXOUT
2200 INPUT #3,RULES(I,J,NODE)
2210 NEXT
2220 NEXT
2230 NEXT NODE
2240 CLOSE
2250 GOTO 20
2260 REM Examine Rules and Examples:
2270 FOR NODE=1 TO N
2280 PRINT "Node ";NODE
2290 PRINT "The current examples are :":PRINT
2300 FOR I=1 TO VAR(NODE)
2310 PRINT VAR$(I,NODE);
2320 FOR J=1 TO EXS(NODE)
2330 PRINT TAB(20+J*3);EXAMPLES(I,J,NODE);
2340 NEXT
2350 PRINT
2360 NEXT
2370 PRINT:PRINT "Outcome";
2380 FOR J=1 TO EXS(NODE)
2390 PRINT TAB(20+J*3);EXAMPLES(MAXVAR+1,J,NODE);
2400 NEXT:PRINT:PRINT
2410 PRINT "The current rules are :"
2420 FOR J=1 TO OUTCOMES(NODE)
2430 PRINT TAB(20+J*3);OUTCOMES$(J,NODE);
2440 NEXT
2450 PRINT
2460 FOR I=1 TO VAR(NODE)
2470 PRINT VAR$(I,NODE);
2480 FOR J=1 TO OUTCOMES(NODE)
2490 PRINT TAB(20+J*3);RULES(I,J,NODE);
2500 NEXT
2510 PRINT
2520 NEXT
2530 PRINT "Press any key to continue":X$="":WHILE X$="":X$=INKEY$:WEND
2540 NEXT NODE
2550 GOTO 20
2560 REM Subroutine to get the value of Variable BESTVAR on Node NODE:
2570 PRINT "Variable ";BESTVAR;" (";VAR$(BESTVAR,NODE);") is ";:
     INPUT VALUE(BESTVAR,NODE)
2580 IF VALUE(BESTVAR,NODE)<MINI(BESTVAR,NODE)
     OR VALUE(BESTVAR,NODE)>MAXI(BESTVAR,NODE) THEN
     PRINT: PRINT "Input is out of range":
     PRINT "You gave minimum ";MINI(BESTVAR,NODE):
     PRINT "and maximum ";MAXI(BESTVAR,NODE):GOTO 2570
2590 VARFLAG(BESTVAR,NODE)=0
2600 RETURN
2610 REM Subroutine to get find the Outcome CORRECT on Node NODE:
2620 PRINT: PRINT "Which Outcome is it :"
2630 FOR QQ=1 TO OUTCOMES(NODE)
2640 PRINT QQ;" ";OUTCOMES$(QQ,NODE)
2650 NEXT QQ
2660 INPUT"Answer by number : ";CORRECT
2670 RETURN
2680 REM Subroutine to adjust RULES(J,I,NODE):
2690 FLAG=0
2700 FOR I=1 TO OUTCOMES
```

```
2710 IF DECISION(I)>=DECISION(CORRECT) AND
I<>CORRECT THEN
     FOR J=1 TO VAR:RULES(J,I,NODE)=RULES(J,I,NODE)-VALUE(J,NODE):NEXT:
      FLAG=1
2720 NEXT
2730 IF FLAG THEN
     FOR J=1 TO VAR:
     RULES(J,CORRECT,NODE)=RULES(J,CORRECT,NODE)+VALUE(J,NODE):
     NEXT
2740 RETURN
2750 REM Screen Header Subroutine :
2760 CLS
2770 PRINT "E X P E R T"
2780 PRINT "            "
2790 PRINT: PRINT: PRINT
2800 RETURN
2810 REM Subroutine to DIMemsion arrays :
2820 IF INIT% THEN
     PRINT "This system has already been initialised":
     PRINT"There may be an error message":
     PRINT"Start the run again to avoid it"
2830 DIM VAR$(MAXVAR,N),VALUE(MAXVAR,N),VARFLAG(MAXVAR,N),RULEVALUE(MAXVAR,N),
     MINI(MAXVAR,N),MAXI(MAXVAR,N),EXAMPLES(MAXVAR+1,50,N),VAR(N),
     OUTCOMES(N),OUTCOMES$(MAXOUT,N),RULES(MAXVAR,MAXOUT,N),
     DECISION(MAXOUT),POSSIBLE(MAXOUT),OUTFLAG(MAXOUT,N),EXS(N)
2840 INIT%=1
2850 RETURN
```

Program Notes:

Figure 7.3 is the only program code in this book which uses disc files in any way. The code, as with all of the code in this book, is designed to work under IBM's Advanced Basic (Basica) and the disc input/output is written with that in mind. By and large, the rest of the program code should run under most versions of Basic, including the Locomotive Basic 2 provided on the Amstrad PC 1512. However, if you do encounter problems with this program when attempting to save and load the expert system to disc (options 6 and 7) the lines containing disc input/output are the places to look to see if modifications have to be made. For the benefit of owners of the Amstrad PC 1512 running Locomotive Basic 2, the only two lines which need changing to make this program run under that particular interpreter are lines 1780 and 2020 which should read :

```
1780 OPEN #3 OUTPUT "EXPERT.DAT"
2020 OPEN #3 INPUT "EXPERT.DAT"
```

And, in case anyone's curious, the reason why I chose #3 as a file number is because this is the maximum file number that can be used by Advanced Basic without altering the defaults for that language and the minimum that can be used by Locomotive Basic 2 for disc files—which means that #3 works pretty effortlessly under either interpreter.

7.8 Some Examples

If you actually managed to key in that program then the first thing you'll want to do is to go off somewhere quietly by yourself and nurse your bleeding fingers for a week or so.

But, having done that, you might like to try running it – in which case some examples could be handy so that you know if it's working or not.

So, here's some examples of what it will do, complete with actual run-time output so that you can see what it will look like on the screen if you happen to have keyed it in correctly.

Note, though, that the *precise* output you get may vary slightly from what's shown here simply because the results returned by the RND function when you Exercise the Expert will depend on the state of the random number generator inside your computer at the actual time of the RUN.

7.8.1 A Single Node Example

First, RUN the thing and you should get a menu of 9 items. Choose the first option to initialise it. Tell it you have one node. Tell it the maximum number of variables and outcomes is two.

```
E X P E R T
_____


1. Initialise Expert
2. Input Examples
3. Exercise Expert
4. Training Session
5. Normal Running
6. Save Current Expert
7. Load Current Expert
8. Examine Rules and Examples
9. Quit


Choose an Option? 1
E X P E R T
_____


To set up an Expert System
Please answer the following :-

How many Nodes have you ? 1
What is the maximum number of Variables at any one Node ? 2
What is the maximum number of Outcomes at any one Node ? 2
```

At this node you have two variables. Name them as Wings (with minimum value 0 and maximum value 1) and Engine (minimum 0, maximum 1). Tell it you have two outcomes. Name them as Bird and Plane.

```
E  X  P  E  R  T
_____


Node 1
How many Variables have you at this Node ? 2
Please name these Variables :-

Variable 1 is ? wings
It has minimum value = ? 0
It has maximum value = ? 1
Variable 2 is ? engine
It has minimum value = ? 0
It has maximum value = ? 1
E  X  P  E  R  T
_____


Node 1
How many Outcomes have you at this node ? 2
Please name these Outcomes:-

Outcome 1 is ? bird
Outcome 2 is ? plane
```

Now you should get the menu back and you can do one of two things. Either, go to a Training Session and let it learn slowly; or, go to the Input Examples option to give it a slab of examples to work from. We go to the Input Examples to keep things simple. Give it two examples. It will ask about the variables and the outcomes so, for the first example, give it a Bird and, for the second example, give it a Plane.

```
E  X  P  E  R  T
_____


1. Initialise Expert
2. Input Examples
3. Exercise Expert
4. Training Session
5. Normal Running
6. Save Current Expert
7. Load Current Expert
8. Examine Rules and Examples
9. Quit


Choose an Option? 2
E  X  P  E  R  T
_____


Node 1

Input some Examples

How many Examples have you at this Node? 2
```

```
E X P E R T
_____


Example No. 1 on Node 1

Variable 1 (wings) is ? 1
Variable 2 (engine) is ? 0
Which Outcome is it :
 1 bird
 2 plane
Answer by number : ? 1
E X P E R T
_____


Example No. 2 on Node 1

Variable 1 (wings) is ? 1
Variable 2 (engine) is ? 1
Which Outcome is it :
 1 bird
 2 plane
Answer by number : ? 2
```

Then go to Exercise Expert and put your feet up for a minute or two while it works
out its rules for you.

```
E X P E R T
_____


1. Initialise Expert
2. Input Examples
3. Exercise Expert
4. Training Session
5. Normal Running
6. Save Current Expert
7. Load Current Expert
8. Examine Rules and Examples
9. Quit


Choose an Option? 3
E X P E R T
_____


Expert is working on it
```

When it comes back go to option 8 to have a look at the rules it has developed. You
should get array EXAMPLES holding the examples you gave it as follows:

```
1   1     —this line is Wings, both Yes
0   1     —this line is Engine, only on the second example
1   2     —this line is Outcomes, 1 for Bird, 2 for Plane
```

And you should have array RULES as follows:

```
 1  -1  -this line for Wings
-2   2  -this line for Engine
```

Have a look at these rules and satisfy yourself that they will separate the two outcomes the way they should. Once you see that they do you'll feel easier about the prospect of the program as a whole working – although there isn't really any need to do this every time.

```
E X P E R T
_____


1. Initialise Expert
2. Input Examples
3. Exercise Expert
4. Training Session
5. Normal Running
6. Save Current Expert
7. Load Current Expert
8. Examine Rules and Examples
9. Quit


Choose an Option? 8
Node 1
The current examples are :

wings                        1   1
engine                       0   1

Outcome                      1   2

The current rules are :
                            bird
                                plane
wings                        1  -1
engine                      -2   2
Press any key to continue
```

Then press any key to return to the menu.

Go to option 5 – Normal Running.

The program will first ask about Engine. Notice that in array RULES this seems the most important variable (which it really is!). Reply 1 and the expert will guess Plane without asking anything else.

```
E X P E R T
_____


1. Initialise Expert
2. Input Examples
3. Exercise Expert
4. Training Session
5. Normal Running
```

```
6.  Save Current Expert
7.  Load Current Expert
8.  Examine Rules and Examples
9.  Quit


Choose an Option? 5
E X P E R T
```
_____

```
Node 1
Normal Running
Variable 2 (engine) is ? 1
I suggest plane as likely
Do you wish to continue Normal Running [y/n]? y
```

Reply Y to continue.

It asks about Engine again. Reply 0. It now asks about Wings, reply 1. It guesses, correctly, that it is a Bird.

```
E X P E R T
```
_____

```
Node 1
Normal Running
Variable 2 (engine) is ? 0
Variable 1 (wings) is ? 1
I suggest bird as likely
Do you wish to continue Normal Running [y/n]? n
E X P E R T
```
_____

```
1.  Initialise Expert
2.  Input Examples
3.  Exercise Expert
4.  Training Session
5.  Normal Running
6.  Save Current Expert
7.  Load Current Expert
8.  Examine Rules and Examples
9.  Quit


Choose an Option? 9
Ok
```

If it does all of this the program is working pretty well and you can try something rather more adventurous.

7.8.2 A Two-Node Example

Try two nodes. On the first node set it up to establish whether the object you have in mind is a Machine or an Animal.

For instance:

Variables: *Outcomes:*
Feathers   Animal
Metal   Machine

On the second node set it up to establish whether or not the object is a Bird or a Plane.

For instance:

Variables: *Outcomes:*
Feathers   Bird
Metal   Plane
Animal
Machine

Like this :

```
RUN
E X P E R T


_____


1. Initialise Expert
2. Input Examples
3. Exercise Expert
4. Training Session
5. Normal Running
6. Save Current Expert
7. Load Current Expert
8. Examine Rules and Examples
9. Quit


Choose an Option? 1
E X P E R T

_____


To set up an Expert System
Please answer the following :-
How many Nodes have you ? 2
What is the maximum number of Variables at any one Node ? 4
What is the maximum number of Outcomes at any one Node ? 2
E X P E R T

_____


Node 1
How many Variables have you at this Node ? 2
Please name these Variables :-

Variable 1 is ? feathers
It has minimum value = ? 0
It has maximum value = ? 1
Variable 2 is ? metal
It has minimum value = ? 0
It has maximum value = ? 1
```

```
E X P E R T


Node 1
How many Outcomes have you at this node ? 2
Please name these Outcomes:-

Outcome 1 is ? animal
Outcome 2 is ? machine
E X P E R T


Node 2
How many Variables have you at this Node ? 4
Please name these Variables :-

Variable 1 is ? feathers
(feathers) already occurs on Node 1
with minimum value 0 and maximum value 1
Is it the same here [y/n]? y
Variable 2 is ? metal
(metal) already occurs on Node 1
with minimum value 0 and maximum value 1
Is it the same here [y/n]? y
Variable 3 is ? animal
It has minimum value = ? 0
It has maximum value = ? 1
Variable 4 is ? machine
It has minimum value = ? 0
It has maximum value = ? 1
E X P E R T


Node 2
How many Outcomes have you at this node ? 2
Please name these Outcomes:-

Outcome 1 is ? bird
Outcome 2 is ? plane
```

Note the way it was able to detect variables which you'd already mentioned previously, such as Feathers and Metal on Node 2.

Now input some examples. When you input examples on node one, think first of an Animal and answer the questions with this in mind. Then think of a Machine and answer the questions with that in mind. Two examples in all.

Then give two examples on node two. One with a Bird in mind and another with a Plane in mind.

Take particular care to spell the words the same everytime you key them in or the string matching will go wrong.

```
E X P E R T
_____

1. Initialise Expert
2. Input Examples
3. Exercise Expert
4. Training Session
5. Normal Running
6. Save Current Expert
7. Load Current Expert
8. Examine Rules and Examples
9. Quit


Choose an Option? 2
E X P E R T
_____


Node 1

Input some Examples

How many Examples have you at this Node? 2
E X P E R T
_____


Example No. 1 on Node 1

Variable 1 (feathers) is ? 1
Variable 2 (metal) is ? 0
Which Outcome is it :
 1 animal
 2 machine
Answer by number : ? 1
E X P E R T
_____


Example No. 2 on Node 1



Variable 1 (feathers) is ? 0
Variable 2 (metal) is ? 1
Which Outcome is it :
 1 animal
 2 machine
Answer by number : ? 2
E X P E R T
_____


Node 2

Input some Examples

How many Examples have you at this Node? 2
```

```
E X P E R T
_____


Example No. 1 on Node 2

Variable 1 (feathers) is ? 1
Variable 2 (metal) is ? 0
Variable 3 (animal) is ? 1
Variable 4 (machine) is ? 0
Which Outcome is it :
 1 bird
 2 plane
Answer by number : ? 1
E X P E R T
_____


Example No. 2 on Node 2

Variable 1 (feathers) is ? 0
Variable 2 (metal) is ? 1
Variable 3 (animal) is ? 0
Variable 4 (machine) is ? 1
Which Outcome is it :
 1 bird
 2 plane
Answer by number : ? 2
```

Then exercise the expert.

When it comes back send it off into Normal Running. The first thing it asks about is Feathers. Suppose we' re thinking of a Bird and reply 1. It then asks about Metal so we Reply 0. It then suggests Animal as likely and immediately moves on to Node 2 where it suggests Bird as likely without asking any more questions.

What happens is that once Node 1 is settled and it has deduced that the object is an Animal it then has the following information : It has Feathers, isn' t Metal, is an Animal and isn' t a Machine. Now, if we look at Node 2, we see that this covers everything it might want to know on that Node so it can then solve Node 2 correctly to guess Bird.

```
E X P E R T
_____


1. Initialise Expert
2. Input Examples
3. Exercise Expert
4. Training Session
5. Normal Running
6. Save Current Expert
7. Load Current Expert
8. Examine Rules and Examples
9. Quit
```

```
Choose an Option? 5
E X P E R T
```

```
Node 1
Normal Running
Variable 1 (feathers) is ? 1
Variable 2 (metal) is ? 0
I suggest animal as likely
E X P E R T
```

```
Node 2
Normal Running
I suggest bird as likely
Do you wish to continue Normal Running [y/n]? y
```

Give it another try, thinking of Plane.

Feathers? Reply 0. Metal ? Reply 1. It deduces a Machine and can then move immediately to Node 2 where it deduces that it is a Plane.

```
E X P E R T
```

```
Node 1
Normal Running
Variable 1 (feathers) is ? 0
Variable 2 (metal) is ? 1
I suggest machine as likely
E X P E R T
```

```
Node 2
Normal Running
I suggest plane as likely
Do you wish to continue Normal Running [y/n]? n
```

Have a look at the examples and rules that you can see with Option 8 :

```
E X P E R T
```

```
1. Initialise Expert
2. Input Examples
3. Exercise Expert
4. Training Session
5. Normal Running
6. Save Current Expert
7. Load Current Expert
8. Examine Rules and Examples
9. Quit
```

```
Choose an Option? 8
Node 1
The current examples are :

feathers                        1   0
metal                           0   1

Outcome                         1   2

The current rules are :
                              animal
                                    machine
feathers                        1  -1
metal                          -1   1
Press any key to continue
Node 2
The current examples are :

feathers                        1   0
metal                           0   1
animal                          1   0
machine                         0   1

Outcome                         1   2

The current rules are :
                              bird
                                    plane
feathers                        1  -1
metal                          -1   1
animal                          1  -1
machine                        -1   1
Press any key to continue
```

7.8.3 And Now For Something Useful

Hopefully, by now your aching fingers are recovering and you feel a bit better about the effort involved.

And the question is: Can it now do anything useful? Something other than an apparently trivial game. Well, we can give it a try with a real life problem – like trying to diagnose faults on a cassette recorder.

We'll suppose that there are the following faults which you could observe on your recorder:

1.No Lights
2.Tape won't move
3.Unit won't record
4.Intermittent sound
5.Distorted sound
6.Erratic speed
7.Hum

These could arise from any combination of the following causes:

    1.Not switched on
    2.Deck in Pause

3.Tape jammed
4.Tape inserted wrongly
5.Erase tab removed
6.Dirty head
7.Stretched tape
8.Poor recording
9.Amplifier problem
10.Dirty capstan
11.Wrong leads

And the remedial action could be any one of the following:

1.Switch on power
2.Press Pause
3.Replace cassette
4.Re-insert cassette
5.Clean Heads
6.Re-record tape
7.Check amplifier
8.Clean capstan
9.Check leads

Set up a two node system. The first node is to find out what is wrong so it has as its variables the seven faults and, as its outcomes, the 11 causes.

The second node is to suggest remedial action so it has 11 causes as its variables and, as its outcomes, the 9 remedial actions.

Now input examples.

For the first node give 11 examples, one for each cause, and answer the system's questions with the specific cause in mind. For the second node give 9 examples, one for each remedial action, and answer questions on the causes in such a way that you reply 1 for each cause that might be helped by the remedial action and 0 for each cause that would not be helped by it.

Then exercise the expert (or, alternatively, instead of inputting examples and exercising, you could have had a training session instead). It's only fair to point out that, as the system gets bigger, the training and exercising will take longer – so don't think the computer has gone and died on you if it goes away for a while to work on the problem.

When it comes back, having worked out a rule set, you can then use Option 8 to look at the rules and examples. These are the ones it was trained on :

E X P E R T
_____

1. Initialise Expert
2. Input Examples
3. Exercise Expert
4. Training Session
5. Normal Running

Choose an Option? 8
Node 1
The current examples are :

	1	2	3	4	5	6	7	8	9	10	11
No lights	1	0	0	0	0	0	0	0	0	0	0
Tape won't move	1	1	1	1	0	0	0	0	0	0	0
Unit won't record	1	1	1	1	1	0	0	0	0	0	1
Intermittent sound	0	0	0	1	0	1	1	1	0	0	0
Distorted sound	0	0	0	0	0	1	1	1	1	1	0
Erratic speed	0	0	1	0	0	0	1	1	0	1	0
Hum	0	0	0	0	0	0	0	1	1	0	1
Outcome	1	2	3	4	5	6	7	8	9	10	11

The current rules are :

	Not switched on	Deck in Pause	Tape jammed	Tape inserted wrongly	Erase tab removed	Dirty head	Stretched tape	Poor recording	Amplifier problem	Dirty capstan	Wrong leads
No lights	3	-3	-1	-2	-1	-1	-1	-1	-1	-1	-1
Tape won't move	-5	-3	-5	-4	-7	-6	-6	-5	-4	-6	-6
Unit won't record	-8	-6	-8	-8	-5	-8	-8	-8	-8	-8	-7
Intermittent sound	-5	-6	-6	-2	-5	-4	-4	-4	-6	-8	-5
Distorted sound	-5	-5	-7	-8	-6	-4	-6	-7	-4	-3	-7
Erratic speed	-5	-7	-2	-7	-5	-7	-3	-4	-6	-3	-5
Hum	-3	-3	-3	-3	-4	-4	-5	-1	-1	-5	-1

Press any key to continue
Node 2
The current examples are :

	1	2	3	4	5	6	7	8	9
Not switched on	1	0	0	0	0	0	0	0	0
Deck in Pause	0	1	0	0	0	0	0	0	0
Tape jammed	0	0	1	1	0	0	0	0	0
Tape inserted wrongly	0	0	1	1	0	0	0	0	0
Erase tab removed	0	0	1	0	0	0	0	0	0
Dirty head	0	0	0	0	1	0	0	0	0
Stretched tape	0	0	1	0	0	0	0	0	0
Poor recording	0	0	0	0	0	1	0	0	0
Amplifier problem	0	0	0	0	0	0	1	0	0
Dirty capstan	0	0	0	0	0	0	0	1	0
Wrong leads	0	0	0	0	0	0	0	0	1
Outcome	1	2	3	4	5	6	7	8	9

```
The current rules are :
                        Switch on power
                          Press Pause
                            Replace cassette
                              Re-insert cassette
                                Clean heads
                                  Re-record tape    -
                                    Check amplifier
                                      Clean capstan
                                        Check leads
Not switched on         1 -1 -1 -1 -1 -1 -1 -1 -1
Deck in Pause          -1  1 -1 -1 -1 -1 -1 -1 -1
Tape jammed            -2 -2 -1  1- 2- 2- 2- 2- 2
Tape inserted wrongly  -2 -2 -1  1 -2 -2 -2 -2 -2
Erase tab removed      -1 -1  2- 2 -1 -1 -1 -1 -1
Dirty head             -1 -1 -1 -1  1 -1 -1 -1 -1
Stretched tape         -1 -1  2 -2 -1 -1 -1 -1 -1
Poor recording         -1 -1 -1 -1 -1  1 -1 -1 -1
Amplifier problem      -1 -1 -1 -1 -1 -1  1 -1 -1
Dirty capstan          -1 -1 -1 -1 -1 -1 -1  1 -1
Wrong leads            -1 -1 -1 -1 -1 -1 -1 -1  1
Press any key to continue
```

If you actually key that lot in then you'd better make use of Options 6 and 7 to save and load the expert. Those options just write all the data to disc and read them back in again so that you can re-RUN the same expert without having to re-key everything.

Then send it to Normal Running when it will try to figure out what's wrong with your cassette recorder.

Exactly how it runs will depend on the examples you gave it to work on but, by way of illustration, this is what happened with the above rules and examples :

```
E X P E R T
_____


1. Initialise Expert
2. Input Examples
3. Exercise Expert
4. Training Session
5. Normal Running
6. Save Current Expert
7. Load Current Expert
8. Examine Rules and Examples
9. Quit


Choose an Option? 5
```

It asked if the speed was erratic—Reply 0 for No. It asked about Distorted sound, Intermittent sound and Hum—again, Reply 0. It then asked about No Lights and, on getting the Reply 1 (Yes, we have No Lights) it immediately deduced that the deck wasn't switched on and moved straight to Node 2 where it recommended that you switch on the Power. Which is nothing if not reasonable.

```
E X P E R T
_____


Node 1
Normal Running
Variable 6 (Erratic speed) is ? 0
Variable 5 (Distorted sound) is ? 0
Variable 4 (Intermittent sound) is ? 0
Variable 7 (Hum) is ? 0
Variable 1 (No lights) is ? 1
I suggest Not switched on as likely
E X P E R T
_____


Node 2
Normal Running
I suggest Switch on power as likely
Do you wish to continue Normal Running [y/n]? y
```

Moving onto another example, on hearing that you've got Distorted and Intermittent Sound it deduces that you've got a Dirty head and advises you to Clean the head. Again, pretty reasonable.

```
E X P E R T
_____


Node 1
Normal Running
Variable 6 (Erratic speed) is ? 0
Variable 5 (Distorted sound) is ? 1
Variable 1 (No lights) is ? 0
Variable 4 (Intermittent sound) is ? 1
Variable 2 (Tape won't move) is ? 0
Variable 3 (Unit won't record) is ? 0
I suggest Dirty head as likely
E X P E R T
_____


Node 2
Normal Running
I suggest Clean heads as likely
Do you wish to continue Normal Running [y/n]? y
```

And, with yet another example, when the Tape won't move it suggests that the Deck is in Pause and advises you to Press Pause.

```
E X P E R T
_____


Node 1
Normal Running
Variable 6 (Erratic speed) is ? 0
Variable 5 (Distorted sound) is ? 0
Variable 4 (Intermittent sound) is ? 0
```

```
Variable 7 (Hum) is ? 0
Variable 1 (No lights) is ? 0
Variable 2 (Tape won't move) is ? 1
I suggest Deck in Pause as likely
E X P E R T
```

```
Node 2
Normal Running
I suggest Press Pause as likely
Do you wish to continue Normal Running [y/n]? n
```

Once you have had this example up and running it soon begins to seem possible that something useful could actually be done with this system—after all, the program as it stands would take a lot more nodes, a lot more variables, and a much more complicated set of interconnections for it all.

You may well feel that it would be more natural, in many of the examples given so far, to reply Yes or No rather than 0 and 1—and you're probably right. In fact, you could tailor the program quite extensively to behave in a more natural way for any given subject. So, a brief reminder that the input variables do not need to be all ones and noughts.

They could also be any real numbers—like rainfall figures, for example. Bear this in mind when you are developing an idea for the expert system and it could help to improve the performance.

Chapter 8

How can you use your Expert?

8.1 Choosing a problem

Suppose that now you want to build your very own expert system. You don't want to build the system described earlier in this book, you want to build something which is peculiarly yours. Well, the first thing to decide is: About what shall this system be expert?

You can, if you like, reply that it has to be expert about absolutely everything in The Entire Known Universe. There's no harm in such an aspiration. But, if you do, you'll be likely to come up with something that looks a bit like the system described in the previous chapter. After all, to be expert in everything you need a very general design with an absolute minimum of preconceptions. The snag with this approach is that, whilst it might work on a wide range of problems, it might not be outstandingly good at any of them in particular.

Ideally, you might choose an area of intending expertise which is not too broad – and not too narrow. Which sounds a bit vague (and is) but has some reason behind it.

Suppose that you choose too narrow a field to work in. Like, for instance, diagnosing a fault in a motor car. Now you might think that this field would be fine – after all, motor mechanics charge a lot and to get a computer to take their place could be handy. But look at the problem more closely.

Say your car won't start in the morning. What you want is for the computer to diagnose what's wrong with it. So: look in the owner's handbook and you'll probably find that it won't start for one or more of the following reasons. It might be out of petrol; have a flat battery; have water in the distributor; or, have dirty spark plugs. So put that on an expert system. Now run (mentally, as it were) that system and on the screen is the question: Is there petrol in the tank? And you trudge out to the car to have a look and get an answer. If there was, you might be asked: Is there water in the distributor? And, again, you trudge out to look. And, if there isn't, five minutes later you're out there unscrewing a spark plug to see if it's dirty...

And, all in all, you really didn't need to switch the computer on just for that. You could have just taken the owner's manual out to the car with you and saved electricity.

The reason for this is that diagnosing why a car won't start is very trivial. The real effort lies in poking around the car trying to get the information you need in the first place.

The computer can't poke around the car for you – so what you really need is a car mechanic to help you.

Certainly, there might be some tasks in car mechanics which could benefit from an expert system. Suppose that you ran a workshop and regularly had relatively inexperienced mechanics checking out different vehicles and carrying out (fairly) complex work on them. Then you might think it worthwhile to have a screen set up to advise them on how to proceed. Alternatively, you could just give them the workshop manual. But, if it's simply a matter of a car that won't start, that really does seem like a problem which is much too narrow to be worth tackling. The problem has to be 'large' enough to actually give the computer some useful work to do. And it will be most useful if the task isn't already accomplished in some other medium – such as a workshop manual.

At the other end of the scale the problem shouldn't be too large. The reasons for this are practical ones again – primarily, the practical problem of getting an expert system built with enough expertise in a large area. As the size of the problem area increases so does the amount of effort on your part necessary to carry out a thorough implementation. And, if the implementation isn't thorough, the usefulness of the system is pretty dubious.

Real Life Expert Systems aren't expert in, for example, the whole field of medical diagnosis. They are experts in a narrow field – and are good in that field. An all-singing, all-dancing system that frequently makes the wrong diagnosis is liable to kill as many patients as it cures.

Finally, the system will have the most chance of being useful if there appears to be some method of getting it to work. This sounds rather silly but suppose you had a system which you intended to be expert in the field of winning the football pools. Now how, even roughly, would you produce such a system? Some sports and games of chance might be amenable to a bit of computerised prediction. But football? All you need is a few key players to stagger onto the pitch with hangovers and the result of the game can be very different from any results the computer might dream up. The problem is too diffuse to be handled by computer. It isn't at all clear what sort of rules govern the actual play of the game and it isn't at all clear that there's any method by which you could uncover any rules.

In general, you can get an idea as to whether you have a likely field for an expert system (or any program) by asking yourself whether or not there's anything much in the problem that can be measured.

If there is, then you're in with a chance. If not, forget it.

By 'measured', of course, one doesn't necessarily mean length, breadth and width. A Yes/No response is a measure which will keep a computer happy. But, overall, you must be able to describe the problem area in terms of a series of measures of some sort. If there is something in the situation that can't really be reduced to a measurable quantity (like the fine footwork of player X) then you have something which is unlikely to be convertible to computer.

8.2 Analysing the problem

Once you've hit upon a problem area which looks worthwhile the next thing to do is to start analysing it.

First, you need to get a broad overview. Typically, you already have this. After all, most systems don't get written by accident. They tend to arise because a specialist in some field thinks a computer could help or because a computer person knows a specialist with a problem. If you don't have this overview then this is the time for gently poking around in the area – primarily to see if you were right to think that this is something which could be done on a computer. To check that it really was a suitable problem to choose.

And then – the typical next step – you grab an expert and pick his brains on the subject. And you can divide this up into a fairly orderly sequence consisting of the outcomes, the measurable evidence (variables) and the reasoning that links them.

The outcomes may be very simple – Gold In Them Thar Hills, Bronchitis In Them Thar Lungs. That sort of thing. Is it, though, the presence or absence of an outcome which is important? Or is there some other measure associated with the outcome? A probability, for instance. It's important to sit down and work out what, ideally, you want to get out of the system and in what form you want it. A list of possible diagnoses, or conclusions, or recommendations, and an indication of how these results are to be measured.

The variables are the pieces of evidence that the human expert has at his disposal. You have to find out what they all are and how they are measured. Having asked the expert what he hopes to find out you need to know what he considered in coming to his conclusions.

The linkages between these items are the rules the expert applied. What 'internal program' was the expert working through when he came to his conclusions? This can easily be the hardest bit. Quite possibly, the human expert won't be fully aware of what rules he uses. So all you can do is to get a first crack at finding out what he thinks he does and then go away and implement it to see what happens.

Once you've got all this initial information together you may find that a form for the program naturally presents itself.

For instance, with our totally general-purpose system the requirement of generality of purpose dictated that it had to be self-learning, producing its own rules from examples.

It also became evident that the particular inferencing structure used wasn't too critical – because what might be right for one application might be of less use for another (so, we produce a system that's only of marginal use in any situation...)

But if you have a known list of outcomes and a known list of variables and a known list of rules in front of you – then the situation is different. If the rules are of very widely varying type then you might have to write specific code for each one. If they can be reduced to a common format you can store them on file as if they were data and then write a routine for working through them. If they all rely on logical connectives you can write fairly simple deductive code to arrive at definite conclusions. If they have probabilistic elements associated with them you need some method of keeping track of the probabilities.

It seems a bit feeble to say that one can't advise in great detail on what you should do—that you should work it out for yourself. But, in fact, this actually is what you have to do. You can look at some of the ideas in this book and they may give you ideas to help in working out an approach. But just as a general-purpose expert system falls down on fine details so will a general-purpose method of building an expert system. Each application area will have its own peculiarities which suggest a special treatment.

People who have built expert systems of their own frequently report that the hardest stage was the initial accumulation of outcomes, variables and rules. Once they had derived this information from a human expert and set this information down on paper the rest began to fall into place before them. But even if no absolute structure appears at this stage there is a further reported fact which makes things slightly easier. Namely, that the process doesn't stop there.

Using the initial information you set something up to run on the computer—a tentative sort of program which you think might work. You then run it on a few examples and hand the results to the human expert for comment. Usually, the system makes mistakes and between computer person, human expert, and computer a process of feedback sets in wherein the program rules are progressively altered until the thing starts working reasonably.

In some ways you could feel that the process is pretty sloppy. After all, if you set out to write a payroll program without much idea as to how payrolls were calculated then people might feel you were in the wrong business and should try, say, chicken farming instead.

But, this is how expert systems seem to be developed. And one could argue that it's a reasonable method in a situation in which nobody really knows exactly how the thing should be done. After all, if it eventually works the means used probably justify the end.

And one has to admit that, in fact, one does know people who have written even such things as payroll programs by a method not entirely different from this and have managed to sell the end product.

The really hard part of the problem to analyse, actually, is why any human expert should spend his or her, apparently valuable, time giving away the secrets of their art to someone who's going to put it on disc, make a million copies, and sell them to anybody at £5 a time. Such an expert must, surely, be mad. It's as if the experts think that one of two things were likely to happen: One, that the system won't embody their expertise, will be fairly useless, and therefore do no harm to their business; or, Two, that they really don't mind having their expertise devalued and being put out of business. Not a new situation. For ask yourself : where have all the payroll clerks gone? Perhaps they're standing in the dole queue wishing they could meet that nice computer person one more time? The one to whom they explained the intricate task of payroll calculation.

Maybe you should be generous and offer your human expert a cut of the royalties on your system. Maybe you should be generous and offer me a cut of the royalties, too.

Chapter 9

Large-Scale Expert Systems

9.1 MYCIN—medical diagnosis

So far, all we've considered is the one expert system—our very own, totally general-purpose, home-made expert system. There are, of course, others. So, to what extent does our system resemble existing systems? Well, the best answer is to describe a few others and see just where the similarities, if any, lie.

MYCIN is an expert system designed to carry out medical diagnoses. Specifically, it's designed to work in the area of blood and meningitis infections—making an appropriate diagnosis from evidence presented to it and recommending a course of drug treatment for any diagnosed infections. It consists of a total of 450 rules developed with the help of the Infectious Diseases group at Stanford.

Its most fundamental point—and the one which can give rise to the most complications—is the use of probabilities. Medical diagnosis is an inexact science. If a patient exhibits a particular set of symptoms then these might well indicate a particular illness, but the connection is rarely total. Consider the contrast between a medical diagnosis system and a system which was expert in, say, the field of chemistry. To make it easy, let's consider hypothetical systems—because, apart from anything else, this helps to avoid trespassing on the preserve of real, human, experts.

Suppose I have an expert system for chemical analysis and one of the pieces of information I give it is the result of a litmus paper test. That is: on adding litmus paper to the solution in question it goes, for instance, red. Now, from this the expert can 'diagnose' that what I have is acidic. Easy. There are no doubts present.

Now switch on the medical diagnosis system and inform it that the patient under consideration has a bad cough. Well, that might mean that there is a case of bronchitis, tuberculosis, or, well... just a bad cough. There is no absolute certainty about the meaning of the evidence.

And, somehow or another, the expert system has to be able to cope with this uncertainty. Our own system did this to some extent—but not very precisely. And if you recall the earlier discussion on probabilities you'll recall just how difficult it is to deal with a problem like this.

The way MYCIN tackles the problem is to assign a Certainty Factor to every one of its 450 rules. So you can think of MYCIN as containing a series of rules of the form IF...THEN with certainty P.

And now, note that we used the phrase 'Certainty Factor' rather than the word 'Probability' and the question is: Why? Are they different?

Well, you know all about probabilities by now if you've read the earlier sections of this book but what you didn't realise is that there can be more than one type of probability. The type we've looked at so far (and which we'll continue to look at) are statistical probabilities. The whole theory of statistical probability is based on the assumption that, if only you had enough examples, these statistics would accurately describe the behaviour of the system you're looking at. It is the frequency approach to probability.

Some people, however, maintain that this is the wrong approach to use for inferencing systems – systems which modify their degree of belief in an outcome depending on the inputs they receive. For these systems, it is claimed, a theory of Logical Probability is better than a theory of Statistical Probability because, in the case of an inferencing system, there isn't really an external frequency model for what is happening. To go into the detail of Logical Probability is somewhat beyond the scope of this book but, by way of slight compensation, this author would suggest that if you stick to a statistical model then you won't, really, go far wrong and that the theorists of Logical Probabilities are not, in fact, particularly good at pinning down the details of the calculations you should make, even if you did accept their theories. In other words, even if you knew the theory backwards it probably wouldn't improve your program much. (This criticism of Logical Probability is known as the Sour Grapes Theory).

Anyway, Logical Probability is the approach used by MYCIN and the practical effect is that MYCIN's Certainty Factors are, roughly, what most people would think of as Conditional Probabilities of the form $P(H:E)$ – the probability of this hypothesis given this evidence. Because they aren't really probabilities in the sense we've discussed them the calculations which we've used so far don't really apply – and MYCIN uses a fairly *ad hoc* method of summing up its Certainty Factors as it proceeds through the program.

So, to start at the beginning, where did these Certainty Factors come from? In the case of MYCIN they came from the human experts who provided the rules in the first place. When they suggested a rule they stated their degree of confidence in that rule on a scale from 1 to 10.

And the point we made earlier concerning probabilities arises – how do we know that these probabilities are correct? Well, we don't really. Doubtless they're fairly correct (and the fact that MYCIN gives good results supports the suggestion that they are pretty good) but the method is essentially *ad hoc* – which means it wouldn't make a statistician happy.

Having set up these rules with their associated certainties MYCIN works by backward chaining from a possible outcome to see if this outcome can be believed or not. Once it's established all of the items it needs concerning a particular outcome it makes a judgement on that outcome calculated on the basis of the certainty factors associated with all of the rules which had to be used to reach that particular outcome.

For instance, if the outcome were item Z, it might have been necessary to establish both X and Y in order to deduce Z. But the rules used to establish X and Y might have had certainties P and Q associated with them. Now if P and Q were each of value 1.0 say, then Z would necessarily follow. If P and Q are less than 1.0 (which, in general, they are) then Z doesn't necessarily follow. It only follows with a certain amount of certainty.

And, recalling the earlier discussion of probabilities, it is no mean task to calculate just what the certainty of Z will be under these circumstances. So much depends on the exact form of all the items concerned and how they interrelate.

So MYCIN, instead of trying to get an exact solution to this problem, simply cumulates all of the certainties concerned to give an idea of the sort of relative magnitude of the answers.

Probably the important point to note is that MYCIN doesn't come up with a diagnosis and disclose the exact certainty of that particular diagnosis being true. What it does is to come up with a whole series of diagnoses each of which has some kind of certainty 'score' associated with it. Above a certain – *ad hoc* – value all of these diagnoses are accepted as being, to some extent, likely and the user is presented with a list of possibilities.

Mathematically the procedure is somewhat shaky but, against that, the evidence is that it works very well in practice. So much, of course, for mathematics...

Medical diagnosis, though, is itself something of a shaky procedure. A doctor doesn't give an exact probability statement about each of his patients – he simply reckons that a particular diagnosis seems kind of likely with, maybe, some other diagnoses being additional possibilities. Further, a patient might not be suffering from just one complaint – he might be suffering from several things simultaneously. In this case, to work out the one, best, exact, diagnosis is to exclude the perfectly valid possibility that there just isn't one best, exact, diagnosis, but several.

It has been reported that members of the medical profession, encountering MYCIN, have been quite happy with it reckoning its abilities as good as theirs. Possibly that is where the real proof of the pudding actually lies.

The next point to make about MYCIN is its use of the English language. When it wants information from the user it asks for it in an English language way. When the user enters information he does so in a way which appears fairly natural and English-like. This sounds handy – but is it anything more than that?

There are two parts to the matter – the part that concerns user acceptance of the finished product (was it worth doing?) and the part that concerns the actual implementation (was it easy to do?).

Taking the first part it's reckoned that one of the advantages of expert systems is that anyone can use them with very little previous knowledge of computers. Certainly, it's easy to see that users would respond more favourably to a system that used their language than a system which forced them to talk in, say, BASIC. Doctors, for instance, using MYCIN found the language easy to work with and, conceivably, wouldn't have wanted to waste their time evaluating a system that was hard to use. And, if nobody's willing to waste their time using a system then one might argue that its long-term usefulness was pretty non-existent.

But what about implementation? After all, everyone knows that natural language processing is one of the most difficult jobs around – how do you get around the problem?

The answer, really, is a bit of a cheat because, in fact, MYCIN doesn't carry out full natural language processing at all.

The trick is that every profession tends to play its own little language game. It has special words, stereotyped ways of saying things, that are quite particular to that profession. There are lots of reasons for this, some of them good reasons. At the semi-malicious level one could point to the fact that even small children often have their own private language which they use to exclude outsiders from their conversations and which increase solidarity amongst their friends. Adults have these private languages too (including computer people – they're the worst of the lot). At a more significant level, when one is talking about precise concepts one has to use words in a precise way and in the same way every time you use those words. This leads to a specialised subject language which might look the same as normal English to an outsider – but which is actually very different.

Take for instance the words 'chronic' and 'acute'. In medical parlance these words simply refer to the duration of an illness – whether it has been around for a long time (chronic) or only a short time (acute). So, clearly, when a doctor says his patient has a chronic cough he doesn't mean that it's simply awful. Nor, if he says that a cough is acute, does he mean that he thinks the patient is going to drop dead any minute. He's simply making a statement about the length of time the patient has been coughing like that.

All of this might seem like an unnecessary diversion – but it can help a lot in implementing an expert system. For MYCIN it was found that doctors working in this area of diagnosis used words in very precise ways and uttered very stereotyped comments. Much more so than most people would do in the course of a normal conversation. And the advantage of this was that it was possible to easily define a very limited subset of English which would express everything that might be said on the subject with very few complications. Standard phrases and forms of grammar were readily adapted into the program and the result was a highly stunted subset of English which was easy to program.

The doctors were happy with the result because, possibly without realising it, they too spoke in a highly stunted subset of English. At least when they were discussing their work they did. For all one knows they turned into famous orators once they got home of an evening – but that is beside the point.

In a way this all ties in with the comments on DENDRAL which, you'll see later, doesn't use any English language at all. What it uses is a graph language suited to the particular activities of chemists. That is a very restricted subset of English – but the point is similar. Model the system into the language of the human experts who will use it and you increase its chances of user acceptance and can more readily take advantage of the knowledge that already exists in that field which will, to some extent, have shaped the language used to describe that knowledge.

The Bad News though (there's always some Bad News) is that, having done this, you have an expert system which is more difficult to adapt to other areas of expertise, simply because of the differences that exist in the language used to describe expertise in other fields.

On the subject of user-acceptance MYCIN has a capability which many other expert systems possess and which is frequently commented upon – its ability to explain to the user why it is doing what it is doing.

As a simple example, suppose that you have an expert system and it asks you if you have a cough. Instead of simply replying Yes or No you could ask the expert: Why? That is, Why has it asked that question. The system could then display a message pointing out that a cough sometimes indicates lung trouble. Or some such comment.

Now, at its very simplest level, programmers will realise that this is nothing more than a simple program comment. Every time a rule is programmed into the system all you need to do is to program in a brief piece of text giving an explanation of the purpose of that rule. So, when the system asks a question involving that rule it can invoke this piece of text as an explanation if the user wants it. It resembles the REM, in BASIC.

In other words, it's not very clever. So why the interest in it?

Well, in the finished product the reason for doing this is simply user acceptance. Users, particularly those who don't know much about computers, are impressed with a system that acts in such a human fashion that it can explain itself when asked to. And, as noted before, there's not much point in writing a system that nobody's going to use.

But there's rather more to it than that. Consider the programmer (you, for instance, writing the system). Program REMs are all well and good. They certainly assist in debugging and design because they remind you of why it was you included that bit of code and of what it is supposed to do. But the snag with REMs is that you have to list the program in order to read them. It sounds rather a trivial complaint but in a long program which might have finished up almost anywhere there might be a better way of recording what's going on.

And that's, to some extent, what the Why? of the expert systems represents. They are 'live' REMs that can be called at any time and remind you of what's going on without actually interrupting anything else.

Now stand back a little further from the actual program and recall the problems that are usually encountered in building up an expert system – problems of knowledge acquisition and engineering. The program contains a series of rules and reasons for those rules and, typically, the program doesn't work perfectly as yet. The human expert is sitting at the screen working through an example. Suddenly, as it were, the machine asks a stupid question. At this point the (human) expert can now ask Why? and get some idea of what's gone wrong with a view to putting it right by adding another rule or modifying some old rules.

All of which would not be very earth-shattering if, really, all the system did was to print out a standard comment. Something a bit more sophisticated would certainly help.

In the case of MYCIN this something-more-sophisticated is TEIRESIAS – a system for modifying the MYCIN rule set and explaining the actions of MYCIN. In essence it's very much like a trace and dump facility with the big advantage that it's somewhat more user-friendly than the traditional technique of filling a box of lineprinter paper with the contents of main memory in hexadecimal.

With our human expert sitting at the MYCIN screen it's possible to ask *Why?* in response to a request for information and receive a summary of the line of reasoning that has been followed so far. Specifically, it can display the current rule that has asked for information and show the status of any or all of the other inputs to that rule.

If you think of the system in the early part of this book you might have given it the problem of identifying an object as either a Bird, a Plane or a Glider. The system, at some point, asks you if the object has an Engine and you ask: Why?

Obviously, it would be fairly easy to check through the current node to see what the state of the other variables was. In which case the system might point out that it has already determined that the object has Wings, and doesn't have a Beak, and (with an extra piece of coding) it could calculate that if it got a Yes response to Engine then it could conclude that the object was a Plane but a No response to Engine would cause it to conclude that the object was a Glider.

And if the rules it was working from were faulty it might announce its intention of deducing Glider if the object had an Engine – which would be wrong, thereby letting the user know that this particular rule needed modifying.

Naturally, a system like MYCIN needs more code to enable it to tailor its statements, but the principle is the same. *Why?* provides a snapshot into the current reasoning position of the system which is a useful aid in initial development and debugging as well as serving to reassure the eventual users that it isn't just working at random.

Another facility of TEIRESIAS is the question: How? applied to any given statement. Thinking again of our Bird/Plane/Glider example one might have introduced code to enable the user to ask *How? Wings*. In other words, the system believes that the object in question had Wings – how has it come to believe this. The answer would be simple in this instance – because the user told it so. And it would be simple to print a short message to that effect.

More complex systems need more complex methods though because, typically, the user wouldn't ask about the validity of some statement which he himself had made. He would be asking about some intermediate conclusion drawn by the system itself. In this case the technique is to step backwards through the chain of reasoning that leads up to this intermediate conclusion showing what rules were used and what information was used to reach this intermediate conclusion. The obvious application of this facility is again in program development at the point where the system has made a mistake – by asking an inappropriate question, for instance – and the human expert wants to know how it managed to get to where it now is. If Why? is the snapshot facility then How? is the trace.

It's fairly easy to see that enhancements like those offered by TEIRESIAS can be useful in developing an expert system but, even with a system that works perfectly, they have some use.

For, if the system can work well, and if the system includes the means to explain its actions in fairly English-like terms, then you have a system that could be used to teach others about its area of expertise.

After all, if you have a medical student who isn't very good at diagnosis and a computer system which is very good at it then you might as well sit the one down with the other and let them get on with it. A technique such as this could, one supposes, dramatically reduce the incidence of apoplectic fits amongst those who would formerly have been landed with the onerous task of educating the young.

This approach has, in fact, been tried.

A program, called GUIDON, has been developed to work with MYCIN in order to exploit MYCIN's knowledge about diagnosis for teaching purposes. And, again using GUIDON, the set of rules in PUFF (see next section) has been adapted to MYCIN so that teaching work can be carried out in the field of breathing disorders.

Obviously, it would have been possible to use these expert systems as they stand for teaching purposes. But some modification can enable the system to act as a more closely-involved monitor of the students' behaviour with a higher degree of interaction than would be possible if the students just sat there staring at the screen until it was time to go home.

With all the work that's been done in the field of expert systems for medical diagnosis you'd think that there was no need for doctors anymore really. Doubtless there's some truth in this belief but as yet no medical authority has suggested that an expert system could be licensed to practice in its territory despite the reported comments that these systems are as good as the human experts. And (one supposes) if there's got to be a licensed (human) expert on hand one might as well save some money and get him to carry out the diagnosis as well rather than splash out on a computer.

A bit of a pity, really. The idea of an expert system with a pill dispenser just below the keyboard is rather a nice idea. Unless, of course, one happens to feel unwell oneself. That would then be a very different matter.

9.2 PUFF—breathing disorders

Having considered MYCIN, consider the following:

What would happen if one took MYCIN and shook it over the wastepaper basket until all of the domain-specific knowledge fell out leaving only the basic reasoning mechanism?

The answer is that you would have EMYCIN—Empty MYCIN—which would be a more-or-less general purpose expert system that, temporarily, wasn't expert in anything at all. So that's what the scientists at Stanford did. And having got an Empty MYCIN they then proceeded to fill it up with something else.

That Something Else was a set of 50 or so rules concerning pulmonary disorders and, once put into EMYCIN, they gave rise to PUFF a, rather happily-named, program for diagnosing breathing disorders.

The idea is that a patient staggers into the doctor's surgery and breathes into a machine. There's nothing new in this—the machine simply records the volume of air the patient breathes and how fast the air moves when he breathes it. From this record a doctor can make some kind of diagnosis of the patient's condition.

For instance, he might be normal, he might be sick, the sickness might be bronchitis, it might be emphysema, it might be a number of things.

Whatever it is, the idea is to input data into PUFF and have PUFF work out a diagnosis.

For a start, it's worth noting that PUFF doesn't receive its data straight off the machine into which the patient breathes. Doubtless it could be modified so it did, but it doesn't

What happens is that the breathing machine presents the doctor with several, possibly relevant, pieces of information about the patient's breathing. The doctor also has to hand certain, possibly relevant, pieces of information about the patient in general. For instance: the patient's sex, age and smoking habits.

At this point you can forget about the breathing machine and turn your attention strictly to the computer, ready-loaded with its expert system. For all that we have now is a list of variables and certain values associated with those variables and the machine has to make a diagnosis.

As a trial run 150 sets of patient data were presented to PUFF to see how it got on – and the results were that PUFF made the same diagnoses as a human doctor about 90 per cent of the time.

Now, at this point, it's possible to see that this is the sort of thing which could be set up on our own expert system, described earlier.

Taking all of the variables to be considered we could have set these up and listed all the possible outcomes (perfect health, bronchitis, etc.). We could then have presented the system with the 150 sets of data in a training session and let the expert develop its own rules for forming diagnoses. We might then have found that it was, occasionally, right in making subsequent diagnoses.

However, it would be pretty unfair to the scientists at Stanford to suggest that the systems are identical in every respect because they aren't.

For a start PUFF doesn't work out its rules for itself. The Stanford scientists got together with others from the Pacific Medical Centre who actually told them how to make the diagnoses and, for most expert systems currently in use, this approach is far more usual. One reason for this could be that they don't like to trust the program to do too much by itself – but a more likely reason is that it's usually possible to build a more efficient system if you know, in advance, just how you want it to proceed.

So the medics came up with a set of rules by which diagnosis could be carried out. And the computer scientists implemented these rules in PUFF. Put like that it sounds fairly easy and, in fact, Stanford makes no claims to the effect that it was hard.

About the form of these rules, it's worth making a few points. For a start, like MYCIN its rules are in the IF...THEN... format. So, we might have (in strictly non-medical language) IF (the patient can hardly breathe) AND (he smokes 200 ciggies a day) AND (he can't stop coughing) THEN (he has a smoker's cough).

Now this (apart from the specifics of the items in brackets) is how many workers describe their expert systems – as a set of IF...THEN rules. This way of describing things has one prime advantage – that anybody who uses computers knows what

IF...THEN means. You could even write a BASIC program in which you actually code in terms of IF...THEN. (There is no disgrace at all in doing this – in fact, PUFF is one example of an expert system that actually has been re-coded into BASIC.)

But it's as well to avoid the trap of thinking that this is exactly how it must be done. All the IF...THEN statement consists of is a proposition – a statement in logic. And there are many ways of making the same statement without using the words IF...THEN at all.

For instance, our expert system doesn't store its rules in IF...THEN terms but it holds exactly the same information as if it did. The expert generates its own rules and, every time it applies them, it effectively performs the same logic as if there were an IF...THEN statement there whose conditions corresponded to the rules it has developed.

There's quite a range of terminology associated with the rules in expert systems. Commonly, they're called 'production rules' because they can produce an outcome, or conclusion. Often the first part of the statement, following the IF, is called the 'antecedent' and the second part, following the THEN, the 'consequent'. But you can also call them: fact and hypothesis, assertion and deduction, variables and outcomes, or whatever suits you. The only good reason for standardising on terminology is so that other people can understand you but in a fairly new field like this there isn't yet much standardisation of terms to provide many guidelines as to what other people will understand.

In its early days PUFF had only 55 rules embedded in it – which is quite encouraging because most computers (one would think) can cram 55 rules into them and it's nice, therefore, to think that most computers can be made to contain something useful.

Now, before we go on to think about what PUFF does with its rules there's a few more things to say. For a start, PUFF didn't work too well at first. A typical complaint of most programs under development, this should give the amateur cause for cheer. The problem was that the medics didn't supply perfect diagnostic rules in the first place. The rules they gave the people at Stanford simply weren't logically capable of diagnosing everything that came along. And this is where the Knowledge Engineer comes in.

PUFF produces a faulty diagnosis. The medics say it's a bad diagnosis. So (says the Knowledge Engineer) what should it have been? And then: Why? Which of the existing rules was wrong? What new rule should be added?

So the medics think about it and come up with a few suggestions which are added into PUFF's rule base. It sounds a trivial procedure, this process of fiddling around with the rules until the thing works, and, intellectually, maybe it is. But it isn't a trivial problem as far as building an expert system is concerned. In fact, it's one of the most commonly-reported problems there is.

On the mechanical level, there has to be a facility for tinkering with the system to get it working better – an easy way of modifying and adding rules. This is because almost every system will need altering sometime and the danger is that if it's hard to do then it won't be done as often as it should be or as thoroughly. A practical point, but a worthwhile one.

On the more abstract level, you would think that a bunch of medics could have got their rules right in the first place. And, again, it's an important point to note that they couldn't. The human expert working on a problem usually has some idea of how he or she solves a problem – but most people are agreed that, initially, they don't have any very exact idea. Certainly not exact enough to get a computer to copy it straight off first time.

What happens is more like a process of mutual learning in which both the computer program and the human expert find out how the human expert has been working over the years. Possibly aided by the efforts of the Knowledge Engineer standing between the expert and the program, the program gets more sophisticated as the exact methods used by the expert are gradually untangled.

All of this points up the basic problem of how to get the expert knowledge into the machine in the first place. In many ways it's not strictly a computer problem. It's a problem of finding an expert and understanding what he's talking about sufficiently well to be able to write a program to do what he can do. Rather more like systems analysis than anything else. But it's not a problem which can be ignored altogether because it is often regarded as the biggest (smallest?) bottleneck in the whole business of building an expert system.

We cheated, of course. By designing a system which formed its own rules we sidestepped the problem of finding and understanding a human expert – but this may well have been done at the expense of the finished product.

The important point to note is that, apart from the simplest systems, it should be fairly easy to add new rules and modify old ones.

Exactly how the rules are held isn't too important. They could be explicitly coded (with the hazard that this can make extensive alterations difficult) or they can be stored as an antecedent/consequent list as if they were data. This latter method is one which, theoretically, expert system builders favour. By treating the rules as data it makes it, theoretically, possible to modify them easily whilst retaining the same program for handling the rules.

Having built up a set of rules, it's reasonable to ask what PUFF does with them. If it had been our own expert system it would have gradually wandered through these rules drawing what conclusions it could as and when it could. PUFF (and MYCIN), however, don't work like that for they are much smoother.

In general, there are two methods of handling sets of rules – usually referred to as forward and backward chaining.

The system we described earlier used forward chaining inasmuch as it worked out what it could from what it had and, having done that, it then went on to work out a bit more on the basis of what it had just done. Forward chaining, as its name implies, involves moving forward through the rules all the time driven by the features which are present in the data it's given.

Backward chaining, on the other hand, works backwards (surprise!) and is much more purposeful in its behaviour.

It starts off by putting up a hypothesis – Is the patient suffering from bronchitis? for instance – and attempts to work out whether or not this is the case. To do this, it finds a rule one of whose outcomes is bronchitis and checks to see what the antecedents of this consequent are (i.e. what variables would give the outcome 'bronchitis'). If it doesn't have data on these variables it chooses just one of them and tries to get data on it. Obviously, it can do this by either asking the operator to provide that item of data or it can do it by stepping back through the rules to find another rule which, if satisfied, would provide the data as one of its outcomes.

The method is essentially recursive and (in case you were thinking of it) it isn't particularly easy to code recursive techniques in BASIC.

But, conceptually, if you think of our own system, it's a bit like going to the last node in the system (or some node which has an outcome labelled as a goal state) and then trying to get values for all of its inputs by stepping backwards through all of the preceding nodes that provide input to this final node.

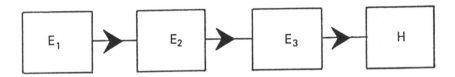

Fig.9.1 Forward chaining

If E_1 is true then E_2 is true then E_3 is true then H is true so all of E_1, E_2 and E_3 have to be established as true in order to establish H.

In a *forward chaining*, or *data driven*, strategy this is exactly how it does proceed. The system is given E_1, after which it is given E_2, after which it is given E_3 – after which it can deduce H.

In a *backward chaining*, or *goal driven*, strategy the system first considers H and wishes to establish whether or not H is the case. Looking backwards it finds it needs to know E_3 to establish H. And to know E_3 it needs to know E_2 and to know E_2 it needs to know E_1. So it requests data on E_1, E_2 then E_3. After which it can proceed forwards again to H.

The difference is most apparent when there are a large number of different conclusions (goals, or outcomes, or hypotheses, H) at which the system could arrive and a variety of routes to each goal.

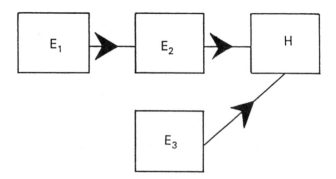

Fig. 9.2 Alternative reasoning

Here, H is most readily established by asking for E_3 rather than by starting with E_1.

In this case Forward Chaining might start with E_1 to give E_2 to give H. Backward Chaining would start with H and, then, look to E_2 or E_3. Seeing E_3 as the quicker route it would obtain E_3 to give H, ignoring E_1.

The argument in favour of backward chaining is that it gives the system a sense of direction. It isn't just trying to find out anything it can in an *ad hoc* fashion – it's specifically trying to establish whether or not a number of important things are the case.

With a well-formulated set of rules it's highly arguable whether it matters much which method is used. But if you happen to have an expert system that has been collected over a period of time and which contains (to put it charitably) a wide assortment of rules of varying degrees of usefulness with a wide variety of outcomes of varying degrees of interest then it could well be an advantage to have a system which could get to the point as quickly as possible rather than trying to establish the truth or otherwise of absolutely everything under the sun every time you used it.

As a final point on PUFF, one might wonder what benefits were gained by writing the program. Why not just leave a subject like this to human experts?

The obvious answer is that there's a bit of a shortage of experts in some fields. And, in many ways, this answer is too obvious.

After all, they could have written a book, or manual, on the subject and left it at that. Why bother with a computer program?

Well, in part that's a reasonable suggestion and there's probably also some truth in the suggestion that expert systems are being written simply because they're interesting to write.

But it's very interesting to note that early versions of PUFF, as with other expert systems, didn't work too well. Doubtless the human experts thought they knew what they were doing when they formulated the initial rule set – but, apparently, they didn't know all that well. So: if they'd written a book on the subject, what would it have been worth?

In a way, one could make this general-purpose point about computers as a whole: That they are really great Thought Machines. If you can think of something, some way of doing things, you can try to program it on a computer. If the program doesn't work too well then you can be sure that you have been unable to express what you wanted it to do – which implies that you didn't really understand the matter yourself. Or not as well as you might have done.

Only when the program is working can you really feel that you understand the problem fully – which makes the exercise of programming not just an exercise in educating the computer. It's also an exercise in educating oneself.

It is sometimes said that a person really has to understand a subject thoroughly to be able to teach it. By a similar token, one has to have a very good grasp of a subject to be able to teach a heap of chips the essence of that subject.

9.3 DENDRAL – chemical structures

Seeing as how expert systems are the latest thing it might come as a bit of a surprise to hear that DENDRAL dates back to 1965. There were, of course, computers in 1965 but it was the age of the transistor, paper tape and punched cards rather than the age of the chip and the screen.

All of which has nothing to do with DENDRAL itself – except to note that this must be the oldest, best-established, expert system in the world. Or, at least, the oldest system that's advertised as being 'expert'.

Like PUFF, it comes from Stanford University and is a joint effort between the computer scientists and a bunch of human experts – this time in the field of chemistry. And the basic idea is this:

When a chemist has prepared a substance he frequently wants to know what its chemical structure is and there are a number of ways he can find out. First, he can make some intelligent guesses using his own expert knowledge. Next, he can put some of it in a spectrometer and study the resulting spectrum lines to refine his initial guesses. In many cases this will enable him to pin down the exact structure of the substance and everybody's happy. The problem is that this all takes time and a fair bit of expertise of the human variety. And this is where DENDRAL comes in – it's an attempt to automate the process of deducing the correct chemical structure.

In very broad outline the process is just the same as that used by our own system or by PUFF. The user presents DENDRAL with some information about the substance plus the spectrometer data (infra red, nuclear magnetic resonance and mass spectrometry) and DENDRAL comes up with a 'diagnosis' in the form of an appropriate chemical structure. But you only need to go marginally deeper into the workings of DENDRAL to find that the differences are so great as to almost mask the similarities altogether. The problem really arises because of two main facts. One, the structure of chemical substances can't easily be described in simple words. Two, the number of possible structures is enormous – literally millions of possibilities exist.

So, let's look at the first item – the description of the structures.

If you've got just a passing familiarity with chemistry you'll have come across pictures of chemical structures. Those graph-like drawings that show atoms and bonds. You might, for instance, have seen a picture of a benzene ring – if so, then you know roughly what it's like. If you only had a benzene ring and one or two other structures you could refer to them by name and proceed very much as if you were diagnosing the presence of, say, bronchitis given certain data. The problem is that there are so many different interconnection possibilities for chemical structures that it just isn't feasible to name them all. The only way to proceed is to draw them. And some of them are so complex that the drawings are very far from simple. The way around this problem is to describe each structure in terms of a graph with a variety of nodes and links. This is the 'language' of chemistry.

So far so good. But a point worth noting is that, having done this, the same 'language' could not readily be used to describe, say, medical conditions. The language of the chemist simply wouldn't be appropriate here. It is often said that the idea of an expert system is to provide a general-purpose reasoning program so that the expert system could become expert in any area you chose simply by unplugging a set of rules on one subject and plugging in a new set of rules on another subject. DENDRAL is a very good example of the extent to which this ideal would be hard to realise because it highlights the extent to which one descriptive language might suit one problem and not another. It would be a major inconvenience (if not a practical impossibility) to either force medical diagnosis into the language of the chemist or to force the description of chemical structures into the language of medicine. And to the extent that different subject areas are best suited to different languages we find that it is necessary to adopt a specialised approach for each subject area.

The second point concerns the number of possible structures. In medical diagnosis it's more or less feasible to hold all of the possible outcomes in memory all of the time and the same is true of some other fields. But when the number of possible outcomes runs into millions this clearly is never possible. So the problem then becomes one of choosing the correct structure when the machine doesn't 'know' in detail just what structures are possible.

The way DENDRAL solves this problem is to generate possible chemical structures at run time and then test them to see if they're the right ones. If it did this with no constraints on its behaviour it could generate all possible chemical structures and would be faced with the initial problem – simply, that there are too many of them. It gets around this problem by generating only a small subset of all possible chemical structures.

Effectively, you can think of DENDRAL as being in two parts. Almost, two separate expert systems in one.

The first part contains a set of rules for generating possible chemical structures. The input data to this part consists of a series of statements made by a chemist which provide some clues about what structures are likely in this instance. This is, in a way, very similar to the systems we've looked at so far.

The output from this first part, though, is not one single answer. It is, usually, a whole series of possible structures – the program is unable to say exactly which is the right one.

The second part of DENDRAL then takes each of these structures in turn and uses a second expert system to work out, for each, what spectrometer results it would give if this substance actually existed and was actually placed in a spectrometer. The input to this second expert is some program-generated chemical structure; the rules it uses are a series of rules derived from real chemists which express the behaviour of a spectrometer; and, the output is a simulated spectrometer response. At this point we recall that a further input to DENDRAL was the actual spectrometer readings which actually came from the substance under investigation – and DENDRAL compares its hypothesised simulation results with the actual results to see if they're the same. If they are then this might be the right structure – if not, this structure can be discarded and another one generated.

The process, which is often called *Generate-and-Test*, is one of constant pruning to keep the number of possibilities under consideration as small as possible at any one time. Unlike some expert systems, DENDRAL isn't a 'toy'. It doesn't exist just to test a theory about expert systems – it actually has a real use in identifying chemical structures and over two dozen scientific papers have been written using the results of DENDRAL working on real problems. In its field it is said to rival human experts. As such, it certainly gives cause for optimism that other, useful, systems can be produced for use in other fields. But the extent to which they could make use of DENDRAL's methods is debatable.

Certainly, the overall Generate-and-Test scheme of narrowing the search area down with a few initial constraints, generating possible solutions, and testing these possible solutions against some other criteria – that might be applicable in other fields.

But the precise DENDRAL code in which solutions are described in terms of the 'graph theory like' language of chemists and tested by means of spectrometer simulation – that might be a bit difficult to transport to another field.

And this seems to be a fairly general point: That simple expert systems can be fairly easily converted to work in another field but are only of limited use in any field. And expert systems which have a very real use often have this usefulness because of their complexity and are very domain-specific. By making them solve one particular set of problems really well they become highly specific to that particular problem area and become difficult, if not impossible, to adapt to other areas.

As a further illustration of this point, consider META-MENDRAL. You recall that DENDRAL has a system for simulating spectrometer results from a given chemical structure – well, META-DENDRAL is an expert system which was used to build that simulation. The problem was: How to simulate spectrometer results? What are the rules which an expert system should have so that it could do this? And that's what META-DENDRAL was built to find out. It works, roughly, the same as DENDRAL inasmuch as it is able to generate a whole series of possible rules which it then reapplies back to the input data to see if each rule would explain the results.

Specifically, it receives as data some spectrometer output and a graph description of the substance that gave rise to that output. It then starts to generate a series of rules which might be applied to that spectrometer data and, for each rule, applies it and checks its own output to see if it's the same as the given structure. If it isn't, it generates a different rule. If it is, then that rule is a possible rule.

By working over a large number of examples META-DENDRAL was able to generate a set of rules which would show the likely spectrometer output from a given structure.

In a (very rough) way this is similar to the system described in the early part of the book in which we just presented the expert system with a series of examples with known outcomes and let it work out a set of rules for itself. And it goes close to the heart of one of the main problems in the field – that when you start building an expert system you often don't really know what rules should be used at all and need some, preferably simple, way of finding out.

We noticed, with PUFF, that human experts' knowledge of the rules they use in real life is often pretty shaky – and that's in a field in which there actually are human experts. But why should there be any human experts in the field of META-DENDRAL? What person would spend his time working out the likely spectrometer output from a substance of which he already knew the molecular structure? After all, if you have such a substance, you could always put it into a spectrometer and solve the problem that way. And, if you don't have such a substance, who cares what sort of output it would give? The need to have an expert in META-DENDRAL's field only arose because of the existance of DENDRAL itself and there wasn't really any expert to turn to for help – so everybody started from square one.

The problem is an interesting one. Most expert systems carry the knowledge of human experts in some form or another. But a system that can acquire its knowledge in this way relies much less heavily on any pre-existing body of knowledge and is actually likely to increase our store of knowledge – not just about specific cases but about the entire domain in which it operates.

Consider the earlier example of weather forecasting. Maybe you know nothing about weather forecasting. Well, that doesn't matter too much. You can still set up a system and train it with a series of examples of actual weather and, in time, it's likely to get the idea and predict the weather to a reasonable extent. Now, the fact that it can do this means that it actually has a set of rules in there which are better than any rules you yourself have for forecasting the weather. And if you then poke around inside its rule set you would stand some chance of learning something about weather forecasting for yourself. A trivial example, possibly, but an interesting principle – and one which META-DENDRAL puts to good use.

9.4 PROSPECTOR – searching for minerals.

Whereas it must be nice to be able to heal the sick, and doubtless could be nice to be able to deduce a molecular structure, there's not really much doubt that nicest of all would be able to discover gold in them thar hills. Real gold, that is. The sort you can spend.

Now, PROSPECTOR doesn't help in actual prospecting for gold for its originators have confined their activities to much duller though still valuable deposits. But the principle's the same. PROSPECTOR is an expert system designed to help in the hunt for commercially-exploitable mineral wealth. And, as such, it's interesting.

Traditionally – one supposes – the human expert in this field loads his mule with a few pots and pans, makes enough sandwiches to last him through the winter, and heads up into the hills to apply his expertise. Come Spring, having used his expert judgement, he is able to stagger into town exhausted and file his claim to a piece of goldbearing territory. Immediately after he does this he is, usually, shot leaving only his daughter to avenge him and get the gold back. The rest of the plot is pretty familiar (she does get his gold back, along with the hand of one who helped her, and lives happily ever after).

But the real question, which is never satisfactorily answered in most accounts, is this: What did he actually do when he was up in the hills?

So begins the story of PROSPECTOR. For the first stage was – as with all expert systems – to find out what real human expert prospectors do when they're looking for gold (or some duller, but still valuable, deposit). And the answer, in general, is the usual series of inferences and deductions, some certain, some probabilistic, from which the expert forms a judgement on the matter.

Just in case you're wondering, the method doesn't consist of pointing the computer system at a vast tract of territory and asking it where one should look for gold – that's a bit vague for a computer. It consists of specifying an exact location about which certain facts are known and asking for an estimate of the probability of a certain deposit occurring at this location. It's a bit like medical diagnosis in some ways. In medical diagnosis you present the expert (human or machine) with a patient and ask what's wrong with that particular patient. You don't ask the expert for a diagnosis of patients in general.

And, in some ways, the prospector can proceed as does the medic. Like MYCIN, for example, PROSPECTOR contains a large number of rules concerning the various things which might be observed and the things which might be deduced from them. It then proceeds by backward chaining – hypothesising that a particular outcome might be the correct outcome and working backwards through the rules to see if it can justify this outcome.

Unlike medical diagnosis though, the result isn't a simple statement on the matter.

Consider. Given a patient suspected of being ill, what one wants to know is: What is he ill with? One of several outcomes has to be chosen. It's not very important really what the exact probability of the diagnosis being correct should be. It's simple a matter of getting that diagnosis which is the most likely.

Now contrast this with mineral prospecting. In any given situation any given mineral is likely to occur in some quantities – albeit minute – so the conclusion that a certain mineral exists isn't very helpful. What the user of a prospecting system wants to know is just how much of the mineral is present. Maybe the exact quantities aren't too important – it would be quite good enough to know that there was 'a lot'. But the probability of there being a lot there is very important. A simple Yes/No answer won't do when the cost of digging up the terrain to test the system's opinion is so high.

The subject of risk analysis has some bearing on the matter, inasmuch as there is a cost associated with a wrong decision.

Suppose you have a patient and you diagnose an illness in that patient. Now, the diagnosis might be right – in which case, by treating for that illness you've done the right thing. Good. And with some probability the diagnosis might be wrong – but, typically, it won't do the patient much harm if you still treat him for that illness. (Don't amputate limbs on the advice of a computer, though.)

So the essence of medical diagnosis is that it's important to uncover, and treat for, every possibility and it may not matter too much if the possibility doesn't turn out to exist in fact.

With mineral prospecting the situation is slightly different. Obviously, you'd like to dig in all the places where you might find gold just in case you happen to be lucky. But, in some ways, it's more important not to dig for gold in places where there isn't any.

For digging up the scenery takes time and costs money – and while you're digging up one bit, in general, you aren't digging up another bit.

The trick is to find the most likely place and dig there – and that's why an exact estimate of probabilities is important here in a way it wasn't in medical diagnosis. It's not that gold is more valuable than health (even though it is), it's just that the equations on which you take action are different.

Having said this, it's interesting to see how PROSPECTOR handles the matter of probabilities in coming to its conclusions – arguably, its methods are the best worked out of any current expert system.

The simplest cases occur with those rules that express logical relations. These are of the sort IF x THEN z in which z follows necessarily from x. Now that's easy, and it's still easy if you associate a probability with x because you can argue that if the probability of x is p then the probability of z is p also.

But, in general, for x to have a single argument would make that rule quite trivial. More usually we would replace x by a more complex term, say, (x AND y) or maybe (x OR y).

In the case of ANDed relations in which the individual elements have probabilities associated with each of them. PROSPECTOR takes the minimum of the values and assigns this minimum probability to the outcome. So, if the probability of x was 0.1 and the probability of y was 0.2 then the probability of z would be 0.1. It's easy to see why this method is chosen – for z to be true both x and y have to be true, which is a tight constraint so you take the minimum value.

On the other hand, for items joined with OR the maximum value is chosen because either x or y will cause z, which is a very loose constraint.

Actually, this method isn't entirely free from critisism – again, you could glance at the section on Probabilities. To give an idea of the error, if x and y are both independent variables then $P(x \text{ and } y) = P(x)P(y)$ i.e. the product of the two. If x and y aren't independent but are exactly correlated one with the other then $P(x) = P(y)$ and $P(x \text{ and } y) = P(x) = P(y)$. And, in general, for partially correlated variables the truth lies somewhere in between.

Also, for the OR relationship independent variables would give $P(x$ or $y) = P(x) + P(y) - P(x)P(y)$. And, if they were completely correlated then $P(x$ or $y) = P(x) = P(y)$. With the actual value for partially correlated variables lying somewhere in between.

So, PROSPECTOR's method is a bit *ad hoc* but it's still a method which gives an answer in the appropriate range.

The next, and more interesting, method is one in which a series of assertions (rules) occur which each contribute something to the probability of some hypothesis.

For instance, we might say that if there's gold lying around in big lumps on the ground then there's gold in them thar hills with probability 0.9.

By itself this statement is much the same as ones we've come across earlier. The difference here is that we're really only concerned with the one hypothesis – that there's gold in them thar hills – and, therefore, a very great number of statements will occur which have some bearing on that hypothesis, either supporting it or contradicting it. The problem then becomes one of how to keep score of all of these probabilities.

The method PROSPECTOR uses is a neat application of Bayes' formula (see section 2.5) for assessing the prior and posterior probabilities of an event occurring – and 'event' here can be anything, such as the hypothesis concerning gold and hills being true.

In outline, each hypothesis starts off with an initial (prior) probability of being true, say $P(H)$. So, the prior probability of there being gold in them thar hills might be, say, 0.1 and, therefore $P(H) = 0.1$.

Now, there you are in your prospector's hat, sitting at the screen presenting the system with an extra piece of evidence. Having got this extra piece of evidence ("just found a piece of gold the size of your fist", say) the probability $P(H)$ changes to become $P(H:E)$ – the probability of the hypothesis given this new evidence. So the system can update its old probability value with an assignment statement, $P(H) = P(H:E)$, and then proceed to check out a new item of evidence.

The question then is: how to calculate $P(H:E)$.

Well, the Rev. Bayes had an answer. It is:

$$P(H:E) = P(E:H)P(H)/(P(E:H)P(H) + P(E:not\ H)P(not\ H))$$

And in some ways, the best thing to do is to put this into the program and forget it. If you can't persuade yourself to do that, then try:

$$P(H:E) = LS.P(H)/(P(not\ H) + LS.P(H))$$ which, at least, looks easier.

And in that equation :

$$LS = P(E:H)/P(E:not\ H)$$

All of these formulae mean the same thing in fact and the explanation goes like this:

LS is the *Likelihood Ratio* which is a well-known quantity, but only to statisticians. It is the ratio, in this instance, of the probability of receiving this bit of evidence given that the hypothesis is true divided by the probability of getting this same bit of evidence given that the hypothesis isn't true.

So – take the hypothesis that there's gold in them thar hills. Now, if this is true the probability of picking up a piece of gold the size of your fist is, maybe, 0.3. And if it isn't true the probability of the same event falls dramatically to, say, 0.1. So the likelihood ratio has the value 3.0.

If we turn then back to the formula for P(H:E) we get:

$$P(H:E) = 3P(H)/(1 - P(H) + 3P(H)) = 3P(H)/(1 + 2P(H))$$

And, so, if there was a fifty:fifty chance of gold being in the hills beforehand P(H) = 0.5 and P(H:E) = 1.5/(1 + 1) = 0.75

In other words, things are looking up.

This gives a new value of P(H) for this hypothesis and, as more evidence accumulates, new values of P(E:H) will continually modify P(H).

The story doesn't quite stop there though, because there are always a few pessimists around who will note that some evidence points to the fact that there isn't any gold around. Specifically, you might find that there aren't any pieces of gold the size of your fist lying around and you want to be able to allow for this. The calculation is the same as before except that you consider not-E instead of E, to indicate that the evidence was lacking. And you then calculate the likelihood ratio and adjust P(H) as before. The main point to note is that you need a new set of probabilities – a new likelihood ratio because the old one was based on the presence of the evidence. So, if we take :

$$LN = P(not\ E:H)/P(not\ E:not\ H)$$

as the likelihood ratio associated with the lack of a certain piece of evidence we can calculate a new P(H) = P(H:not E) as before except that we use LN instead of LS.

Suppose, for instance, that you haven't found that bit of gold. Then the probability of not finding a lump lying around given that there *is* gold in the hills might be 0.9, say, and the probability of not finding gold lying around given that there actually isn't any gold in the hills might be 1.0. Giving LN = 0.9/1.0 = 0.9. So the absence of gold lying around would reduce the probability of there being gold in them thar hills – but not by very much. In the example above it would reduce P(H) from a value of 0.5 to a value of 0.47 approximately. Of course, if the system asked you about lumps of gold lying around and you said that, yes, there were, then there'd be no need for it to then ask you if it was true that there *weren't* any lumps of gold lying around. Effectively, the reason for having the two values LS and LN is simply to put together the results of the two questions – the positive side and the negative side, without having to be so boring as to ask each question separately.

In general, the rules in PROSPECTOR are all in the form IF...THEN (LS,LN) so that each rule is set up with a likelihood ratio both for a positive response and a negative response. These ratios are calculated as just described and originate in the minds of expert, human, prospectors. The designers of the system having asked the experts questions like:
If there was gold in them thar hills what do you reckon the chances would be of it lying around in big lumps?
And:
If there wasn't gold in them thar hills what do you reckon the chances would be of there not being any actually lying around in big lumps?

Four questions in all to cover the full range of possibilities, to give values for:
P(E:H)
P(E:not H)
P(not E:H)
P(not E:not H)

Although, in practice, we can reduce these four questions to two by noting that :
P(not E:H)=1−P(E:H), and
P(not E:not H)=1−P(E:not H)

Obviously, in order to keep things simple, we've considered a rather special case – that in which the user of the system actually knows the answers to the questions the system asks.

After all, any idiot ought to know if he's got a lump of gold in his fist or not.

But in general, in real life, the answers are much less certain.

Prospectors of other minerals tend to ask pretty specific questions, like: Has hornblende been pervasively altered to biotite?

And, really, one sympathises with anyone who isn't altogether sure of the answer to that one.

The PROSPECTOR solution is to give the user a scale from −5 to +5 in which to answer. A reply of +5 is definite Yes, and −5 is definite No.

Typically, the user will answer somewhere in between and PROSPECTOR takes account of this by readjusting P(H) with a little bit of LS and a little bit of LN by a system of linear interpolation. You can think of it as a linear scale with LN on the left and LS on the right. Accordingly, as the user's response varies between −5 and +5 then P(H) is adjusted with the value, L say, which is picked off from this sliding scale between the two.

As it stands, the system that PROSPECTOR uses is pretty elegant in theory and, according to reports, pretty good in practice. But, like most experts, it isn't quite so modular in design as it first appears.

The main difference occurs when the user starts to respond with answers that aren't simply Yes or No. For instance, the system might want to know the estimated age of a lump of rock and the answer would be a figure in years. This leads to a situation in which the values for LN and LS aren't simple values. In general, likelihood ratios are functions of a variable and these functions have to be stored somewhere and calculated at the time the input is given. It's not a big problem – but it's a departure from strict modularity. Also, the strictly logical questions require a slightly different form of code to the more general probabilistic items.

The result is that, although the principles used in PROSPECTOR could be adapted to other areas, the exact code might not be easily modifiable – a comment that could be made about many expert systems.

But the overall impression (again, with most systems) is that once the human experts have been interrogated and a set of rules drawn up the hardest part of the job is over. For, after this has been done, the form in which the system should be programmed becomes, to some extent, apparent. Or, at the very least, some possible ways of proceeding become very unattractive and some other ways tend to stand out.

It's all a bit like the distinction between systems analysis and programming. If by 'programming' you mean doing the entire job then it can be quite complicated. But if programming simple entails coding up a structure predetermined by systems analysts then it's fairly straightforward. In the field of expert systems the big problem lies in uncovering this overall structure prior to the actual coding for each separate area of expertise.

9.5 Some other examples

The problem with giving examples of expert systems is that the very definition of expert system is sufficiently loose to enable one to add in just about anything. This doesn't mean that the definition is completely useless – it just means that it's flexible. You can stretch it a bit (in which case the list of current expert systems become nearly endless) or hold it rigid (in which there are hardly any expert systems in existence at all).

And it's not just us who have this problem. At the time of writing the First Edition of this book the UK's Central Computer and Telecommunications Agency (CCTA) had got sufficiently jumpy about the prospect of Great Britian being swamped by cheap Japanese expert systems that it commissioned a survey to find out who was doing what in the field. This survey (and no disrespect is intended to any involved parties) consisted of a questionnaire which began with a definition of expert systems (the one given at the front of this book) and then, more or less, asked respondents whether they had one and, if so, what it did. It's a sensible approach in many ways but it would have been more sensibly applied to a subject about whose existence there was less doubt.

For instance, towards the end of this book you'll find a Bayesian inferencing program which can be readily used for medical diagnosis. So: put it on your micro and you then have an expert system and can tell the CCTA about it. If everybody did that UK usage of expert systems would, apparently, rocket. Or, maybe, do the same with the system in the first part of this book. Or, maybe, sinking even lower, just write a program to do something (anything) and decide that that's an expert system. And who's going to argue with you?

The point is that asking someone if they have an expert system isn't the same thing as asking them if, say, they've got a colour TV.

Still, be that as it may, the following is a list of some systems which are claimed to have a large knowledge-based component. The list is now grossly incomplete, of course, because the recent expansion in expert systems applications means that any complete list would be enormous and, also, almost immediately out of date. But it does help to give the general idea.

System Name	Purpose
MYCIN	Medical Diagnosis
PUFF	Medical Diagnosis
PIP	Medical Diagnosis
CASNET	Medical Diagnosis
INTERNIST	Medical Diagnosis

SACON	Engineering Diagnostics
PROSPECTOR	Geology Diagnostics
DENDRAL	Chemistry
SECHS	Chemistry
SYNCHEM	Chemistry
EL	Circuit Analysis
MOLGEN	Genetics
MECHO	Mechanics
PECOS	Programming
R1	Configuring Computers
SU/X	Machine Acoustics
VM	Medical Measurements
SOPHIE	Electronics Tuition
GUIDON	Medical Tuition
TEIRESIAS	Knowledge Acquisition
EMYCIN	Knowledge Acquisition
EXPERT	Knowledge Acquisition
KAS	Knowledge Acquisition
ROSIE	Building Expert Systems
AGE	Building Expert Systems
HEARSAY III	Building Expert Systems
AL/X	Building Expert Systems
SAGE	Building Expert Systems
Micro-Expert	Building Expert Systems

There are a number of interesting points to note in this list. And, doubtless, the first point to note is the number of expert systems which are involved in building other expert systems – and maybe this helps to show the difficulty of definition. Consider, for a moment, compilers. These are computer programs and their function is to help people write computer programs. And, by allowing a definition of expert systems that includes expert systems that help people write expert systems aren't we, somehow, getting a definition that's really about as loose as the term 'computer program'? Maybe it doesn't matter if we are. After all, we could just sit back and say: –They're useful, who cares what they're called?– And that attitude may well, in the end, prove to be the best one to adopt – otherwise there's a danger of being so pedantic that we finish up criticising other people's work simply because it doesn't fit some preconceived label.

The next interesting group of systems are those used in Knowledge Acquisition. We've already noted that getting the expert knowledge into the system is one of the hardest tasks and one for which computer help would be handy – so here's some computer help.

Not, of course, that we haven't got our own help. Our learn-by-example system is a Knowledge Acquisition System in its very own right.

If you've got your own expert system (the one described so far) running you might be interested to see if it can run in any of the problem areas listed above.

Very simple medical diagnosis should be fairly straightforward. Use symptoms as the input variables and illnesses as the outcomes and throw some examples at the system to see how it gets on (though you might find the later, Bayesian, system rather more effective for this).

Engineering diagnostics – yes. You could try buiding up a system to show you why your car won't start.

Geology – maybe. It depends rather on your knowledge of geology. The advantage of medicine is that you can buy medical encyclopaedias fairly cheaply which give information on lots of illnesses to work with. There aren't very many home textbooks on mineral prospecting, unfortunately.

Anyone with an interest in palaeontology could try classifying fossils using our expert though. For instance, a lamellibranch has an asymmetrical shell whereas a brachiopod has a symmetrical shell. So: is it a lamellibranch or a brachiopod? The snag is that, having said that, you hardly need a computer to work out the answer once you've looked at the shell! More complex examples may well spring to the mind of the enthusiast.

Chemistry – yes. Chemical analysis (at school level) does involve a series of tests with specific results. So it could assist in some chemical analyses.

Circuit analysis – again yes. Because the system only deals with Yes/No responses it would be no good with analogue circuits (in which currents vary continuously) but it could very easily represent a digital process. Use a multi-node system and let each node represent one component whose inputs are either 0 or 1. Interconnect the various nodes and you could have an expert system to represent a whole boardfull of chips. If certain conditions were good (i.e. were consistent with the designers' intentions) then these could be monitored by another node designed to judge good conditions from bad ones. So the expert could simulate the 'chip' operations at the same time as monitoring the operation for error conditions.

Many of the applications listed above will tend, however, to leave our own expert system somewhat standing – largely because ours is too general purpose to be able to be tailored to some of these specific applications.

Take MECHO, for instance. This is an expert system which can give intelligent answers to complicated mechanical problems. Suppose, for instance, that you have a system of pulleys, strings and weights. In place of one weight there is an empty pan hanging by a string. With the pan empty the system is not in equilibrium and the question is: What weight should be placed in the pan to bring it into equilibrium? The problem is fairly familiar in school physics. To answer the question the system needs to understand the arrangement of pulleys; the relevant laws of physics; and, be able to use this knowledge to get an answer. MECHO can do this. And in a very, very crude way our multi-node system might also do it. Using each node to represent a pulley the inputs could be the weight hanging from that pulley and the outputs (outcomes) could be the strings supporting that pulley. And the problem is that our system with its Yes/No outcomes could only (once it had got past the first pulley) say whether a given string had a force acting on it or not – not the *exact* force that was acting on it. Which makes an exact solution impossible.

You might try to get around it by 'using' standard weights – like, for instance, presence or absence of a weight altogether. And then add a 'monitoring' node to check for equilibrium at some point(s) as its input and then outputting additional weights here and there according to its inputs until the system balanced. But it might (might!) lack a certain precision.

On the other hand, of course, it might work. There's really no substitute for putting together a system that you think might do something and then watching to see what it actually does. After all, that's what everyone else does. That's what is known as Research.

Chapter 10

A Rule Based BASIC Expert

10.1 A system that works backwards

Although the system described in the early parts of this book may be fine for you, the previous chapter shows that there are some alternative methods that might be more useful in certain circumstances. In this chapter there is a practical alternative for you.

In a sense, one of the main problems in building an expert system seems to be that even if all of the necessary knowledge is readily available it's in a form which is the wrong way round.

Suppose you want to build a system which is expert in the field of medical diagnosis.

Now: you hardly need to build a system based on learning by example, as we did in the case of weather forecasting, because there's lots of information readily available which should allow you to go to a much more direct solution. The problem really is that the information appears to be the wrong way round.

Get a medical encyclopaedia and look up the entry for influenza, say. You'll find that all of the symptoms are given, and that there isn't any argument about these symptoms. In other words, given the symptoms, an accurate diagnosis could be made every time.

But to use information organised in this way rather suggests that what you should do is pick up a patient, decide he has influenza, then look in the encyclopaedia to see if he has the right symptoms and, somehow, this seems all wrong.

What you want to do is to pick up a patient, decide what his symptoms are, and then look these symptoms up to see what he's suffering from – and the encyclopaedia doesn't seem quite the right way of doing things. Instead of one illness with lots of symptoms we want a system which shows a group of symptoms followed by one illness. And that's what we'll put together now. The ideal being a situation in which you can, in some particular field, simply throw a lot of definitions at the machine in such a way that it can use these definitions rather like a human expert might use them.

This, of course, is what programs like PUFF, DENDRAL and PROSPECTOR try to do. So there's no harm in us giving it a try.

We'll use a Bayesian inferencing system to allow for the fact that most information isn't absolutely certain, but probabilistic, and to allow for the fact that it sounds pretty good to say you're using a Bayesian inferencing system when you're telling people about it all. And we'll place the main emphasis on the format of the information you're going to give the program about the field in which it's supposed to become expert because collecting this information is likely to be the hardest part of the job.

So, to get going, we'll start coding.

```
3000 DATA Symptoms
3010 DATA 1,Symptom 1
3020 DATA 2,Symptom 2
3030 DATA END,END
```

This is the form in which we'll keep the symptoms. By saying 'symptoms' it sounds as if we're exclusively concerned with medical work – but it might be anything really. The essence of the matter is that there's a lot of questions the computer might ask and that these questions are held as strings Symptom 1, Symptom 2, etc.

For instance, Symptom 1 might be the string: "Do you cough a lot?" Or, if you were trying to fix a wayward car: "Are the lights dim?"

Organised in this way, you can build up a lot of questions very quickly.

Now we have the illnesses.

```
2000 DATA Illnesses
2010 DATA Illness 1,p,[j,py,pn,]999
2020 DATA Illness 2,p,[j,py,pn,]999
```

This is the form in which we'll keep the illnesses. They needn't actually be illnesses though. They can be any outcomes and each DATA statement contains one outcome and all the information relating to it.

To go through the items one at a time, the first is the name of the outcome – say Influenza. The next item, p, is the prior probability of that outcome $P(H)$ – this is the probability of this outcome occurring given no further information at all. We then have a series of repeated items with three elements. The first element, j, is the number of the relevant symptom (or evidence or variable or question if you want to call it something else). The next two items are $P(E:H)$ and $P(E:not H)$ – the probability of getting a Yes answer to this question given that the outcome is true and the probability of getting a Yes answer if it isn't true. The last item, 999, is a stop code – it's there so that the program can tell when it's come to the end of the list of details on one particular illness.

For example:

```
2010 DATA Influenza,0.01,1,0.9,0.01,2,1,0.01,3,0,0.01,999
```

This says that, in the case of influenza, there is a prior probability $P(H)=0.01$ of any random person having this illness.

172

Now suppose that the program asks question 1 (symptom 1). We have $P(E:H)=0.9$ and $P(E:\text{not } H)=0.01$ which says that if the patient has influenza then nine times out of ten he'll answer Yes to this question and, if he doesn't have influenza, then he'll only answer Yes in one case in a hundred. Obviously, a Yes answer supports the hypothesis that he has influenza. A No answer tends to suggest that he hasn't.

Similarly, for the second symptom/probability group (2,1,0.01). In this case $P(E:H)=1$ which says that, if he has influenza, then he must have this symptom. He might have the symptom without influenza ($P(E:\text{not } H)=0.01$) but it's not very likely.

Question 3 rules out influenza if he gives a Yes answer because $P(E:H)=0$. This could have been a question like – Have you had the symptoms for most of your life? Or some such.

It takes a bit of thought and, if you want good results, a bit of research to come up with reasonable figures for these probabilities. And, to be honest, getting this information in the first place is probably the hardest task – and one in which a computer can't help you much. But if you can get the information in this form then you can write a fairly general-purpose program to sort it all out.

Fundamental to this program is Bayes' Theorem, which states that:

$$P(H:E)=P(E:H)P(H)/(P(E:H)P(H)+P(E:\text{not } H)P(\text{not } H))$$

The gist of this being that the probability of some hypothesis given a certain piece of evidence can be calculated from the prior probability of that hypothesis with no knowledge of the evidence and the probability of the evidence arising given that either the hypothesis is true or that it isn't true.

So, looking at our illnesses, we can calculate:

$$P(H:E)=py.p/(py.p+pn.(1-p))$$

The process is that we start off with $P(H)=p$ for each illness. The program asks a question and calculates $P(H:E)$ depending on the answer. The answer Yes gives the above calculation. The answer No gives the same calculation but with $(1-py)$ instead of py and $(1-pn)$ instead of pn.

Having done this, this question is then 'forgotten' except inasmuch as $P(H)$, the prior probability, is replaced by $P(H:E)$. And the process carries on like that, continually updating $P(H)$ as new information arrives.

Broadly, we can divide the program into a number of parts.

PART ONE
The program searches through the DATA statements to find out how many illnesses there are and how many symptoms. You could have told it this in advance, but it saves you having to count them all up if it can do it for itself.

At this point any arrays that are needed can be DIMensioned.

PART TWO
The program checks the DATA statements to find all the prior probabilities $P(H)$. It also works out some rule values and puts them in array RULEVALUE. The idea of these is to see which questions (symptoms) are the most important so that it knows which to ask about first. If you calculate:

$$\text{RULEVALUE(I)} = \text{RULEVALUE(I)} + \text{ABS}(\text{P(H:E)} - \text{P(H:not E)})$$

for each question you'll get RULEVALUE(I) showing values which represent the amount of change they can make to the probabilities of all the illnesses to which they apply.

PART THREE
The program finds the most important question and asks it. There are a number of ways you can handle the answer – you could just take Yes or No. You could also consider a Don't Know (which produces no change). More complex still – you could have a scale from −5 to +5 to express degrees of certainty in the answer.

PART FOUR
The prior probabilities are updated with the new values given the new evidence.

PART FIVE
New rule values are calculated. Also calculated are minimum and maximum values for each illness based on the current prior probabilities and the supposition that either all the remaining evidence goes in favour of the hypothesis or goes against it. The idea is to see whether any given hypothesis might still be in the running or not. Those which aren't can be discarded. Those whose minimum values are above a certain level can be announced as possible conclusions.

The program then goes around to Part Three and continues until there's nothing more for it to do.

10.2 The BASIC program
Here is the BASIC equivalent of the above steps :

```
10 REM Find number of Illnesses and Symptoms
20 CLS:PRINT "E X P E R T": PRINT''_____''
30 READ A$,A$
40 HYPOTHESES%=0:EVIDENCE%=-1
50 WHILE A$<>"Symptoms"
60 READ P,J%
70 WHILE J%<>999
80 READ PY,PN,J%
90 WEND
100 HYPOTHESES%=HYPOTHESES%+1
110 READ A$
120 WEND
130 WHILE A$<>"END"
140 READ A$,B$
150 EVIDENCE%=EVIDENCE%+1
160 WEND
170 DIM P(HYPOTHESES%),RULEVALUE(EVIDENCE%),QUESTIONS%(HYPOTHESES%),
    MINI(HYPOTHESES%),MAXI(HYPOTHESES%),VAR%(HYPOTHESES%),
    VARFLAG%(EVIDENCE%)
180 FOR J%=1 TO EVIDENCE%
190 VARFLAG%(J%)=1
200 NEXT
```

The code scans the list of illnesses looking for, and counting, the number of stop codes (the number '999') to give HYPOTHESES%, the number of illnesses or hypotheses defined. It then reads the list of symptoms or items of evidence, counting them, until it comes to the word END in the DATA, giving EVIDENCE% as the number of symptoms listed.

The arrays DIM'd are:

P(HYPOTHESES%)   — which is used to keep a record of the current probabilities.

RULEVALUE(EVIDENCE%)   — which is used to keep a record of the 'value' of each item of evidence in terms of the amount of change it can induce in the probabilities of the hypotheses.

QUESTIONS%(HYPOTHESES%) — a list of the number of relevant questions outstanding for each hypothesis, this is reduced by one every time a question is asked

MINI(HYPOTHESES%)   — the minimum possible probability which each hypothesis can achieve.

MAXI(HYPOTHESES%)   — the maximum possible probability which each hypothesis can achieve.

VAR%(HYPOTHESES%)   — a record of the total number of questions listed for each illness.

VARFLAG%(EVIDENCE%)   — a flag which is initially set to 1. After each question it is set to 0 to stop the same question being asked twice.

```
210 REM Find the prior probabilities and rule values:
220 RESTORE: READ A$
230 FOR I%=1 TO HYPOTHESES%
240 READ A$,P(I%),J%
250 P=P(I%)
260 WHILE J%<>999
270 READ PY,PN
280 QUESTIONS%(I%)=QUESTIONS%(I%)+1
290 RULEVALUE(J%)=RULEVALUE(J%)+
    ABS(P*PY/(P*PY+(1-P)*PN)-P*(1-PY)/(P*(1-PY)+(1-P)*(1-PN)))
300 READ J%
310 WEND
320 VAR%(I%)=QUESTIONS%(I%)
330 NEXT
340 REM Find the maximum symptom and query
350 RV=0:BESTVAR%=0
360 FOR J%=1 TO EVIDENCE%
370 IF RULEVALUE(J%)>RV THEN BESTVAR%=J%:RV=RULEVALUE(J%)
380 RULEVALUE(J%)=0
390 NEXT
400 IF BESTVAR%=0 THEN PRINT "No further symptoms": END
9410 READ A$
420 FOR J%=1 TO BESTVAR%
430 READ P%,A$
440 NEXT
450 PRINT: PRINT: PRINT "Question :-": PRINT A$
460 VARFLAG%(BESTVAR%)=0
```

At this point the program has found a question and printed it on the screen. What you have to do now is to answer it.

In this program your response is held in RESPONSE% and is on a scale from −5 to +5.

```
470 REM Obtain user response and adjust probabilities:
480 INPUT "Reply on a scale -5 (No) to +5 (Yes) ",RESPONSE%
490 REM Update the prior probabilities using RESPONSE%
500 RESTORE: READ A$
510 FOR I%=1 TO HYPOTHESES%
520 READ A$,P
530 FOR K%=1 TO VAR%(I%)
540 READ J%,PY,PN
550 IF J%<>BESTVAR% OR QUESTIONS%(I%)=0 THEN 610
560 QUESTIONS%(I%)=QUESTIONS%(I%)-1
570 P=P(I%)
580 PE=P*PY+(1-P)*PN
590 IF RESPONSE%>0 THEN
    P(I%)=P*(1+(PY/PE-1)*RESPONSE%/5) ELSE
    P(I%)=P*(1+(PY-(1-PY)*PE/(1-PE))*RESPONSE%/5)
600 IF P(I%)=INT(P(I%)) THEN QUESTIONS%(I%)=0
610 NEXT
620 READ S%
630 NEXT
```

You might be a bit puzzled by the calculations for P(I%) which vary depending on whether or not RESPONSE% is positive or negative.

The idea is this:

If RESPONSE% were +5 then the answer would be Yes and we calculate :

P(H:E) = P(E:H)P(H)/(P(E:H)P(H) + P(E:not H)P(not H))

and, if it were −5, we calculate :

P(H:not E) = P(not E:H)P(H)/(P(not E:H)P(H) + P(not E:not H)P(not H))

and, if RESPONSE% were 0 we calculate :

P(H:E) = P(H)

And if it's somewhere in between the extremes we have a bit of one and a bit of another – the code given calculates just how much of one bit and how much of another with a bit of simplification and re-arranging thrown in to speed things up a bit.

If P(I%) = INT(P(I%)) then P(I%) either equals 0 or 1 and we can knock QUESTIONS%(I%) down to zero because there's no doubt left concerning this hypothesis – so no more questions are needed on this item.

```
640 REM Find new rule values and minimum and maximum probabilities
650 RESTORE
660 READ A$
670 MAXOFMIN=0:BEST%=0
680 FOR I%=1 TO HYPOTHESES%
690 P=P(I%)
700 A1=1:A2=1:A3=1:A4=1
710 READ A$,PRIOR
720 FOR K%=1 TO VAR%(I%)
730 READ J%,PY,PN
740 IF VARFLAG%(J%)*QUESTIONS%(I%)=0 THEN 810
750 IF PN>PY THEN PY=1-PY:PN=1-PN
760 RULEVALUE(J%)=RULEVALUE(J%)+
    P*PY/(P*PY+(1-P)*PN)-P*(1-PY)/(P*(1-PY)+(1-P)*(1-PN))
```

```
770 A1=A1*PY
780 A2=A2*PN
790 A3=A3*(1-PY)
800 A4=A4*(1-PN)
810 NEXT
820 MAXI(I%)=P*A1/(P*A1+(1-P)*A2)
830 MINI(I%)=P*A3/(P*A3+(1-P)*A4)
840 IF MAXI(I%)<PRIOR THEN QUESTIONS%(I%)=0:PRINT "We can ignore ";A$
850 IF MINI(I%)>MAXOFMIN THEN BEST%=I%:MAXOFMIN=MINI(I%)
860 READ S%
870 NEXT
```

Of this, probably the calculation of the new rule values looks easy, but the bit about MINI(I%) and MAXI(I%) probably isn't so clear.

First, notice that we tested PY against PN to see which was the biggest. If PY is the biggest – fine, that means that a Yes answer increases P(H) and a No answer decreases it. It it's the other way around we want the opposite of these answers and that means, when you're working with probabilities, taking the complement, i.e. 1−PY and 1−PN. This way we can phrase our questions any way around we like and, as long as we got the probabilities right, the program knows whether it has supporting evidence for a hypothesis or not.

What we do now is to consider MAXI(I%) – the maximum probability possible and we calculate this by assuming that all the unanswered questions will eventually be answered in such a way as to support the hypothesis.

We still calculate P(H:E) in exactly the same way as we would have done if we'd been adjusting the probabilities. But, for the maximum possible value, we regard E as not just the answer to one question but the answer to *all* the outstanding questions. So P(E:H), for instance, is the probability that *all* the supporting evidence occurs given the hypothesis is true. And, assuming that each question is independent of every other question, this is the product of all the outstanding values of P(E:H).

P(all supporting evidence occurs: H) = $P(E_1:H)P(E_2:H)P(E_3:H)...P(E_n:H)$

which is the value we stored in A1.

So, we have:

> A1 = P(all supporting E:H)
> A2 = P(all supporting E:not H)
> A3 = P(no supporting E:H)
> A4 = P(no supporting E:not H)

And, frankly, anyone that starts to get a little mixed up at this point isn't alone. The procedure I usually adopt is to write down what I think it means then go and mow the lawn. Then I come back and write down what I should have written down if I'd been thinking straight in the first place. Then I go and mow the lawn again. Then I realise that I hadn't seen it quite straight that time and alter the equations a bit. Then I go and mow the lawn again. And so on.

At the end of the day, the lawn looks magnificent and I have a few drinks at which point I realise I've got it wrong and, just before passing out, see what I should have done and forget to write it down.

177

The next day the process resumes.

At the end of the week I am nearly down to bedrock where once there was a fine lawn and am trembling with what might well be fatigue.

I then realise that the very first set of equations I wrote down were right but that I've lost the piece of paper I wrote them on.

You, too, can spend your life this way. It has the great benefit of qualifying you for a disability pension around age 35 or less. Or, I suppose, you can plan the whole thing systematically in the first place.

Anyway, having got A1, A2, A3 and A4 you can calculate the minimum and maximum possible values as shown. All you need do is copy out the code and reflect on the fact that this treatise is built on human suffering beyond average comprehension.

Finally, we deduce the most likely conclusion, like this:

```
880 REM Search for a clear winner
890 FOR I%=1 TO HYPOTHESES%
900 IF MINI(BEST%)<=MAXI(I%) AND I%<>BEST% THEN MAXOFMIN=0
910 NEXT
920 IF MAXOFMIN=0 THEN 340
930 RESTORE: READ A$
940 FOR I%=1 TO BEST%
950 READ BEST$,A$
960 FOR K%=1 TO VAR%(I%)
970 READ J%,PY,PN
980 NEXT
990 READ A$
1000 NEXT
1010 PRINT: PRINT: PRINT "The most likely outcome is ";BEST$
1020 PRINT "With a probability ";P(BEST%)
1030 END
2000 DATA Illnesses
2010 DATA Illness 1,0.01,1,0.8,0.1,2,0.2,0.9,999
2020 DATA Illness 2,0.5,1,1,0.5,2,0,0.1,999
3000 DATA Symptoms
3010 DATA 1,Symptom 1
3020 DATA 2,Symptom 2,END,END
```

What this does is to take the maximum of the minimum values possible and see if it's greater than the maximum of any of the other values.

If it is, you stop, having finished.

If it isn't this is because some other outcome could, just possibly, be more probable than this particular outcome and, as this is currently the most probable outcome, you can't draw any firm conclusion yet and you have to go back and query another item.

If this sounds a bit too much like hard work you could simply pick that outcome with the greatest P(I) on the basis of the questions asked so far and, if it's a high enough probability to satisfy you, decide that this is the correct conclusion. Or, correct enough, anyway.

Anyway, just so that you know whether or not you've got it all working, here's an example of the actual run-time output you can expect to see on your screen if you give the same responses :

```
RUN

E X P E R T
_____


Question :-
Symptom 1
Reply on a scale -5 (No) to +5 (Yes) 5

Question :-
Symptom 2
Reply on a scale -5 (No) to +5 (Yes) 5
We can ignore Illness 2


The most likely outcome is Illness 1
With a probability 1.764057E-02
Ok
RUN

E X P E R T
_____


Question :-
Symptom 1
Reply on a scale -5 (No) to +5 (Yes) -5
We can ignore Illness 2


The most likely outcome is Illness 1
With a probability 2.239642E-03
Ok
```

Although this program works reasonably well (a miracle of modern technology, really) a great deal of its performance depends on the list of questions you supply it with.

On a theoretical level, the calculations all proceed on the assumption that each question is independent of every other question – and if they aren't the performance will deteriorate.

For instance, if you ask "Do you have a temperature?" and also ask "Are you feverish?" it's obvious that the two questions are very highly correlated. There simply isn't any point in asking both questions but, if you do, it will have the effect of upsetting the probabilities you'd associated with these items because, effectively, the same evidence will get counted in twice.

Also, you have to provide enough questions to be able to actually make some sort of diagnosis. To actually enable the system to come to a conclusion. That sounds obvious, but suppose you gave details of the Common Cold and Influenza and reckoned that both made you feel unwell, with a runny nose and a cough. Maybe the probabilities would be a bit different in each case – but they have to be sufficiently different to enable the program to actually see the difference. The trick is to go for clear, unambiguous, questions which don't overlap each other and are capable of splitting up the problem as cleanly as possible.

179

Typically, you'll find yourself working like any other person who's developed an expert system.

You'll write the program and throw a handful of likely-looking rules at it. (The rules are those definitions you gave in the DATA statements.)

You'll then pretend that you have pneumonia (if it's a medical system, maybe, a flat battery if you've been producing an expert mechanic) and answer the questions the system asks you with this in mind.

The system will then produce a wrong answer or ask some stupid questions – so you start fiddling around with the questions and the probabilities until the performance improves. And, really, this process has nothing much to do with computers at all. It's all to do with understanding the subject in which you want the computer to become expert – and it can be quite interesting in its own right.

And if it isn't you can always revert to the system described in the earlier part of this book – just sling a few examples at it and let it work it out for itself.

10.3 A medical knowledge base

If you set up the Bayesian Inferencing scheme just described then there will be one thing lacking before it will do anything useful – a Knowledge Base. Now, strictly speaking, that's your job to provide it with some domain-specific knowledge. But doing so can be pretty time-consuming. So, just to help things along a bit, here is a Knowledge Base for the Domain of Medical Diagnosis. If you load this code into line 2000 and forwards and line 3000 and forwards it will provide the expert system with knowledge on nearly 100 different diseases and their diagnosis. The figures given are, roughly, accurate and although it won't enable you to practice medicine it will enable you to indulge in some very exotic fantasies of hypochondria. It will also serve to give you an idea about how you might build up a Knowledge Base in other fields and will demonstrate how the expert runs when it has a real slab of knowledge inside it.

Once you have loaded this try altering some of the items to see how it affects the expert's skills.

For instance, you might want the expert to take account of the fact that Chronic Bronchitis (illness 10) is more common in men than in women (Symptom 53). So you could add to illness 10: –

   53,0.8,0.5

i.e. If the patient has chronic bronchitis then he is male with probability 0.8 – and, if the patient does not have chronic bronchitis then the probability of male is 0.5.

In other words, the healthy population is an even mixture of males and females.

Many diseases are sex-related in their incidence so question 53 could usefully be added to a number of illnesses in the Knowledge Base.

If you add symptom 53 to enough illnesses then you are likely to find that RULEVALUE(53) rises and one of the questions the expert asks very early on in a consultation will be to determine the patient's sex. Which seems reasonable – few human doctors would be willing to carry out a diagnosis without this, very basic, item of knowledge.

Then try adding other illnesses – bubonic plague, for instance, and see if the expert can diagnose that. If you need to add more symptoms (questions) these can easily be tacked on to the end of the list and referenced by their number in the same way as existing symptoms.

Then try writing a Knowledge Base of your own with questions, symptoms and 'illnesses' relating to the problem of why, for instance, your car won't start in the morning (it's probably got bubonic plague).

```
2000 DATA Illnesses
2010 DATA Common Cold,0.02,1,0.9,0.05,2,0.8,0.02,3,0.8,0.02,5,0.6,0.01,
     6,1,0.01,7,0.2,0.01,8,0.5,0.01,15,0.8,0.01,34,0,0.01,999
2020 DATA Allergic Rhinitis,0.01,1,1,0.01,2,1,0.01,6,0.9,0.01,10,0.7,0.01,
     11,0.7,0.01,12,0.6,0/.01,20,0.9,0.01,999
2030 DATA Sinusitis,0.01,14,0.8,0.01,13,0.9,0.01,15,0.8,0.01,7,0.6,0.01,
     22,0.5,0.01,2,0.5,0.001,6,0.5,0.01,63,0.9,0.01,999
2040 DATA Pharyngitis,0.02,3,1,0.01,16,0.9,0.01,8,0.5,0.01,11,0.9,0.01,
     37,0.8,0.3,64,0.4,0.01,999
2050 DATA Tonsillitis,0.001,3,1,0.01,7,0.9,0.01,15,1,0.01,16,0.7,0.01,
     19,0,0.5,8,0.8,0.01,34,0,0.01,64,0.8,0.01,999
2060 DATA Influenza,0.01,3,0.9,0.01,1,0.9,0.01,6,0.5,0.01,7,0.7,0.01,8,1,0.01,
     15,1,0.01,17,0.8,0.01,18,0.6,0.01,34,0,0.01,999
2070 DATA Laryngitis,0.01,4,1,0.01,8,0.6,0.01,15,0.05,0.01,16,0.17,0.01,
     37,0.8,0.3,999
2080 DATA Tumour of the Larynx,0.00004,4,1,0.01,34,0.99,0.01,37,0.8,0.3,999
2090 DATA Acute Bronchitis,0.005,5,0.1,0.01,8,1,0.01,12,1,0.01,15,1,0.01,
     18,0.5,0.01,21,1,0.01,31,0.9,0.01,34,0,0.01,22,0.9,0.01,999
2100 DATA Chronic Bronchitis,0.005,5,1,0.01,12,0.9,0.01,14,0.5,0.01,
     21,1,0.01,22,0.8,0.01,34,1,0.01,36,0.9,0.01,37,0.8,0.3,999
2110 DATA Asthma,0.02,12,0.8,0.01,22,1,0.01,23,0.5,0.01,24,0.5,0.01,
     25,0.5,0.01,26,0.5,0.01,31,0.8,0.01,999
2120 DATA Emphysema,0.01,22,1,0.01,5,0.001,0.01,26,0.8,0.01,12,0.001,0.01;
     21,0.01,0.01,37,0.8,0.3,999
2130 DATA Pneumonia,0.003,8,1,0.01,15,1,0.01,18,0.8,0.01,22,1,0.01,
     23,0.5,0.01,26,0.5,0.01,28,1,0.01,29,0.02,0.01,27,0.2,0.01,31,
     0.9,0.01,36,1,0.9,7,0.9,0.01,17,0.9,0.01,32,0.5,0.001,999
2140 DATA Pleurisy,0.001,31,0.8,0.01,32,0.8,01,22,0.5,0.01,5,0.8,0.01,
     8,0.9,0.01,15,1,0.01,0,0.01,999
2150 DATA Pneumothorax,0.0002,18,0.8,0.01,22,0.8,0.01,32,0.8,0.01,999
2160 DATA Bronchiectasis,0.00001,21,1,0.0,27,0.5,0.01,5,1,0.01,14,0.5,0.01,999
2170 DATA Lung Abscess,0.00001,33,0.9,0.01,18,0.5,0.01,21,0.5,0.01,
     27,0.5,0.01,999
2180 DATA Pneumoconiosis,0.001,22,1,0.01,36,1,0.01,21,0.8,0.01,9,1,0.001,999
2190 DATA Lung Cancer,0.001,5,1,0.01,21,0.8,0.01,27,0.5,0.01,22,0.5,0.01,
     18,0.8,0.01,12,0.5,0.01,37,0.99,0.3,999
2200 DATA Interstitial Fibrosis,0.00001,22,0.8,0.01,35,0.8,0.01,21,0.6,0.01,999
2210 DATA Pulminary Oedema,0.001,22,0.9,0.01,25,0.9,0.01,30,0.5,0.01,
     27,0.5,0.01,26,0.5,0.01,12,0.8,0.01,999
2220 DATA Gastritis,0.01,41,0.8,0.01,43,0.8,0.01,42,0.5,0.01,8,0.4,0.01,
     37,0.9,0.5,999
2230 DATA Hiatus Hernia,0.001,18,0.9,0.01,32,0.5,0.001,42,0.8,0.001,
     57,0.9,0.01,16,0.9,0.01,41,0.8,0.01,999
2240 DATA Duodenal Ulcer,0.01,37,0.8,0.2,42,0.99,0.001,41,0.8,0.01,999
2250 DATA Peptic Ulcer,0.01,42,0.9,0.001,18,0.5,0.01,20,0.8,0.01,
     41,0.7,0.01,56,0.9,0.01,62,0.0001,0.01,999
2260 DATA Diverticular Disease,0.001,42,0.6,0.001,43,0.5,0.01,41,0.5,0.01,
     8,0.5,0.01,49,0.5,0.01,999
2270 DATA Crohn's Disease,0.0001,42,0.9,0.001,43,0.9,0.01,15,0.9,0.01,
     8,0.7,0.01,62,0.00001,0.01,999
2280 DATA Intestinal Obstruction,0.00001,42,0.9,0.00,43,0.8,0.01,41,0.5,0.01,999
```

```
2290 DATA Appendicitis,0.001,34,0.1,0.9,42,0.9,0.001,41,0.8,0.01,8,0.8,0.01,
     44,0,0.5,999
2300 DATA Food Poisoning,0.001,42,0.5,0.001,41,0.9,0.01,43,0.9,0.01,
     7,0.8,0.01,999
2310 DATA Gastroenteritis,0.01,41,0.8,0.01,42,0.7,0.001,43,0.9,0.01,
     8,0.5,0.01,999
2320 DATA Kidney Stones,0.001,42,0.7,0.001,999
2330 DATA Acute Pyelonephritis,0.001,42,0.9,0.001,8,0.8,0.01,41,0.7,0.01,
     67,0.9,0.01,999
2340 DATA Gallstones,0.01,42,0.5,0.001,41,0.5,0.01,57,0.9,0.01,999
2350 DATA Cholecystitis,0.001,42,0.8,0.001,8,0.9,0.01,41,0.8,0.01,
     45,0.8,0.001,999
2360 DATA Shingles,0.001,42,0.5,0.001,18,0.5,0.001,60,0.9,0.01,59,0.9,0.01,
     2,0.6,0.01,46,0.5,0.01,999
2370 DATA Deep Vein Thrombosis,0.0005,40,0.8,0.01,999
2380 DATA Rheumatoid Arthritis,0.001,15,0.8,0.01,17,0.8,0.01,
     40,0.5,0.001,999
2390 DATA Heart Failure,0.001,22,0.9,0.01,36,0.5,0.01,25,0.5,0.001,
     12,0.6,0.01,18,0.5,0.001,32,0.3,0.001,40,0.5,0.01,42,0.5,0.01,
     28,0.3,0.001,47,0.9,0.01,999
2400 DATA Anxiety,0.01,46,0.9,0.01,28,0.3,0.01,47,0.6,0.01,39,0.8,0.01,
     23,0.6,0.01,48,0.6,0.01,16,0.3,0.01,43,0.2,0.01,22,0.5,0.01,
     50,0.5,0.01,57,0.5,0.01,58,0.5,0.01,15,0.5,0.01,7,0.5,0.01,
     4,0.5,0.01,999
2410 DATA Depression,0.01,47,0.5,0.01,7,0.5,0.01,49,0.5,0.01,50,0.5,0.01,
     15,0.5,0.01,62,0.8,0.01,999
2420 DATA Coronary Thrombosis,0.01,18,0.5,0.01,32,0.9,0.001,20,0.5,0.01,
     36,0,0.2,38,0.5,0.01,22,0.5,0.01,23,0.5,0.01,41,0.5,0.01,
     15,0.9,0.01,999
2430 DATA Angina,0.01,37,0.8,0.37,18,0.9,0.01,36,0.9,0.01,22,0.5,0.01,
     27,0.5,0.01,38,0.5,0.01,41,0.3,0.01,999
2440 DATA Pulmonary Embolism,0.0001,22,1,0.01,18,0.7,0.01,21,0.6,0.01,
     27,0.5,0.001,25,0.5,0.001,26,0.4,0.0001,999
2450 DATA Stroke,0.001,28,0.8,0.01,38,0.7,0.01,51,0.8,0.001,58,0.9,0.01,
     61,0.9,0.01,999
2460 DATA Transient Ischaemic Attack,0.001,28,0.8,0.01,38,0.7,0.01,
     51,0.8,0.001,34,01,0.01,20,0.5,0.01,58,0.9,0.01,
     61,0.9,0.01,999
2470 DATA Tuberculosis,0.0001,7,0.5,0.01,8,0.5,0.01,12,0.5,0.01,
     15,0.5,0.01,18,0.5,0.01,5,0.5,0.01,30,0.5,0.01,27,0.5,0.001,
     22,0.5,0.01,62,0.0001,0.01,23,0.5,0.01,999
2480 DATA Haemorroids,0.01,52,0.9,0.001,49,0.8,0.01,56,0.9,0.01,
     59,0.5,0.01,999
2490 DATA Hypothyroidism,0.001,49,0.8,0.01,17,0.5,0.01,24,0,0.01,
     23,0.001,0.01,39,0.001,0.01,4,0.5,0.01,43,0,0.01,46,0.001,0.01,
     48,0.001,0.01,62,0.9,0.05,999
2500 DATA Irritable Colon,0.0007,43,0.5,0.01,49,0.5,0.01,42,0.8,0.001,
     41,0.3,0.01,57,0.9,0.01,999
2510 DATA Cancer of Large Intestine,0.001,43,0.9,0.01,49,0.9,0.01,
     52,0.5,0.001,42,0.5,0.001,56,0.9,0.01,62,0.001,0.01,999
2520 DATA Ulcerative Colitis,0.0004,42,0.8,0.001,43,0.8,0.01,52,0.6,0.001,
     23,0.5,0.01,41,0.5,0.01,8,0.5,0.01,34,0.4,0.01,
     56,0.9,0.01,999
2530 DATA Meniere's Disease,0.0005,38,0.9,0.001,41,0.8,0.01,34,0.5,0.01,
     20,0.9,0.01,999
2540 DATA Cervical Spondylosis,0.006,54,0.9,0.01,7,0.5,0.01,38,0.5,0.01,
     58,0.9,0.01,61,0.5,0.01,999
2550 DATA Subdural Haemorrage,0.000001,55,0.99,0.0001,28,0.9,0.001,
     7,0.9,0.01,41,0.9,0.01,38,0.9,0.01,20,0.5,0.01,
     34,0.5,0.01,999
2560 DATA Brain Tumour,0.000001,7,0.9,0.01,41,0.9,0.01,38,0.8,0.01,
```

```
      50,0.8,0.01,34,0.5,0.01,999
2570 DATA Meningitis,0.000001,8,0.9,0.01,7,0.9,0.01,41,0.9,0.01,
      28,0.7,0.01,54,0.9,0.01,2,0.9,0.01,60,0.5,0.01,999
2580 DATA Subarachnoid Haemorrage,0.000001,7,0.99,0.01,54,0.9,0.01,
      38,0.7,0.01,28,0.7,0.01,41,0.8,0.01,2,0.8,0.01,999
2590 DATA Acute Glaucoma,0.01,2,0.9,0.01,7,0.9,0.01,41,0.7,0.01,
      20,0.8,0.01,0.34,0.8,0.01,63,0.8,0.01,68,0.9,0.01,999
2600 DATA Temporal Arteritis,0.001,7,0.9,0.01,17,0.7,0.01,2,0.8,0.01,
      63,0.99,0.01,999
2610 DATA Dyspepsia,0.1,18,0.7,0.01,57,0.7,0.01,42,0.7,0.01,41,0.7,0.01,
      46,0.5,0.01,20,0.9,0.01,999
2620 DATA Heart Block,0.0003,22,0.5,0.01,58,0.8,0.01,39,0.6,0.01,
      18,0.6,0.01,999
2630 DATA Pernicious Anaemia,0.0004,22,0.9,0.01,58,0.9,0.01,39,0.9,0.01,
      36,0.9,0.01,45,0.5,0.01,42,0.5,0.01,50,0.5,0.01,
      28,0.4,0.01,999
2640 DATA Migraine,0.1,7,1,0.01,15,0.9,0.01,41,0.9,0.01,43,0.5,0.01,
      20,0.9,0.01,34,0.9,0.01,63,0.99,0.01,999
2650 DATA Hypertension,0.15,7,0.5,0.01,39,0.5,0.01,15,0.5,0.01,34,0.9,0.01,999
2660 DATA Eczema,0.3,59,0.9,0.01,60,1,0.01,999
2670 DATA Urticaria,0.03,59,0.9,0.01,60,1,0.01,46,0.5,0.01,999
2680 DATA Scabies,0.001,59,1,0.01,60,1,0.01,999
2690 DATA Measles,0.02,15,1,0.01,8,1,0.01,6,0.9,0.01,2,0.9,0.01,11,0.9,0.01,
      5,9,0.01,43,0.5,0.01,6,0.8,0.01,7,0.5,0.01,34,01,0.01,999
2700 DATA Rubella,0.01,8,0.5,0.01,60,0.9,0.01,54,0.2,0.01,34,0,0.01,
      64,0.5,0.01,999
2710 DATA Chickenpox,0.001,60,1,0.01,59,1,0.01,8,0.8,0.01,7,0.5,0.01,
      15,0.5,0.01,34,0,0.01,999
2720 DATA Psoriasis,0.02,46,0.6,0.01,3,0.5,0.01,60,0.99,0.01,59,0.5,0.01,999
2730 DATA Pityriasis Rosea,0.01,60,1,0.01,59,0.9,0.01,34,0.5,0.01,999
2740 DATA Acne Rosacea,0.01,60,0.9,0.01,2,0.5,0.01,34,0.8,0.01,999
2750 DATA Thyrotoxicosis,0.0001,46,0.9,0.01,47,0.8,0.01,48,0.9,0.01,
      23,0.9,0.01,39,0.9,0.01,22,0.8,0.01,43,0.8,0.01,
      62,0.00001,0.01,2,0.5,0.01,24,0.9,0.01,64,0.3,0.01,68,0.3,0.01,999
2760 DATA Diabetes Mellitus,0.01,62,0.0001,0.01,61,0.5,0.01,2,0.5,0.01,
      66,0.99,0.01,68,0.1,0.01,999
2770 DATA Stomach Cancer,0.0003,41,0.5,0.01,42,0.7,0.001,62,0.0001,0.01,
      52,0.6,0.001,56,0.5,0.01,999
2780 DATA Atrial Fibrillation,0.001,39,0.8,0.01,38,0.5,0.01,42,0.4,0.01,
      58,0.5,0.01,999
2790 DATA Hodgkin's Disease,0.0001,23,0.5,0.01,63,0.6,0.01,54,0.8,0.01,
      59,0.7,0.01,64,0.99,0.01,999
2800 DATA Glandular Fever,0.001,8,0.9,0.01,7,0.9,0.01,3,0.9,0.01,
      15,0.9,0.01,64,0.8,0.001,54,0.8,0.01,45,0.5,0.001,
      60,0.5,0.01,999
2810 DATA Lymphoma,0.0001,64,0.9,0.01,54,0.8,0.01,15,0.8,0.01,
      62,0.001,0.01,8,0.8,0.01,23,0.5,0.01,59,0.8,0.01,999
2820 DATA Mumps,0.01,64,0.99,0.01,8,0.8,0.01,15,0.9,0.01,16,0.7,0.01,
      54,0.6,0.01,3,0.8,0.01,999
2830 DATA Bell's Palsy,0.0003,51,0.9,0.01,63,0.5,0.01,999
2840 DATA Parkinson's Disease,0.001,48,0.9,0.01,51,0.8,0.01,42,0.3,0.01,
      50,0.2,0.01,28,0.1,0.01,999
2850 DATA Rheumatic Fever,0.01,3,0.8,0.01,15,0.8,0.01,0.8,0.8,0.01,
      64,0.8,0.01,60,0.5,0.01,59,0.001,0.01,48,0.1,0.01,999
2860 DATA Cystitis,0.01,66,0.9,0.01,65,0.9,0.01,67,0.9,0.01,8,0.5,0.01,999
2870 DATA Kidney Tumour,0.001,8,0.6,0.01,62,0.0001,0.01,0.41,0.5,0.01,
      42,0.5,0.01,65,0.7,0.01,999
2880 DATA Bladder Tumour,0.0004,65,0.9,0.01,42,0.5,0.01,66,0.5,0.01,
      67,0.5,0.01,8,0.3,0.01,999
2890 DATA Iritis,0.0005,2,0.9,0.01,68,0.9,0.01,999
2900 DATA Acute Hepatitis,0.001,8,0.8,0.01,15,0.8,0.01,17,0.5,0.01,
```

```
      42,0.5,0.01,45,0.5,0.01,41,0.5,0.01,999
3000 DATA Symptoms
3010 DATA 1,Are you sneezing a lot ?
3020 DATA 2,Are your eyes painful or watering a lot ?
3030 DATA 3,Do you have a sore throat ?
3040 DATA 4,Is your voice hoarse ?
3050 DATA 5,Are you coughing a lot ?
3060 DATA 6,Do you have a runny nose ?
3070 DATA 7,Do you have a headache or-in general-do you
     suffer from headaches at all ?
3080 DATA 8,Do you have a high temperature ?( over 100 F say)
3090 DATA 9,Do you spend a lot of your time in a very dusty atmosphere ?
3100 DATA 10,Does your skin itch ?
3110 DATA 11,Do you have a dry throat ?
3120 DATA 12,Is your breath 'wheezy' ?
3130 DATA 13,Is your nose very 'blocked up' ?
3140 DATA 14,Have you had a cold or similar infection recently ?
3150 DATA 15,Do you feel generally ill ?
3160 DATA 16,Do you have trouble swallowing ?
3170 DATA 17,Do your muscles ache ?
3180 DATA 18,Do you have any pain at all in your chest ?
3190 DATA 19,Have you had your tonsils removed ?
3200 DATA 20,Do you have any symptoms which tend to occur in 'attacks'
     rather than being present all the time ?
3210 DATA 21,Do you have a 'productive' cough-a cough in which you bring
      something up ?
3220 DATA 22,Are you rather breathless ?
3230 DATA 23,Do you sweat a lot-not just when you exert yourself but
     when you are apparently relaxing as well ?
3240 DATA 24,Is your pulse rate high ? Normally it should be about
     60 to 80 beats each minute and slightly faster for people
     over 70 or under 20.
3250 DATA 25,Do you have severe attacks of breathlessness-enough to
     seriously worry you ?
3260 DATA 26,Does your skin have a bluish tinge ?
3270 DATA 27,When you cough is your phlegm stained with blood ?
3280 DATA 28,Are you confused-muddled about what's going on around you ?
3290 DATA 29,Are you (or the patient) delirious-talking incoherently with
     poor muscular coordination ?
3300 DATA 30,Do you have a dry (non-productive) cough ?
3310 DATA 31,Is it painful when you breathe or cough ?
3320 DATA 32,Do you ever have any really severe pain in your chest ?
3330 DATA 33,Do you swing between feeling chilled and feeling feverish ?
3340 DATA 34,Do you have any symptoms which have been present for
     some time-possibly six weeks or more ?
3350 DATA 35,Do you have 'clubbed fingers' ?-These are fingers in which
     the cuticles have almost disappeared and the nails curve over
     at the fingertips.
3360 DATA 36,Do you have any symptoms which mainly occur when you exert
     yourself ?
3370 DATA 37,Do you smoke ? To reply divide the number of cigarettes you
     smoke by 5-use this number to reply (if you smoke 20 a day
     reply 4). 5 is the maximum reply and -5 means you do not smoke.
3380 DATA 38,Do you suffer from feelings of dizziness ?
3390 DATA 39,Do you have palpitations ?-The feeling that your heart is
     beating more strongly or faster or more unevenly than it should.
3400 DATA 40,Is either of your ankles unduly swollen ?
3410 DATA 41,Are you vomiting or do you have strong feelings of nausea ?
3420 DATA 42,Do you have any abdominal pain ? This is pain anywhere between
     the bottom of the ribcage and the groin.
3430 DATA 43,Do you suffer from diarrhoea ?-Passing unusually runny faeces.
```

```
3440 DATA 44,Have you had your appendix removed ?
3450 DATA 45,Do you have jaundice ? This is not a disease but a
     symptom of disease. Often it is most obvious in the eyes-
     the whites become yellow.
3460 DATA 46,Are you rather tense and apprehensive ?
3470 DATA 47,Do you find it hard to get to sleep or do you often wake
     in the middle of the night ?
3480 DATA 48,Do you have any involuntary twitching or trembling ?
3490 DATA 49,Do you suffer from constipation ? Passing faeces infrequently
     or with difficulty.
3500 DATA 50,Do you have a poor memory ? That is-difficulty remembering
     individual facts either occasionally or regularly.
3510 DATA 51,Have you totally or nearly lost the power of speech ?
3520 DATA 52,Have you experienced any bleeding from your back passage ?
3530 DATA 53,Are you male or female ? Answer 5 for male or -5 for female.
     If you'd like the analysis to be general
     (for either sex) reply 0.
3540 DATA 54,Is your neck stiff and/or painful ?
3550 DATA 55,Have you sustained any kind of head injury over the last
     few weeks ? Even a very slight injury can be important.
3560 DATA 56,Have you recently been passing abnormal-looking faeces ?
3570 DATA 57,Are you passing large quantities of wind-either by belching
     or flatulence ?
3580 DATA 58,Do you have sudden feeling of faintness-feeling weak and
     unsteady maybe even losing consciousness ?
3590 DATA 59,Does any part of your body itch-with or without the presence
     of any rash ?
3600 DATA 60,Do you have a skin rash of any sort ?
3610 DATA 61,Is any part of your body numb-or do you have a tingling
     'pins and needles' sensation anywhere ?
3620 DATA 62,Are you overweight or underweight ?
     Reply 5 for definite overweight and -5 for definite underweight.
     Reply 0 if your weight is just right.
3630 DATA 63,Do you have any pain in your face or forehead ?
3640 DATA 64,Do you have any swelling under the skin ?
3650 DATA 65,Is your urine abnormally coloured ?
3660 DATA 66,Are you urinating unusually frequently ?
3670 DATA 67,Is it painful when you urinate ?
3680 DATA 68,Is your vision impaired in any way-blurring or double vision
     or seeing flashing lights ? (This does not include defects
     which can be corrected by spectacles).
3690 DATA END,END
```

Anyway, again to check that you've got the thing keyed in correctly and, also, so that
you can see for yourselves that I enjoy perfect health—here's a sample of the actual
run-time output obtained using this particular knowledge base :

```
RUN

E X P E R T
_____

Question :-
Do you have any abdominal pain ? This is pain anywhere
between the bottom of
the ribcage and the groin.
Reply on a scale -5 (No) to +5 (Yes) -5
We can ignore Kidney Stones
```

```
Question :-
Do you feel generally ill ?
Reply on a scale -5 (No) to +5 (Yes) -5
We can ignore Tonsillitis
We can ignore Influenza
We can ignore Acute Bronchitis
We can ignore Pneumonia
We can ignore Pleurisy
We can ignore Kidney Stones
We can ignore Measles


Question :-
Do you have a skin rash of any sort ?
Reply on a scale -5 (No) to +5 (Yes) -5
We can ignore Tonsillitis
We can ignore Influenza
We can ignore Acute Bronchitis
We can ignore Pneumonia
We can ignore Pleurisy
We can ignore Kidney Stones
We can ignore Eczema
We can ignore Urticaria
We can ignore Scabies
We can ignore Measles
We can ignore Chickenpox
We can ignore Pityriasis Rosea


Question :-
Are you vomiting or do you have strong feelings
of nausea ?
Reply on a scale -5 (No) to +5 (Yes) -5
We can ignore Tonsillitis
We can ignore Influenza
We can ignore Acute Bronchitis
We can ignore Pneumonia
We can ignore Pleurisy
We can ignore Duodenal Ulcer
We can ignore Kidney Stones
We can ignore Eczema
We can ignore Urticaria
We can ignore Scabies
We can ignore Measles
We can ignore Chickenpox
We can ignore Pityriasis Rosea


Question :-
Are you rather breathless ?
Reply on a scale -5 (No) to +5 (Yes) -5
We can ignore Tonsillitis
We can ignore Influenza
We can ignore Acute Bronchitis
We can ignore Asthma
We can ignore Emphysema
We can ignore Pneumonia
We can ignore Pleurisy
We can ignore Pneumoconiosis
We can ignore Duodenal Ulcer
We can ignore Kidney Stones
```

```
We can ignore Pulmonary Embolism
We can ignore Eczema
We can ignore Urticaria
We can ignore Scabies
We can ignore Measles
We can ignore Chickenpox
We can ignore Pityriasis Rosea


Question :-
Do you have a headache or-in general-do you suffer from headaches at all ?
Reply on a scale -5 (No) to +5 (Yes) -5
We can ignore Tonsillitis
We can ignore Influenza
We can ignore ....
```

And so on and so forth until you really *do* have a headache and strong feelings of nausea.

Anyway, that's what it looks like and you'll probably have noticed that it has a cumulative style of reporting in which it keeps on adding to the list of things which it can't find wrong with you very much along the lines of *Old Uncle Tom Cobley And All*. You can cure this complaint by fiddling around with the code so that it only reports on hypotheses which have actually been discounted as a result of the last-asked question; and, you can also cure it of its slowness if you want by smoothing up the code a little. Mainly, you could bear in mind that all of that data in the DATA statements could be accessed much faster if it was placed into arrays and that RULEVALUE doesn't need to be completely re-calculated after each question but only needs adjustment for those hypotheses which have actually been affected by the last-asked question.

But, as it is, at least the code is fairly clear which makes it a useful starting point for anyone who's feeling a little more adventurous.

Chapter 11

The Tower of Babel

Once upon a time, a long time ago, a group of computer scientists were sitting round a table deep in thought. And, in between thinking, they were counting how many transistors they had between them

"Do you know," said one, "if we fastened *all* of these transistors together we'd have a computer that could do *anything?*" To which statement the others (in between swigs of beer) readily agreed. And, later that same evening, they got out their soldering irons and started work.

Time passed and the machine they were building got bigger and bigger until it was soon apparent that it, really and truly, would be able to carry out any task to which they set it. A more powerful computer had never been built and they dreamed of the day when they would switch it on and, in a matter of seconds, discover the complete answers to every problem in the Entire Known Universe.

As the machine rose skywards vast armies of programmers were recruited to write the programs that would control the new monster and each of these was initiated into the secret rites of machine code programming because, at that time, that was the only programming language that anyone had ever thought of.

The day of the great switch-on drew near and word of the great new computer spread far and wide causing not a little apprehension amongst the population as they thought of the awful cognitive power that was soon to be unleashed.

And, on the very night before the machine's completion, that self-same group of computer scientists again sat around a table, swigging beer, and debating which program should have the honour of being the first program to be written for the new machine.

"Y'know," said one sagely, "it doesn't really matter what program is first." At which the others nodded their own heads wisely. "What really matters is the language it is written in."

At which point the others carried on nodding their heads and began to wonder what other languages there could possibly be, other than machine code.

But the speaker held his ground and pointed out that machine code is difficult to write and difficult to understand. It is machine-orientated, not orientated towards the problems that want solving. And, it had that greatest of all flaws – it was academically unsatisfying.

So, that night, each of the computer scientists went home and wrote a high level language definition and a compiler to go with it. And when the next day dawned bright and clear they reassembled themselves at the foot of the great machine and decided that, before they switched it on, they'd settle for once and for all which was the best of the new languages to use. And, being gentlemen, they decided to settle the matter by discussion.

As far as is known they're still discussing the matter and the machine never got switched on, because the real problem was that none of them would ever understand the languages the others had developed.

And, even if that story isn't one hundred per cent historic fact, there's still a lot of truth in it.

For when the only language around was machine code (or Assembler, which is a bit easier to understand but, essentially, the same) then every computer person understood, more or less, what every other computer person was doing. There are now so many programming languages available that it's more or less impossible to be familiar with them all – yet if ideas are sketched out in an unfamiliar language you'll have difficulty in understanding those ideas. The language becomes a hindrance rather than a help.

That's why the examples given in this book are in BASIC – because it's a language that most people have readily available and that most people understand. But the real question is: Is BASIC the best language to use? Would it be better to have a crack at another language?

Intuitively, you might think there were strong arguments for using, say, LISP because that's the language in which many early expert systems were written. Or, maybe, Prolog – a more recent derivative of LISP in which a large number of expert systems have now been written.

To get at this question we need to consider just what a programming language can and cannot do – and the first point to note is that it really and truly can't do anything which can't be done in machine code. For most people this might be obvious but it's still worth noting that any language is always compiled down into machine code prior to execution and it is the machine code which defines the machine on which the program is run. If an instruction cannot be reduced to machine code then, on that machine, it is unexecutable. So, in machine code it's possible to do everything of which the machine is capable and, in any other language it is impossible to do any more than that.

So: if a language cannot do more than machine code can do, can it be such that it prevents the programmer from doing as much as is possible in machine code? That is: Can a language reduce the range of possible activities? The answer is: Yes. And, for an example, consider BASIC and pretend that there aren't any such things as PEEK and POKE. Now suppose that, for some reason of your own, you wanted to look into byte 3096 in RAM, see what was there, and then alter only one bit in that byte. That would be impossible except by using the weirdest contortions imaginable because BASIC gives you no way (without PEEK or POKE) of accessing an absolute address and no way of 'bit-twiddling'.

In fact, this example isn't particularly unusual. Many high level languages don't give much scope for absolute addressing and yet there are plenty of applications for which absolute addressing is essential.

So a language can never do more than machine code and can, often, do much less. In which case, what are other languages good for?

Two things: One, they are easier than machine code. Two, they can (but don't always) act as an aid to thought.

The first point is obvious. BASIC is easier then machine code both to learn and to use. That's true of most high level languages.

But the matter of an aid to thought isn't quite so obvious and, even when it is, it can be rather a two-edged sword. Staying with BASIC, consider the FOR loop. That is certainly an aid to thought. You can conjure it up in your head, look at it on paper, display it on the screen, and it's quite clear what it does. So you can forget it and concentrate on what's inside the loop. At which point the second edge of the sword starts to appear – because we rather presupposed there that, with BASIC, you are definitely going to use FOR loops. In fact, such a strong aid to thought is the FOR loop that, when faced with a programming problem, the temptation is to try to work out how best to arrange FOR loops to solve that problem rather than to ask whether or not FOR loops are, in fact, a good way to proceed in this instance. And if they weren't a good way to proceed then the odds are that you'd still use them anyway.

To make this point clearer consider the dichotomy between the computer and the problem the computer has to solve.

Machine code is exclusively computer-orientated. If you simply want to drive the machine then machine code is the most efficient way of programming in terms of getting a short, fast program.

But, to a greater or lesser degree, high level languages are problem orientated – they look after the machine and let you concentrate on solving the problem. And with, say, BASIC if you want to work on a matrix of numbers then FOR loops provide an ideal way of accessing the various elements of those matrices so that you can do so. The mistake to avoid though is to think that because a language is problem orientated it is ideally orientated towards each and every one of the particular problems that you might want to solve. There are different types of problems which can be solved in different types of ways – as the names of some of the programming languages reveal. COBOL, for instance, is an acronym for Common Business Oriented *(sic)* Language – it's aimed at business problems. ALGOL is an acronym for Algorithmic Language – and it's aimed at problems for which an algorithmic solution is handy (an algorithm is a recipe for solving problems primarily in the field of logic and maths). FORTRAN is an acronym for Formula Translator – a language designed for evaluating formulae. And BASIC? That's Beginners All-Purpose Symbolic Instruction Code – a language designed, actually, for the problem of beginners who don't know how to program at all well!

Back to the expert systems though and the question: Is there a language aimed at these?

Obviously, to answer that question you need to know the sort of problems that arise when you're building an expert system. And that's difficult to specify because of the wide variety of problems which are subsumed under the heading 'expert systems'.

However, there are a few points which can be made. For a start think of that multi-node expert system we dreamed up. In BASIC the nodes were connected to each other by means of labelling them with a string variable and then searching through all the string variables to see if there was a matching string to determine the connections. Now that was pretty messy – and it wouldn't be helped any by the fact that those variables are data and will be likely to be lost as soon as you switch the machine off unless you write a routine to specifically save them to disc.

This is the sort of problem that LISP was designed to get around for what we have is a series of lists (LISt Processing Language, you see!). Suppose now, for example, we have two nodes, Node 1 and Node 2 with inputs and outputs to each.

Define a list for Node 2. This list contains all the inputs and outputs to that node. Define two sub-lists in Node 2, Input and Output, to show which is which. Do the same for Node 1. Now, if Node 1 has an Output 1 which contains X which is the same element as Node 2 Input 2 then it's possible to define that in a LISP program also.

We can define a structure something like Fig. 11.1.

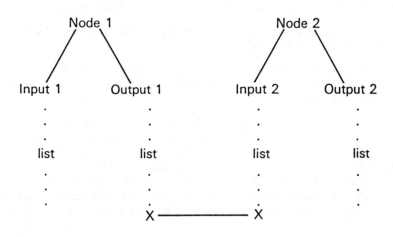

Fig. 11.1 List Processing

And all of this is contained in the program code – not as data as such (although, to be honest, the distinction between program and data isn't very strong in LISP anyway).

Having defined the above structure it is fairly easy then to write code to ask if any of the inputs on Node 2 are outputs from Node 1. That's a fairly simple example and the real value of LISP is that it allows these structures to be defined in as complex a fashion as you like. You can just go on and on making things more and more complicated – something which would make the average head hurt if it was tried in BASIC.

Consider a further point – that all of the systems we have given have been forward chaining. They collected items of data and then worked forward through the program to see what could be done with that data. Suppose that we'd wanted a backward chaining program? In the above example the distinction goes like this:

In forward chaining we provide the program with, say, Input 1 on Node 1 which produces output which is passed to Node 2 as input so that Node 2 can produce output.

In backward chaining the program looks at Node 2, thinks it will see if it can produce a specific output, looks backwards to see what inputs it needs, sees Node 1 is needed for some of these inputs and then goes back to Node 1 and asks for input to that. Not very easy in BASIC. The main reason why it's hard is because most BASICs don't offer recursion – the ability of a procedure to call itself.

The most usual example of recursion (in case you're not sure what it is) is the evaluation of a factorial – say, $3! = 3*2*1 = 6$. So, if we had the recursive procedure FAC(N) we could say that :

```
FAC(N)=N*FAC(N-1) if N is greater than 1
       =1 if N less than or equal to 1
```

So

```
FAC(3)=3*FAC(2)
      =3*2*FAC(1)
      =3*2*1
      =6
```

It isn't always so easy to give examples for less simple matters but suppose we had a recursive procedure called NODE(N). This procedure tries to evaluate Node N and does it by considering the inputs to that node. While it is considering these inputs it also checks to see if any of them are the outputs from Node (N−1) and, if they are, it calls NODE(N−1). Which then checks Node (N−2) and so on until the method has got back to the front of the chain.

Now, that could be useful. Writing NODE(N) might take some thought but, once written, it could be used on the arbitrarily complex structures we mentioned earlier. But, of course, the fact that most BASICs don't support recursion doesn't completely rule out recursive code. It would be possible to write BASIC code which did behave like this – but it would be fiddly.

Using LISP or Prolog makes life easier if activities like this seem like a good idea for solving the problem in hand.

In a way, the advantages of these languages lie largely in the fact that they are organised to help deal with very complicated symbolic structures which, largely, have very little to do with ordinary mathematics. And the application to expert systems lies in the fact that, when we try to make our expert system behave like a human expert, we are often trying to make it work with a large amount of rather complicated, non-numeric, structures.

The point about non-numeric or non-mathematical structures helps to display another side to the coin. The fact that if you need to do maths these languages can be rather laborious. Take for instance the BASIC statement $X = 2 + 2$ and consider the LISP alternative which is (SETQ X ADD(2 2)). Not too complicated, but consider what a real calculation might look like if that's just the starting point!

What's happened is that LISP was designed to help solve a particular type of problem – and it was not the type of problem associated with maths expressions. But some LISP users might want to do a bit of maths so that side of it was provided but was expressed in just the same way as the rest. With the result that the maths is somewhat on the weird side! In BASIC we find the opposite. Beginners maybe did want to do lots of maths – so design a language aimed at those problems. And, of course, you find that the language so designed is somewhat weak in other areas.

But now consider Prolog. Prolog stands for Programming in Logic and makes it very easy to write programs using what logicians call the First Order Predicate Calculus although, frankly, you don't have to know what logicians call it in order to use it. To my mind it's much easier to use than LISP and, in the field of expert systems, it has a lot of supporters. So, an example of Prolog, to give you the idea :

```
mortal(X):-man(X).
man(socrates).
```

What this says is that X is mortal if it is true that X is a man; and, also, that Socrates is a man. The first line being a rule and the second being a fact. When this small program is run it's possible to ask the system the question whether or not Socrates is mortal and the program will answer Yes. The way this might look on the screen when you respond to the Prolog prompt (?–) is :

```
?-mortal(socrates).
Yes
```

Effectively, what you have asked the system is whether or not there is a Socrates such that Socrates has the property of being mortal. The program then notes that in its first line it can put X equal to Socrates and that this would be true if the same X was such that there was an X which had the property of being a man. In the second line of the program it actually finds the fact that there is a value of X which is 'socrates' such that it is true that X is a man and it can then go on to answer 'Yes'– with X equal to Socrates it is true that X is mortal.

A simple example, but enough to show the attraction to many people of using Prolog to build expert systems – because you can simply sling in a whole load of rules and facts and the Prolog system itself will do all the hard work of slogging through these in a logical sequence. But what the Prolog system has done is to automatically implement a system of backward chaining in which a goal state is set up and the program automatically chains backwards from this goal state in order to try to establish the truth or otherwise of that goal. All of which is fine if that's what you want to do. But if you'd rather have a forward chaining system or, worse, use the Rule Value approach described in this book – then you've got problems, because Prolog is not necessarily ideal once you try to move away from backward chaining.

And this is, really, a very good example of language influencing thought because you can almost invariably tell when an expert system has been written in Prolog on account of the fact that it will use backward chaining; and, one of the main reasons I developed the Rule Value approach was because it was readily implemented in Basic.

All of which probably helps to explain why there's some slight trend nowadays towards building expert systems in another language altogether – C.

C doesn't stand for anything at all. In fact, the only reason it's called C is because an earlier version of the same language was called B which is, of course, one of those little-known facts that nobody really needs to know. However, the main point to note about C is that it's actually very much like a slightly smoothed up version of Assembler – in other words, it's very close to machine code. And that's its attraction. That it places very few, if any, restrictions on what you can make the machine do. Rather hard to program in, but it lets you program what you want without tending to push you too hard in any one single direction.

Of course, what we ideally want is one, big, language that does everything under all circumstances and isn't too hard to program. But we'll be unlikely to get it simply because nobody knows what it might look like. Even our very own English isn't up to every task – witness the large number of specialist sub-languages that have been evolved over the years to extend English into new fields – like, for instance, the language of the mathematician or the doctor. If we wish to produce a language that would be perfect for, say, medical diagnosis we would need English (to communicate with the patients), Doctor-ese (to communicate with the medics – maybe Latin would do), and Mathematics (to work out any calculations). And there's no harm in saying that this is rather more than many practising physicians have!

In a way the problem of languages isn't really so bad as might be made out though for the simple reason that most computer users only have access to a limited number of choices – and that settles most arguments about which language should be used. There's also the fact that, often, the best language to use is the language you're good at. A great deal of research in artificial intelligence has relied on LISP and Prolog but one reason for this is that students of artificial intelligence are often taught these languages and, after that, the habit is bound to die just as hard as does the BASIC habit in someone else.

But certainly the language you use influences, one way or another, the way you think about problems and the BASIC programmer is likely to find himself implementing an expert system in quite a different way to the way a LISP or Prolog programmer might do it.

In the end the value of each approach lies simply in the quality of the end result and, in the final extreme, you can always go back to machine code. The only danger of which is that you might die of old age before you finish writing the program.

Chapter 12

Summary and Technical Overview

As this book reads rather like a story, the plot of which involves getting you to do something, you may well be sitting there and saying something like:

"Fine, I can see how these systems work. I could even write my own expert system now but I can't remember how this Naylor character defined 'rules' or.."

Well, you could look it up in the index or consult those notes you've been making. But, to make it really easy, here is a list of the important terms that you'll need to know:

12.1 Events

An Event can be almost anything.
Let H be the event that a given Hypothesis is true.
Let E be the event that a given piece of Evidence occurs which may, or may not, support the given Hypothesis.

12.2 Probabilities (see also pages 16−21)

$P(H)$ is the probability that H is true.
$P(E)$ is the probability that E occurs.
Probabilities are numbers in the range 0 to 1.
If the probability is 0 then the event never occurs.
If the probability is 1 then the event always occurs.

$P(\text{not } H) = 1 - P(H)$ and is the probability that H is not true.

Two events are independent if their joint probability of occurrence equals the product of their separate probabilities of occurrence.

$P(E_1 \& E_2)$ is the joint probability that both E_1 and E_2 occur.

E_1 and E_2 are independent if, and only if, $P(E_1 \& E_2) = P(E_1)P(E_2)$.

P(H:E) is the conditional probability of H occurring given that E has already occurred.

If H and E are independent P(H:E) = P(H).

In general: P(H:E) =   P(H&E)/P(E)

Similarly,   P(E:H) =   P(E&H)/P(H)

So: P(H:E) =   P(E:H)P(H)/P(E)

12.2.1 Bayes' Theorem
(see also pages 27, 160−166, 171−174)

P(H:E) = P(E:H)P(H)/(P(E:H)P(H) + P(E:not H)P(not H))

The Question of P(H:E) versus P(E:H):

It might, initially, seem much more sensible to work always with P(H:E) − after all, we want to know what the probability is for each hypothesis given the evidence, not the other way round.

The problem is that P(H:E) is not at all an obvious quantity. If you knew P(H:E) to start with there would be very little point in writing a computer program to work it out for you.

P(E:H), on the other hand, is usually much more apparent when data is being collected on the problem in hand.

You ask the question: If H is true, what is the probability of observing this particular piece of evidence?

And, for P(E:not H): If H is not true, what is the probability of observing this particular piece of evidence?

These two questions enable the program to calculate P(H:E), successively improving the estimate as each new piece of evidence comes in.

For two, or more, events E_1 and E_2:

If E_1 and E_2 are independent:

$P(E_1 \& E_2 : H) = P(E_1 : H)P(E_2 : H)$

Note: it is never correct to say:

$P(H : E_1 \& E_2) = P(H : E_1)P(H : E_2)$

If E is the event 'all E_i occur', and the E_i are independent of each other, then we can calculate:

$P(E:H) = P(E_1 : H)P(E_2 : H)...P(E_n : H)$
$P(\text{not } E:H) = P(\text{not } E_1 : H)P(\text{not } E_2 : H)...P(\text{not } E_n : H)$

12.2.2 Prior and posterior probabilities

Suppose we have a hypothesis H and some evidence, for or against H, which we call E.

Then:

P(H) is the prior probability of H. It is the probability of H with no knowledge of E.

P(H:E), or P(H:not E), is the posterior probability of H. It is the probability of H once we know the truth about E.

From Bayes' Theorem, we have:

P(H:E) = P(E:H)P(H)/(P(E:H)P(H) + P(E:not H)P(not H))

Or, if E were found to be absent, we would have:

P(H:not E) = P(not E:H)P(H)/(P(not E:H)P(H) + P(not E:not H)P(not H))

Suppose that, for some H, there are a larger number of items of evidence which become progressively available to either support H or deny H. Call them E_1 to E_n.

If they were all available at once, and if they were all independent of each other, we could calculate P(E:H) as the product of the individual $P(E_i:H)$ and then find P(H:E) where E is the event 'all E_i occur' . Similarly, we could calculate P(not E:H) as the product of all the $P(not E_i:H)$.

But, instead, we might find it more convenient to work in stages, totting up the evidence and its effects as we go through the E_i. We can do this using prior and posterior probabilities in the following way:

1. P(H) is the prior probability of H
2. For given evidence E_i we have $P(E_i:H)$ and $P(E_i:not H)$
3. Using Bayes' Theorem we can calculate $P(H:E_i)$ or $P(H:not E_i)$ depending on the outcome of E_i. This is the posterior probability of H.
4. We can now disregard E_i altogether and call the posterior probability of H the (new) prior probability of H. So: put $P(H) = P(H:E_i)$, or $P(H:not E_i)$ depending on the value of E_i.
5. Select a new E_i to consider. Go to 1.

12.2.3 Odds

The odds in favour of an event may be calculated from the probability of that event:

O(E) = P(E)/(1 − P(E))

And:

P(E) = O(E)/(1 + O(E))

12.2.4 Approximations (see also pages 162−163)

P(A AND B) = min(P(A),P(B))
P(A OR B) = max(P(A),P(B))

These results are not strictly true and the extent to which they are in error depends on the extent to which A and B are independent or otherwise. If information concerning the independence is not available they may, however, prove useful. Note that :

$$\min(x,y) = x, \text{ if } x \text{ is less than } y$$
$$= y, \text{ if } y \text{ is less than } x$$
$$\max(x,y) = x, \text{ if } x \text{ is greater than } y$$
$$= y, \text{ if } y \text{ is greater than } x.$$

12.2.5 Combinations (see also page 26)

Given n events, of which we choose x, there are $\binom{n}{x}$

ways of making the selection.

$$\binom{n}{x} = \frac{n!}{(n-x)!x!} \text{ where } n! = n(n-1)(n-2)(n-3)...(n-(n-1))$$

e.g. $4! = 4.3.2.1 = 24$

If there are n items of evidence and any or all of these may occur then there are:

$$\sum_{x=0}^{x=n} \binom{n}{x}$$

possible combinations of the evidence.

12.2.6 Descriptive statistics (see also pages 92−98)

Descriptive statistics are, as the name implies, statistics used to describe or summarise the main features of some data which we have.

Mean m:

$$m = \sum_{i=1}^{i=n} \frac{x_i}{n}$$

often referred to as the 'average' .

Variance, v:

$$v = \sum_{i=1}^{i=n} \frac{(x_i - m)^2}{n}$$

Standard deviation, sd:

$$sd = SQR(v)$$

12.2.7 Normal distribution

Most of the statistical methods used in this book involve the use of non-parametric statistics. Non-parametric statistics make no assumption about the underlying behaviour of the variables being studied and are, consequently, less prone to let you down.

Parametric statistics assume an underlying mathematical model for the behaviour of the variables being studied. One such family of parametric statistics is that group of statistics which assumes that variables basically come from a population which possesses the normal probability distribution function. This is the, well-known, bell-shaped curve. A large body of theory is available for handling normal distributions and it is frequently tempting to use normal distribution theory.

Before doing so it is essential to examine any data to see if it really is normally distributed. In practice, as opposed to theory, many variables are not normally distributed even though many statisticians wish they were. You should vigorously resist the temptation to apply normal distribution theory on variables which are not normally distributed.

12.2.8 Discrete and continuous variables

A discrete variable is one which can only adopt certain fixed values – for instance, Yes/No responses are discrete. Continuous variables are those which can adopt any number as their value – for instance, rainfall figures are continuous. Continuous variables may be made discrete by chopping them up into sections – for example, rainfall over one inch/rainfall under one inch.

You are likely to get into trouble if you use the same methods of working for both discrete and continuous variables together. Decide which you are using at the start and stick to that type of variable. In general, you will find discrete variables much easier to handle than continuous variables. To some extent this is because methods involving continuous variables tend to rely on parametric statistics – and the choice of suitable parametric families can be a vexed question.

12.3 Surfaces (see also pages 36–39)

The general equation of a surface is:

$$y = \sum_{i=0}^{i=n} b_i x_i$$

where the b_i are constants and the x_i are variables.

A table top has a two dimensional surface ($n=2$) and x_1 and x_2 are at right angles to each other. This can be expressed as saying that x_1 and x_2 are independent of each other, or are not correlated with each other. In general, there may be as many variables as you wish. They may be independent of each other, or not. They may be used to describe something which does not exist in real, three-dimensional, space. They may be a description, for instance, of a particular pattern of behaviour, or of disease, or of anything.

A surface is a mathematical convenience.

12.4 Discrimination (see also pages 36−39,113)

Suppose that we have n categories of objects described by measurements on a certain number of variables. We are then given a further object and a set of measurements for this object on these variables. We then have to decide to which of the n categories it belongs. This is the problem of discrimination.

In general, it is only possible to solve the problem completely if the various categories are linearly separable. That is to say, if it is possible to place a surface (or a series of surfaces) between each of the categories. The surfaces are defined in terms of the variables we are able to measure on these objects.

We may decide that the categories are mutually exclusive − that is to say, the object can fall only into one category of the n. In this case we place it in the most likely category.

This might mean that we place it in that category for which P(H:E) is a maximum. Here H defines one category and E is all the evidence relating objects to category membership.

Note that, mathematically, P(H:E) is the equation of a surface. It is a surface which 'points' in the direction of a particular H. The calculations for P(H:E) give, indirectly, the b_i for the surface. And the evidence E on each variable gives the x_i.

We do not, however, have to use probability measures explicitly. Any method that produces a discriminating surface will do. Any method that works is right.

If the categories are not mutually exclusive we may place our object into more than one category. In this case we do not simply choose the most likely category. We have a threshold criterion and the object is placed into those categories for which it exceeds the threshold criterion.

If the discriminating surface is:

$$y = \sum_{i=0}^{i=n} b_i x_i$$

then we can categorise the object for each case in which y exceeds some y_c.

12.5 The learning algorithm (see also pages 30,49)

1. Take n observations x_i on an object to be categorised.
2. Calculate:

$$y_k = \sum_{i=0}^{i=n} b_{ik} x_i$$

for each of the possible categories. Initially, $b_{ik} = 0$ for all i,k.
3. Find that category k for which y_k is the greatest.

4. If the object belongs to category k then this categorisation is correct. No changes are necessary. Go to item 6.
5. If the categorisation is wrong, modify b_{ik} as follows:

$b_{ik} = b_{ik} + x_i$, for that category k to which the object should have been categorised. Do this for all b_{ik} in k.

$b_{ik} = b_{ik} - x_i$, for all categories k to which the object should not have been categorised and for which y_k is greater than the y_k of the correct classification. Do this for all b_{ik} in these incorrect categories.
6. Take another observation. Go to 1.

This algorithm requires a training set of objects with known categorisations to get it going. Once it is working well it can be used on further objects whose correct classification is not known.

12.6 Parallel and sequential procedures (see also pages 51−56)

A parallel procedure takes all of the available information at once and makes one, final, calculation on the basis of this information:

$$y_k = \sum_{i=0}^{i=n} b_{ik} x_i, \qquad \text{for all categories k}$$

A sequential procedure steps through the variables one by one making what use it can of the information as it goes along:

$y_{ik} = y_{i-1,k} + b_{ik} x_i$, sequentially through i for all categories k

A sequential procedure should, once all of the information has been collected, give the same result as a parallel procedure. If all of the information is always needed to obtain a conclusion then the difference between the two methods is purely cosmetic.

If a conclusion can be reached on the basis of less than all the possible information a sequential procedure could be more economical because it would come to a conclusion faster.

12.7 Minimum and maximum values (see also pages 55-56,57-62)

If the variables x_i which are to be provided to the system have minimum and maximum values associated with them then the procedure may be able to come to a conclusion more quickly.

Suppose that all max(x_i) always support a particular categorisation and that all min(x_i) always argue against such a categorisation. Then, for as yet unknown variables x_i calculate two possible outcomes based on max(x_i) and min(x_i) for the outstanding variables. If neither of these overturn the current 'best guess' of the system then that best guess cannot be overturned and can be taken to be correct. Therefore, the outstanding x_i are not actually needed.

12.8 Processing strategies
(see also pages 108-112,155-156)

If all the x_i are required to make a categorisation then any difference in processing strategies is purely cosmetic. If not all x_i are needed then it becomes important to use the most efficient processing strategy possible in order to come to a conclusion as efficiently as possible.

12.8.1 Goal-driven strategies

These work by selecting a categorisation and, staying with that categorisation, checking out the relevant x_i until it is possible to decide whether that particular categorisation is correct or not.

Having done that, the system can then proceed to check out the next category. And so on.

12.8.2 Data-driven strategies

These work by selecting an x_i which, on some grounds, looks like a useful x_i to know. Having got a value for this x_i the system makes what use it can of the information.

Having done that, the system goes on to select another x_i. In the course of this, conclusions are reached about various categories.

12.8.3 Selecting the next variable (see also page 173)

Whether the system works on a goal-driven strategy or a data-driven strategy there will usually be some latitude with respect to which x_i should be examined next. The problem is one of choosing a 'good' question to ask from a series of possible questions and it is hard to be very precise about what constitutes 'good'. However, of any question, we may consider:

1. How many categorisations does it influence?
2. To what extent does it influence those categorisations?
For example:
    1. For each currently unknown x_i we might calculate:
y_{ik} (using the $\max(x_i)$) $-y_{ik}$ (using the $\min(x_i)$) to determine the maximum possible change that can be brought about by a knowledge of x_i.
    2. Using Bayesian probabilities we might calculate:
$P(H:E) - P(H:not\ E)$
where E is the observation x_i, to determine the maximum change that can be brought about by each piece of evidence.

To work out these items for each variable prior to asking a question involves far more processing (on the part of the computer) than simply to ask the next question on a list. The advantage is that it might require, overall, less effort on the part of the person using that computer.

However, as short cuts to speed processing time:

Try: $\max(\max(x_i) - \min(x_i))$ to give an idea of an 'important' question. The snag with this method is that x_i might have a very wide range of variation but might not be, actually, important in any way.

Try: $\max(\text{variance}(b_{ik}))$ to give an idea of the extent to which a variable is used in the categorisations. The snag with this method is that a variable which appears to be widely used might, in fact, have a small $(\max(x_i) - (\min(x_i))$ and the large range in the b_{ik} might simply be to allow for this fact.

12.9 Intermediate conclusions (see also page 103)

Intermediate conclusions aren't always strictly necessary but they can be useful in 'humanising' the system. An intermediate conclusion can be used as an input variable to another stage in the expert process. The use of intermediate conclusions greatly increases the difficulty of writing the system in the first place.

However, there is one point which is worth bearing in mind with respect to intermediate conclusions – and this hinges on the rather vexed question of independence.

Most of the statistical methods used assume independence of the various items of evidence E_i and, frequently, the assumptions of independence are not justified.

If there are n items of evidence supporting a hypothesis H and they are correlated with each other but the calculations are made as if the correlations did not exist then H will receive more, apparent, support than it in fact deserves.

Inserting intermediate conclusions in the reasoning process can help to eliminate this effect.

Consider E_1 and E_2 both present to support H_1.

Let H_1 be an intermediate conclusion which acts as evidence for a further conclusion H_2.

Let E_1 and E_2 be, to some extent, correlated with each other.

Then H_1 receives more support than it should.

However, it might still be reasonable to claim H_1 to be true so no real harm is done at this stage.

But, without H_1, the error in calculating for E_1 and E_2 would be carried forward into H_2, gradually getting more and more serious as more and more, possibly correlated E_i, are added into the calculations.

The presence of H_1 and other intermediate conclusions allows the slate to be wiped clean, as it were. A new set of calculations can be started for H_2 based on a smaller number of items of evidence and reducing the risk of a serious build up of uncertainty.

12.9.1 Explanatory systems (see also page 149)

Intermediate conclusions can be used to give explanations of the current state of the system.

In general, an explanatory system can say where it has got to in its reasoning process and, often, how it got there. The problem is that this tends to force the computer to work in a way which is capable of ready explanation and this may be difficult to achieve or may even lead to a less efficient implementation.

For instance, what sort of explanation would be appropriate if the computer asked for x_i because it had calculated that this particular x_i would influence P(H:E) more than any other x_i?

Most of the strategies in this book for selecting a 'good' x_i consist of finding an x_i which looks kind of important from a mathematical point of view. But a naive user might well feel happier with explanations that involved, say, a listing of which categorisations would be affected most by that x_i irrespective of why that particular x_i was really chosen.

12.10 Linear interpolation of responses (see also pages 165, 174)

Suppose that the user is not certain about his answer to a question. He may wish to reply on a certainty scale from, say, minus 5 to plus 5 corresponding to No (-5), Don't Know (0), and Yes ($+5$).

Suppose now that the prior probability of any response is P(E).

If there is uncertainty in the answer then the system must deal with this by putting a value on P(E) and, also, a value on P(not E) because if the user is uncertain about the existence of a piece of evidence then that evidence might not be there.

Let the user's response be R.
If R is greater than, or equal to, 0 then:
$$P(E) = P(E) + (1 - P(E))R/5$$

If R is less than, or equal to, 0 then:
$$P(E) = P(E) + P(E)R/5$$

Obviously, P(not E) = 1 − P(E)

and, if R = 0 then P(E) remains unchanged at P(E).

Then, to calculate the new P(H:E) we have:

$$P(H:E) = P(H:E)P(E) + P(H:not E)P(not E)$$

In other words, calculate both outcomes and weight the final outcome by the certainty the user expressed for the evidence and against the evidence.

12.11 Data formats

1. Arrays

DIM R(E,H)

	Hypothesis 1	*Hypothesis 2...etc.*
Evidence 1	x	x
Evidence 2	x	x
. . . , etc.		

Where the array R holds a series of equations for surfaces enabling a categorisation process to be carried out.

2. DATA statements (see also Section 10.1)

```
DATA Hypothesis 1, prior probability of hypothesis 1[,evidence j,P(Eⱼ:H),P(Eⱼ:not H)]
DATA Hypothesis 2, etc.
```

and:

```
DATA j, Evidence j
```

The DATA statements hold similar information to the array R – each DATA statement is very much like one column from the array.

The advantage of using arrays is that processing is quicker – but the data can be lost if you don't write code to store it on disc.

The advantage of using DATA statements is that they are less easily lost and more easily modified but can be slow to process.

In general, it is better to make the effort and hold the information in a disc file.

Chapter 13

Select Readings

It's quite a problem producing a list of suggested reading for a subject as diffuse as expert systems because one of the best things to do is to read up on the subject in which you want your system to be expert – and that covers, potentially, everything.

Also, if the list is too long then nobody will ever start to look at the items it contains; and, if it's too short, then it will miss out a great deal. However (in alphabetical order)...

Bailey, N T J. Mathematics, Statistics and Systems for Health. Wiley, 1977.

This has a nice section on medical diagnosis. Because of the medical orientation it doesn't confine itself to theoretically 'perfect' methods but, instead, concentrates on methods that work.

Bratko, I. Prolog Programming For Artificial Intelligence. Addison-Wesley, 1986.

If you don't feel in the mood for Clocksin & Mellish, or just want a different flavour of book, then try this one for an approach to Prolog. It gives an introduction to Prolog programming and then some coverage of various AI problems and how they might be tackled – including expert systems. A bit like a Prolog version of Forsyth & Naylor, in some respects.

Clocksin, W F, Mellish, C S. Programming in Prolog. Springer-Verlag, 1981.

This is *the* definitive work on Prolog – the book which most people regard as defining the language standard itself. So, if you feel like trying your hand at a Prolog approach to expert systems, get a copy of this and stick it on your shelves.

Forsyth, R & Naylor, C. The Hitch-Hiker's Guide to Artificial Intelligence. Chapman and Hall/Methuen, 1986.

A fairly cheap paperback, this presents a round-up of most subjects in the field of Artificial Intelligence including program examples in Basic. There are four versions of the book specifically for the Apple II, Amstrad CPC 6128, BBC and IBM PC – so make sure you buy the right version. The section on expert systems doesn't tell you a lot that isn't in this book you've got in your hand now but the rest of the book is ok.

Higman, B. A Comparative Study of Programming Languages. McDonald/Elsevier Computer Monographs, 1967.

A relatively cheap book, this will be a bit of an eye-opener to anyone who thought there were only three or four different programming languages. Like most books which cover a large number of languages this can cause mental indigestion if you try to read it too quickly.

Hunt, E B. Artificial Intelligence. Academic Press, 1975.

A nice book on AI, though it might seem a bit abstract for the non-mathematical reader in places. It covers the learning algorithm and Bayesian inferencing and is generally interesting on a wide range of subjects.

Kendall, M. Multivariate Analysis. Charles Griffin, 1975.

This is, actually, one of my all-time favourites.
It's a book on statistics and covers the problems of classification and distance. It isn't the most up to date book by any means – in fact, with reference to computers, it several times suggests that the use of VDUs (CRTs) could become widespread one day (!) – but it contains a quantity of good, sound, commonsense which you won't find anywhere else on this subject.

Knuth, D.E. The Art of Computer Programming, Volume 1 Fundamental Algorithms. Addison-Wesley, 1973.

It's pretty well impossible not to have a copy of this. You have to have a copy if you want to mess around with linkages and tree structures although its big disadvantage is that all the examples are given in MIX – a sort of assembler-level language for a fictitious machine.

Michie, D (ed.). Expert Systems in the Microelectronic Age. Edinburgh University Press, 1979.

A useful collection of papers on various systems, such as PROSPECTOR, MYCIN, PUFF, SU/X, MECHO and others. It's especially useful in revealing just how complicated things can get.

Mood, A.M, Graybill, F.A, Boes, D.C. Introduction to the Theory of Statistics. McGraw-Hill, 1974.

So many aspects of expert systems are tied in with statistics that the odd book on the subject is essential. The snag is, of course, that such books can't always confine themselves simply to what you need to know, but give you an entire course in all sorts of statistics. However, you'll find Bayesian inferencing and basic probabilities covered here.

Morrison, D.F. Multivariate Statistical Methods. McGraw-Hill, 1976.

An alternative to Kendall. Rather a dry book but it uses matrix notation in contrast to Kendall's use of subscripted variables and some people may find the one easier than the other (in programming languages they both refer to arrays).

Robinson, J.A. Logic: Form and Function. Edinburgh University Press, 1979.

Some people may find this a difficult book if they don't have too much training in logic but it does have a very nice section on LISP and, if you feel like moving on to more complex systems, you're going to have a hard job avoiding formal logic anyway.

Wani, J.K. Probability and Statistical Inference. Appleton-Century-Crofts, 1971.

Another book on statistics this again gives you Bayes and probabilities.

If possible, it's always a good idea to have at least two books on any given subject – especially if the subject is a difficult one.

That way you can read one version, fail to understand it, read another version, fail to understand that, then go back to the first version – at about which point the light often dawns.

In which case, as you've got one book now in your hand (this one) what is the other book you should rush out and buy?

Kendall, probably. It's not a computer book as such – but it's a wonderful source of ideas for someone with a computer. Or, failing that, Hunt.

Or, better still, Forsyth & Naylor because that way I make yet more money out of you.

INDEX

Other Sigma Press Books

This is a partial list of our professional-level computing books, including those due for publication in 1987. You can order them through your usual bookseller.

Title & Author	Subject	ISBN/ Publication Date
Artificial Intelligence		
Designing Artificial Intelligence Software: A. Bahrami	This provides a collection of AI based programming techniques that can be applied to solving every day programming problems together with descriptions of frontier research.	1-85058-085-5 Winter 1987
Progress in Machine Learning–a European Perspective: I. Bratko & N. Lavrac	A collection of papers written by leading European researchers in many areas of AI with an emphasis on machine learning.	1-85058-088-X Spring 1987
Expert Systems for Personal Computers: M. Chadwick & J.A. Hannah	Emphasises the development of rule-based systems, written in BASIC or LOGO.	1-85058-044-8 Published
Expert Medical Systems: M.K. Chytil (Ed.)	International collection of papers on this emerging subject.	1-85058-047-2 Spring 1987
Amstrads & Artificial Intelligence: P.J. Hall	This transfers many classic AI systems to the popular Amstrad CPC range. Readily transferable to other micros.	1-85058-038-3 Published
Build Your Own Expert System (2nd Edition for IBM PC and Compatibles): C. Naylor	Entertaining view of AI with programs completely re-written and tested for IBM PC, Amstrad PC1512 and compatibles.	1-85058-071-5 Spring 1987
Microcomputer Speech Synthesis and Recognitions: A.S. Poulton	Wide ranging survey from biological background to working systems.	0-905104-39-0 Published
Expert System Development in Prolog and Turbo Prolog: P. Smith	This is a practical book aimed at the development of real systems in the commercial and industrial fields.	1-85058-064-2 Summer 1987

215

| Program Design for Knowledge Based Systems: G. Winstanley | There are very few books aimed at designers of AI systems; this book fills the gap, and will enable any AI worker (or persons new to AI) to produce reliable working systems in the shortest possible time, using LISP as the target language. | 1-85058-066-9 Summer 1987 |

Operating Systems

Exploiting MS–DOS (on the Amstrad PC1512 and all IBM PC Compatibles): N.J. Backhurst & P. Davies	This covers all versions of MS-DOS currently in use (including version 3.2 on the Amstrad PC1512), plus a section on MS-DOS Windows and versions 4.0 & 5.0. Suitable for beginners and experienced users.	1-85058-070-0 Autumn 1987
UNIX–The Book: M. Banahan & A. Rutter	The title says it all!	0-90510-421-8 Published
Understanding dBase III & II: G. Burns	Packed with tested examples of dBase applications.	0-90510-475-7 Published
Parallel Processing– with Occam: Alison Carling	An introduction to parallel concepts for those with some knowledge of computers and computer terminology. No specialist background is necessary.	1-85058-077-4 Summer 1987
A Programmer's Guide to GEM– on the IBM PC & Compatibles: B. Howling & A. Pepper	This is aimed at readers with a reasonable knowledge of high level languages who already understand the basic concepts of GEM.	1-85058-084-7 Winter 1987
Windows on the PC–fundamentals and applications of Microsoft's Windows operating system: J.M. Hughes	John Hughes provides users with an easy-to-understand but comprehensive survey of the Microsoft Windows operating system and compatible applications.	1-85058-082-0 Autumn 1987
PICK–Your System N. Kitt	Equally useful to managers and systems analysts requiring background or detailed knowledge of PICK.	1-85058-031-6 Published
Operating Systems: A. Trevennor	A practical guide to operating systems and how they work, illustrated with DEC systems.	0-905104-66-8 Published
Mastering DOS Plus: Simon Williams	Takes the complete beginner (or the seasoned user of other systems) from booting–up to the mouse and WIMP interface and describes each of the commands available.	1-85058-034-0 Published

CP/M – the Software Bus: A. Clarke, J.M. Eaton and D. Powys-Lybbe	The most popular and authoritative CP/M book in the UK.	0-905104-18-8 Published

Programming Languages

Interactive Learning on the IBM PC: Graham Beech	Comprehensive guide to the methods and practice of computer assisted and computer -managed learning, with examples for the IBM PC.	1-85058-057-X Published
Prolog: Programming for Tomorrow: J. Doores, A. R. Reiblein & S. Vadera	Complete tutorial with numerous practical examples. Covers the Edinburgh/ICL dialect.	0-905104-52-8 Spring 1987
How to Solve it in LISP: IBM PC & Compatibles: P. J. Hall	Emphasises LISP in statistics, general business applications and simulations. Databases and expert systems are also examined.	1-85058-005-7 Summer 1987
Practical C: M. Harrison	Down-to-earth, compact guide to the C language.	1-85058-035-9 Published
Prolog Through Examples: A Practical Programming Guide: I. Kononenko & N. Lavrac	Takes a novel approach to the teaching of Prolog, by presenting a series of graded examples, which are solved in Prolog.	1-85058-072-3 Autumn 1987
Using Locomotive BASIC 2 on the Amstrad PC1512: R. Ransom	The only book on the BASIC 2 programming language to be approved by the people who wrote the software – Locomotive.	1-85058-073-1 Published
Practical COBOL for Microcomputers: K. Sullivan	COBOL tutorial for use with inexpensive micros.	0-905104-60-9 Published
Big Red Book of C: K. Sullivan	Comprehensive tutorial on C with many complete listings of programs for business applications.	0-905104-68-4 Published
Applied Fourth Generation Languages: J. Watt	Introduces 4GLs and shows that the system designer must still use conventional design techniques. Examines potential application areas for 4GLs including sales, distribution, production and finance. Avoid wasting your time with unsuitable software.	1-85058-061-8 Spring 1987
The Complete FORTH: A. Winfield	Long established book for beginners to this exciting language – faster than BASIC, easier than assembler.	0-905104-22-6 Published

| CAD on the PC—
and Compatibles:
H.S. Atherton | How to design and draft reliably with an
IBM PC or compatible. Both 2D drafting
and 3D modelling are explained and
illustrated with representative software
packages. | 1-85058-089-8
Autumn 1987 |

Applications

The Desktop Publishing Companion: Graham Jones	Starts with a discussion of such computers as the Apple Macintosh and IBM PC plus aspects of how to plan a publication including typography, word spacing, selection and the positioning of graphics.	1-85058-078-2 Spring 1987
The SuperCalc SuperBook: E. Lee	Officially approved guide to SuperCalc 2,3 and 4. Complementary to the manuals and packed with examples to clarify advanced topics.	1-85058-080-4 Summer 1987
The PC Compendium, Vol. I: C. Naylor	A wide ranging collection of 50 articles on how to get more from the IBM PC and compatibles. Covers languages, operating systems, expert systems, obscure bugs and much more.	1-85058-087-1 Summer 1987
Interactive Video: E. Parsloe	The definitive book on videotape, disc and interfacing to computers. Particularly strong on design techniques.	0-905104-55-2 Published

Communications

| Cost Effective
Local Area
Networks:
S. Bridges | A complete guide to the theory and
practice of local area networks. | 0-905104-86-2
Published |
| Communicating
with
Microcomputers:
I. Cullimore | Describes how to connect microcomputers
to each other—and to just about anything
else—using commercial packages or hand-
crafted code. | 1-85058-055-3
Spring 1987 |